GOOD CARE

Ethics and Methodology

An Anthroposophical Approach to Child- and Youth Psychiatry and Care of Persons with Developmental Disabilities

Erik Baars (ed.), Pim Blomaard, Marijke Bijloo, Bernard Heldt, Willem de Koning and Martin Niemeijer

TEMPLE LODGE

Temple Lodge Publishing Ltd.
Hillside House, The Square
Forest Row, RH18 5ES

www.templelodge.com

First published by Temple Lodge in 2024

Originally published in Dutch under the title *Goede Zorg, Ethische en methodische aspecten, Een antroposofische benadering van kinder- en jeugdpsychiatrie en zorg voor mensen met ontwikkelingsstoornissen* by Uitgeverij Christofoor, Zeist, Netherlands in 2005. This translation is based on the second edition of 2006

Translated from Dutch by Philip Mees and Marjan Sikkel, with many thanks to Penelope Baring, James Dyson, Jan Goeschel, and Coleman Lyles for their assistance

A CIP catalogue record for this book is available from the British Library

ISBN 978 1 915776 15 0

Cover by Morgan Creative
Typeset by Symbiosys Technologies, Visakhapatnam, India
Printed by 4Edge Ltd., Essex

Contents

1 Introduction

In special education and social therapy and the care and support that are given on the basis of anthroposophy to children and adults with learning disabilities, a caregiving methodology has been developed over the past 100 years, which is practised in a variety of forms in more than 50 countries around the world every day. Explicitly or implicitly, this methodology was developed, on the one hand, out of the spiritual-scientific results of the research work of Rudolf Steiner and others and, on the other hand, on the basis of the experiences of co-workers in the practice of caregiving. It is the experiences of many persons needing care, co-workers, and parents or caregivers that the approach that is based on this methodology is more often than not effective and of high quality.

So far however, no fundamental description and scientific justification of the methodology, including its ethical premises, has appeared. This is no longer appropriate in a time when the cultivation and scientific justification of health care has become common practice. This book aims to fill this void. The guiding question of this book is therefore: What are the hallmarks of the anthroposophical caregiving methodology that are necessary, and also justifiable for the provision of (scientifically) responsible 'good care'?

In order to arrive at an answer to this question, first of all Pim Blomaard presents the ethical premises of caregiving (methodology) in Chapter 2. In Chapter 3 Marijke Bijloo describes a number of learning disabilities from a perspective of a spiritual psychology of development. This lays a foundation on which learning disabilities can be methodically approached and comprehended. In Chapter 4 Willem de Koning and Marijke Bijloo describe the core elements of the practice of special education and social therapy, the 'means' with which caregivers can work in practice. Marijke Bijloo describes in Chapter 5 the professional identity, the core views and competences of the professional caregiver, in order to come to clear insight into the knowledge, insight, proficiencies and mentality that are necessary requisites for good professional work. In Chapter 6, Martin Niemeijer describes the phases of the caregiving process as a whole from a methodological perspective. Finally, in Chapter 7 the caregiving methodology is scientifically substantiated by Erik Baars.

Good Care represents things as they could be described by these authors at this time. Besides description and justification, the purpose of this book is also to give the reader insights and openings for good caregiving to all children and adults with learning disabilities. We therefore hope that it will resound enthusiastically with its readers, and that it will lead to inspiration and application in daily caregiving practice. Finally, it is the great wish of the authors that the content of this book will be further tested and developed in the practice of caregiving. In this sense it is an open-ended book that can 'grow' further as the practice continues to develop.

The Birth of Curative Education and Social Therapy

On 18 June, 1924, Rudolf Steiner, the founder of anthroposophy, visited a house where a month earlier the first initiative for curative education had been taken with nine children. It was *Lauenstein* in Jena, a city in eastern Germany. Rudolf Steiner discussed the children with the co-workers, diagnosed their developmental problems in an anthroposophical and scientific manner, and gave indications for how they should be handled and treated. The date is remembered as the beginning of curative education.

A week later, in Dornach, Switzerland between 25 June and 7 July, Steiner gave twelve lectures for physicians, teachers, and *Lauenstein* co-workers, which were published in English with the title *Curative Education* in 1998. For almost a hundred years, with over 600 organizations in over 40 countries, these lectures have formed an inspiring basis for working with these children. Although they reflect the sphere and culture in the German-speaking part of Europe of their time, as to content they are still as timely as ever.

In the 1920s, ideologies like communism and national socialism were trying to break through the dominant pessimism in Europe; both wanted to force a way to the future with blind power. For the group of people to whom Rudolf Steiner gave his lectures on curative education, neither this pessimism, nor these ideologies formed the basis of their life and work. They wanted to begin with the human being, with themselves, and they were searching for spiritual motives that could offer them a framework in which they could work in a meaningful way on the problems of the time. These were mainly people from German-speaking areas, but also from England and Holland, who were looking for insights that could be applied in practical situations in the daily reality of their work with children with learning disabilities.

The individuals, who were then discovering anthroposophy as a new way of looking at the human being and the world, were fascinated by the far from ordinary remarks Rudolf Steiner made about human development. He said that everything that can occur in children with learning disabilities, may also occur in less obvious ways in healthy children, because a so-called abnormality may be found in some corner of the soul of each human being.[1] He called attention to the fact that what we call 'normal' is nothing more than what we have in mind as normal in the sense of being average. Curing 'abnormality,' said Steiner in 1924 (!), might even amount to 'driving out a fragment of genius', something that deviates from the average. And he continued:

> … and the first thing the doctor and teacher have to do is to reject it and get beyond the stage of making pronouncements as to what is clever or reasonable, in accordance with the habits of thought that prevail today. Particularly in this domain we must refrain from jumping to conclusions, and simply *look at things as they are*. What have we actually before us in the human being?

In his course, Steiner emphasized in a number of ways how important *inner mobility, artistic sense, humour, and an ability to relativize* are. We should not be stuck in a pattern of reactions, but be able, time and again, to offer the child an opening toward development. Out of the anthroposophical conception of the human being an approach that shows respect for the individuality of the other is first and foremost. This view provides us with a frame of reference in which the strength and sometimes the greatness of people with developmental disabilities becomes visible. Even more, the worse the disability is, the more clearly recognizable is the struggle and, therefore, the commitment and dynamic of their existence (see also 2.4.2). Besides the potential to observe these characteristics, Steiner also gave the pedagogical law, leading to very concrete indications for working on yourself as educator (see also 5.1.5).

Steiner indicated precisely what inner attitude is at work. He spoke of the need to have a 'religious feeling towards the cosmos'. He gave wonderful meditations to practise such an attitude and inner liveliness, for instance, the point-circle meditation (see also 5.2.2): 'You have to understand that *a circle is a point, and a point is a circle*. He meant that the educator:

> … takes the plunge into *reality* … is grasping hold of reality. *Devotion to little things*—yes, to the very smallest of all! […] Therefore it is so urgent, my dear friends, if you want to become real educators, and especially educators of handicapped children, that you should cultivate, with the utmost humility, this devotion in the matter of little things. And when you have made a beginning in this way in your own sphere, you can afterwards go on to awaken in other circles of the Youth Movement this same devotion to little things.

A very important aspect of this inner attitude is *courage*. As a curative educator or social therapist you have to act. You directly influence the life of another person. This demands great thoughtfulness and care, but also courage—inner courage, as Steiner expressed it. By exerting influence on someone else's life you influence his karma. You continually awaken possibilities that otherwise would not be awakened. You continually make big and little decisions as to whether you will do something or not (see also 5.2.2).

2 Value-Based Caregiving. Ethical Premises of Anthroposophical Care for Persons with Developmental Disabilities

Pim Blomaard

2.1 Introduction

In this chapter we will name a number of ethical premises that guide the practice of anthroposophical child- and youth psychiatry and the care of persons with learning disabilities. In anthroposophical literature so many subjects are discussed that have an ethical import that simplification is unavoidable. For this reason, we try to condense this abundance into three values, which together can function as an ethical foundation for 'value-based' caregiving. There are, however, other ways to approach this. (Glöckler 2002)

The question addressed in this chapter is therefore the following: What are the fundamental values that guide anthroposophical caregiving, and how can they motivate people to provide 'good care'?

To answer this question, we will first of all introduce the three values that are of central importance. A number of modern ethical premises will be reviewed that will show that the three values also appear in current ethical discussions. Further, we will highlight a number of aspects of the anthroposophical conception of the human being and the world that give substance to these values. For according to this view, these values are grounded in reality. This gives the ethical foundation a foundation in reality as it can manifest in the light of anthroposophy.

Further, a relation is shown between these values and certain attitudes and proficiencies that are of practical and methodological importance. Caregivers have to give inner direction to their deeds. Consciousness of the ethics involved can be of help to take this direction purposefully in hand. Here we have to observe a number of conditions that influence this self-direction. Methodical practice of the fundamental values presumes personal characteristics and capacities that are not arbitrary. In the section about virtue we will indicate a number of such characteristics for each fundamental value.

Next we will go into the difference between current practice in anthroposophical caregiving organizations and the anthroposophical ideal of good care. For ideal and practice do not simply coincide. The question then is to what extent the ethical premises are binding on the co-workers, and to what extent in an organization the individual caregivers are free to make their own decisions. Finally, the age-old theme of the 'good' will be raised in order to examine what significance the word 'good' can have in the expression 'good care'.

2.2 Introduction of the Three Fundamental Values

2.2.1 Equality

In the course of the twentieth century, people with handicaps have emancipated themselves from being so-called inferiors to being equals, at least in Western society. The ethical foundation of this equality, however, leaves much to be desired. Some ethicists, such as Singer[2], relativize the difference between a mammal and a person with serious handicaps. Such relativizing evokes vehement indignation because people have an elementary feeling that this difference most certainly exists, and that people with disabilities have a right to the best possible care and coaching. At the same time, however, it is difficult to formulate a rational basis for this feeling, and to demonstrate the difference. The increasing practice of aborting foetuses with a handicap as undesirable offspring makes the question of equality acute, and the tendency to think about caregiving more and more in economic terms causes fears that the handicapped might one day become too expensive. An explicit statement of the ethical foundation of equality is therefore an urgent necessity.

For anthroposophical caregiving to persons with developmental disabilities, equality has been the most important value from day one. The conviction that a human being, regardless of any disfunction, is fundamentally equal to all other human beings was and is what drives the anthroposophical caregiver. This is the reason why anthroposophical care of the handicapped was the first to develop educational programmes for children, and offer work to adults with intellectual handicaps.

This conviction is based on the insight that all human beings derive their equality from a common origin in a spiritual world, and that all human beings develop as spiritual beings along the same lines of shortcomings and talents. This development encompasses a series of lives on earth. The immortal spirit of the human being goes from incarnation to incarnation—it reincarnates—with the goal of transforming itself into an individual spirit substance. Eventually, in the distant future this being will, also without matter, continue spiritual evolution based on spiritual decisions of will. For a good understanding of this view of the human being, we have to make a distinction between being and appearance, between spirit and soul, between reincarnation and destiny (karma). These distinctions form part of a conception of reality, which is unusual for many people, but in itself consistent and coherent, and which raises equality into a fundamental value.

2.2.2 Sense of Service

The realization that human beings are equal as spiritual beings also gives a foundation to the second fundamental value in caregiving to persons with developmental disabilities: a sense of service. It is a hallmark of many workers in health care that they experience a call to their profession. They feel called to do something to or for the vulnerability and dependence of the other. They enter into the life of the other; they 'live his life with him', and out of this empathy arises the intention to want to give effective help to the other.

Another word that we encounter in ethical literature is *beneficence*, in the sense of doing good.[3] This value includes love, friendship and solidarity, in which the relationship with the other always stands in the centre. Justice, in the sense of doing justice to the other, can also be included. In addition, service also includes the virtue of selflessness, which indicates that you have the well-being of the other in view, and are not looking for your own advantage.

In anthroposophical caregiving the perspective for 'beneficence' is the development of the other into a spiritual individuality who can make individual decisions out of free will. This may be a long-term perspective, but it gives great weight to one's actions in the here and now. Service is a development-oriented willingness to help, out of the realization of a shared destiny with far-reaching perspective. We humans are related to each other; my development is linked with yours, and vice versa. What has become my share, was kept from you, and vice versa. My destiny is linked with that of all other human beings.

Service means entering into a relationship out of an awareness of shared destiny. For this reason, the cultivation of community life is often made an objective in itself in anthroposophical organizations (see also 4.3.5). The concrete form this will take is diverse. It can be a community in which co-workers live together with a number of persons with disabilities which, however, only rarely happens these days. Or co-workers become residents on the organization's property and open their private life to all kinds of encounters.

The ability to be of service without in the long run shortchanging yourself and the other demands a number of personal skills—'virtues'—that have to be practised. In other words, besides using and further developing the skills I already possess, I also, and especially, have to transform my own shortcomings in a process of self-education. By reflectively dealing with my own shortcomings I learn to deal with those of others. I will also have to lower my own inner thresholds if I want to truly meet the other. Doing good for another therefore means actively working on myself.

2.2.3 Spiritual Presence of Mind

Equality and service can only become fully effective if they are joined by a third fundamental value, namely spiritual presence of mind. In common parlance this means a true presence of your self. You are spiritually fully present in the situation, you are awake and alert, your judgement is sharp, and you have yourself in hand. I call such wakeful presence a value here. It is a manner of being that is not simply a given, and it is also a manner of acting that is not simply self-evident.

In ethical literature it is more common to name freedom and responsibility as values. Out of what follows it will become clear that spiritual presence of mind is a prerequisite for both of these. Exercising one's own freedom presumes that the person is mentally present; respect for another person's freedom means that one has that person's spiritual presence of mind in view.

To realize this fundamental value you have to practise self-reflection. You ask yourself: In what state am I in this moment, or was I at that time? When you are in a position of power—and someone working with a person with intellectual limitations is in a position of power—you have to reflect regularly on your own condition. Which motives are guiding you when you are directing the other? What is driving you in your treatment of the other? You must also dare to face your own inner impotence in the situation. Your inability to fully understand or adequately guide the other may grow in you into an inner conflict. It may, for instance, lead to annoyance, a form of aversion. In such an inner condition you may yourself become unfree; you may let yourself too much be guided by your antipathy.

The consequence of inner unfreedom may be that you no longer form a sound judgement on the actual situation. You get swept along in a stream of emotion and prejudice and lose spiritual presence of mind. Reflection is therefore necessary to test your inner (un)freedom. Due to this reflection and a willingness to criticize yourself and allow yourself to be criticized, you develop the ability to bear the responsibility for the situation. Self-knowledge and adequate judgement of the situation presume an active perceptive attitude. This requires learning to observe with an open mind and learning to think clearly.

2.3 Ethical Context

The fundamental values discussed above are in this chapter considered as values that belong together. Without equality, service cannot be mutual and has no shared perspective in life. Without service, spiritual presence of mind has no awareness of people's shared destiny. And without spiritual presence of mind, service and equality can become principles that cause unfreedom. Each of the three values may be individually recognized in the practice of caregiving and in existing ethical theories about caregiving. What is new is that they are here presented as an integrated whole, and in their reciprocal fullness.

2.3.1 Virtue

Practising these three fundamental values in the form of virtues (see section 2.7) is a reflection of a growing emphasis on character traits of caregivers. Thus ethicist J. S. Reinders writes:

> The conception of ethics presented here turns against the trend to externalize ethics through procedures and protocols, and take it out of the hands of the caregivers in their daily practice. It is their task and responsibility—and that of their teachers—to reflect on the question of how one can learn the profession in such a way that one can bear the responsibility

> for the daily work. The specifically ethical moment in such thinking about that responsibility lies in the question of which qualities one has to have for it as a person.[4]

And in an article about physicians as 'good caregivers':

> In reaction to regulation-ethics—which is primarily focused on the actions of the caregiver and the rights of the patient—Pellegrino and Thomasma are pleading for more attention for 'the good physician'. These authors acknowledge the importance of a bio-ethics based on rules and rights, but they emphasize the fact that the view becomes one-sided when the entire situation and the character traits of physicians and other caregivers are not taken into account. They advocate a new appreciation of the old ethics of virtue, which has also left its traces in the Hippocratic Oath.[5]

Regulation-ethics, which sets strict standards for the way one has to act, is evidently insufficient to assure professional action in caregiving. Ethicists have observed that basing moral decisions—which have to be made in complex caregiving situations—on a single ethical principle or fixed standard does not suffice. Ethical theory falls short in making responsible choices possible, whereas daily practice demands more and more self-knowledge on the part of the caregivers. Reinders points to the importance of moral sensibility, and sets the ethical approach of Aristotle as an example.

> Caregivers have to develop an approach that enables them to learn to regard their clients with fresh eyes again and again. [...] In other words, the quality of care begins with the qualities of those who have to do the work. [...] Developing the qualities of good caregiving means 'working hard on yourself', because these are properties one only develops in the course of many years' practice.[6]

Anthroposophical caregiving follows this approach by making the development of 'virtues' and working on 'self-education' central objectives. In its methodology this also receives an explicit place (see the following chapters).

2.3.2 Relationship

The emphasis on personal qualities is also an emphasis on the personal relationship, in which the giver and receiver of care are equal in their own individualities. The personal relationship is important in caregiving, as is the attitude one has when giving care. Ethicist Meininger thus writes evocatively about respect for the individuality of the other—the 'who'—which cannot be known except through a personal relationship, and which must not be reduced to the generally known—the 'what'. 'This individuality will primarily be understood in terms of an encounter that implies a question regarding the self-image and self-understanding of the caregiver.' (Meininger 1998) This approach seeks a proximity to the other, 'that opens the potential of true community, of responsiveness', and which seeks a balance between guardianship and distance. Meininger points to the need for caregivers to become conscious of their own vision of the human being, because it determines how they perceive and judge persons with disabilities. This consciousness of one's own convictions may be regarded as an extension of the value 'spiritual presence of mind', in which self-reflection is of central importance.[7]

Caregiving ethics also points to the importance of becoming conscious of one's own vision of the human being, and thus also of one's vision of oneself, in order to arrive at a balanced relationship in caregiving. Joan Tronto thus mentions the relativity of the self-image of the autonomous subject: 'we remain dependent on each other throughout our entire lives'.[8] Dependence and vulnerability are characteristics all human beings share. The modern ideal of the autonomous subject is a caricature of who we really are. In their need for care all people are equal; the caregiving relationship is therefore symmetrical.

Humanist philosopher Manschot adds two side notes to this view. We have to learn to understand the concept of autonomy more broadly. Independence consists in dealing consciously and maturely with the inevitable dependence that arises out of our own neediness, passions and vulnerability. This 'Socratic autonomy' is therefore not invulnerable independence, but the result of effort because the human being conquers his personal independence bit by bit from his infinite dependence. 'People who are called dependent because they need care given by others can, in the Socratic vision, be more independent and autonomous than others, exactly because they are more urgently confronted with the vulnerability of existence.'[9] Where people share the struggle with their own dependencies with each other, they can support each other in mutual engagement.

> The aim of friendly care is not the direct alleviation of needs. Its aim is to foster the existential autonomy of the other. [...] Friends become

> equals to the extent that they are involved in each other's life autonomy to develop a meaningful ('happy') life. [...] Without friendship any help inevitably risks becoming paternalistic, or serving other interests than that of providing care to a human being.[10]

This caregiving ethics can be viewed as an extension of the value 'sense of service'. The definition of care in care ethicists like Verkerk receives a distinctly humane content:

> Care is a feeling and supporting answer to the situation and circumstances of the vulnerable person in need of help. This is care that gives expression to our sympathy and connection with the well-being of the other, to our willingness to identify with the pain and suffering of the other, and to our longing to do what is possible to alleviate their situation.[11]

Duyndam distinguishes this care from service. 'Care has a surplus compared with service.' He points out that good caregivers 'are recognized and welcomed by their clients first of all based on their qualities as human beings, based on their individuality, within which they have integrated their technical-professional qualities in a personal manner'. He continues:

> This experience is fundamental. It is the experience that someone does something for you, or in better words, that in what someone does for you there is something that is 'free, extra', something for which you don't need to do anything in return, a gift that doesn't need to be rewarded or repaid. The 'content' of this gift is the acknowledgement that you matter, that you may be there.[12]

And he names as the value that moves someone to make this gift 'generosity', which he defines as the unconditional readiness to respond to a request for care. Underlying generosity is also the value 'service'.

2.3.3 Suffering

In ethical contemplations about care for handicapped people, suffering has traditionally been an important subject. The technical possibility to diagnose foetuses with an abnormality at an early stage and perhaps abort them has intensified the discussion about the question whether a life with serious handicaps is worth living. Ethics inspired by Christian theology, which places suffering in the context of a created world, often derives its rejection of abortion from the principle of equality.

> Being a person is not bound to any particular characteristic; it cannot be caught in any category invented by humans. This concept of person is of decisive significance for our thinking about the value of the life of handicapped children: they are complete persons, because they too were created in the image and likeness of God. The value of their lives is equal to the value of every other human life.[13]

The author is not blind to the grief of the parents and the suffering of the child, but views it as a shared responsibility of family, neighbours, friends, organizations and government agencies to offer the help that is needed to bear the pain.

On the other hand, there is a utilitarian ethics which, based on self-determination and lessening of suffering, gives the parents the right to prevent the child's suffering, and decide on their own capacity to bear grief.

> The rationality I plead for rests exclusively on the argument that it is a moral duty to lessen suffering, certainly in health care. [...] One person may find a life of a mentally retarded person in an institution a valuable life; another may see it differently. The parents are the ones who have to decide. [...] At any rate, it is a misunderstanding to think in the case of a newly born baby that his life has to be spared because he still has so much life to live. Exactly *because* he has so much life to live, the quality of that life is all the more important. Parents who opt for the death of their seriously handicapped newborn child deserve no blame. On the contrary, psychologically as well as morally such a choice is utterly understandable and justifiable.[14]

There exists no anthroposophical ethics that makes general pronouncements about the question of abortion of foetuses with serious disabilities. The freedom of the individual to choose his own way, and along that way increase his individual freedom, is the principal premise Rudolf Steiner worked out in his ethics. In his philosophical analysis of suffering Steiner arrives at the conclusion that a person can bear more suffering as he is more motivated by a certain striving in his will. Will power determines the power to bear.[15] Anthroposophy as spiritual science sets no standards, but offers the potential of relating more consciously to reality. Anthroposophical embryology, which goes together with a view of (re)incarnation, offers a distinct insight into the reality of being born. Biologist W. Schad says about this:

> There are experiences of mothers who enter into conversation with their unborn child. That would mean, if one does not regard this as a projection but as a real fact, that there exists an identity of the unborn child, which is independent of whether the body is alive or not. If you really accept this as experience, as evidence, then you have to dare to think further. There exists a body-free identity, which means post-existence, and therefore also pre-existence. Without asking these two questions, we cannot gain insight into what it means to be born.[16]

Such insight can help people give direction to their own striving.

This demonstrates that the way we deal with ethical dilemmas (Abortion or not? Allowing suffering or not?) is intrinsically connected with the vision we have of the human being and the world. Ethics without a vision of the human being makes no sense. This view is widely shared. For instance, Dupuis posits:

> The human being himself, meaning his well-being, his life, his existence and his interests form a criterion for morality. [...] If we want to give more content to this criterion we have to consult our vision of the human being. [...] Thus an image of the human being shows itself in which there is room for many sides of the human being, but in which in any case one aspect of being-human stands out: that the human being most of all is a rational being, or would have to be. [...] It is therefore impossible to separate a vision of the human being and morality from each other; they are two sides of the same coin. In other words, vision of the human being and morality are two perspectives on the same reality.[17]

It is therefore of crucial importance that anthroposophical caregiving is based on an explicit view of reality that understands itself as a methodologically and theoretically solidly grounded, rationally justified vision.

2.3.4 Person

In the ethics of caregiving we time and again run into the question: When is the human being a person? Is a damaged foetuses a person? Is an adult with an incompetent will a person? Is a senior with dementia a person? These questions indicate a presumption that being a person is a feature of someone with certain properties like rationality, judgement and a competent will. Whoever lacks these properties is in that view not a person, and less worthy of protection. Partly based on this reasoning interventions such as abortion, sterilization or euthanasia are being justified.

Pedagogue McGee (see note 4) rejects this reasoning by defining a person as 'a full human being—mind, body, spirit'. A person is no less a person when he has mental limitations. Reinders deepens this view by defining being a person 'not in terms of individual capacities, but of interpersonal relationships. [...] Being a person is not an essence, but an *existence*. As a person you only exist out of and facing the other.' Ethicist Vedder calls attention to the existing morality in our culture:

> Common parlance and our moral intuitions come to our aid here: it is very difficult for us to deny that individuals from the above categories (the disabled, comatose, demented) are persons. [...] Even though they may not be factually autonomous persons, they nevertheless share the special moral status of autonomous persons. They have that special status because, even if they will never grow into competent persons, based on their distinctive genetic constitution the above-mentioned inner natural goal-orientedness of the human being can be ascribed to them. For this reason, also a deeply disabled individual is called a person and is just as worthy of protection as a competent adult.[18]

Philosopher Spaemann[19] also comes to the conclusion that the criterion for personality lies in biologically belonging to the human species. In his opinion, all human beings are persons, irrespective of their limitations, and he gives six reasons. All human beings are biologically related, and by definition are in personal relationships with each other. There is no sliding transition through which 'something' becomes 'someone', and it is the recognition of the other as 'someone' that is for every child the prerequisite for the development of personal characteristics. Someone with disorders is certainly able to have specific intentions in his actions, even if others cannot clearly identify those. We do not view persons with profound mental limitations as animals, but as 'sick persons'; the fact that we acknowledge them as persons is the real reason for our self-respect. Being a person is not potential, but substance; something can never generate someone; someone is who he was and shall be as long as he lives. Every human being has an unconditional claim on a unique place in the community of human beings.

The question of being a person shows clearly that a judgement on the equality of all persons is inextricably connected with our vision of the human being. Especially in health care, where so many choices have to be made that directly affect people, the vision of the human being must not remain merely implicit.

2.4 Equality

2.4.1 The Growing Awareness of Equality

Between 1900 and 2000 an enormous change has taken place in the care of the disabled. This shows clearly in the changes in terminology. In the first half of the twentieth century people commonly spoke of the retarded, spiritually deficient, and inferior. The retarded was later called spiritually handicapped and later as mentally handicapped. The problem with these terms is that meaning is not broad enough, and especially that they contain no indication of equality. The new denominations are therefore based on the words 'human being' or 'person' with a descriptive addition, such as 'with mental limitations' or 'with unusual behaviour'. This indicates first of all that we have to do with a human being and that, in addition, there is something 'notably' the matter with this human being.

The search for the right way to name this group, for which a separate sector was even formed—care of the handicapped—is an omen, a sign for the fundamental impossibility to describe people with a deviating development without violating their equality.

Living in normality

Another sign for the striving in society toward explicit equality can be seen in the idea of normality which was advanced in the fifties of the last century. It goes as follows: mentally handicapped people must not be approached and treated differently; they should form part of normal life and be able to lead their lives like everyone else.

The implementation of this idea in practice was reinforced in the 1990s by the call for community care. Society, and first of all government agencies, have to guarantee access for people with handicaps, and encourage their participation.

Equal rights

The strongly growing notion that people with a handicap also have the right to exist and to lead a normal existence has in the past two decades focused primarily on the realm of rights. The United Nations has issued declarations in which discrimination on the basis of a handicap is prohibited. In other countries too, laws have been adopted to add handicap to the list of gender, race, religious conviction, etc. as a quality on which one may not discriminate.

In the field of care for the handicapped the term 'full-fledged citizenship' has come into use to address arrears and abuses. After all, a citizen with a handicap has the same right of access to a public space, transport or public event as anyone else. Out of this conviction an increasing number of laws have been adopted which, although they do not enforce this full-fledged citizenship, do further it. Institutions are enabled to let people with a handicap live among 'normal' people. People with handicaps are stimulated to work in companies. Children with handicaps have a right to education with special support.

In brief, in the twentieth century people with limitations have obtained a more autonomous place in society. They have more and more come to the fore as human beings, and have acquired fundamentally equal rights to participating and functioning in society. The law supports this vision of the handicapped person.

In society it may be called an extraordinary phenomenon that these changes in the way people with disabilities are regarded have taken place. The fact that this emancipation has developed is mostly thanks to the parents. They experience most directly how their child is different and still totally belongs. Equality of people with handicaps has therefore become an important value in the life of rights, and has broad political support.

Who and What?

The question has yet to be been answered on what view of the human being this value is based. A clear feeling has grown that these people must not be discriminated against and that they form part of society. In recent years efforts have also been made in the media, especially in television, to give them a larger role which, however, cannot disguise the fact that resistance against this still exists. This varies from country to country, but is still far from perfect. And abuse continues to be made of people's limitations.

The person with limitations also does not at all correspond with the ideal image of the (Western) human being as presented in the media: this person is beautiful, rich, strong, self-aware and autonomous. He leads his life the way he wants to, and the world is his oyster. The ideal person—the way we are always told—is an independent human being with a self-satisfied smile on his face.

This ideal picture is in sharp contrast with the person who is handicapped. For one or more handicaps will negatively affect his or her appearance. Normal people will decide at first sight that the other is abnormal. Although they will realize that the other is a human being too, they will focus on the abnormality.

In the practice of daily life, we take more notice of someone's secondary characteristics than on the core of his being. The 'what' is easier to catch than the 'who'. The what can be described and shared with others (it is a man with syndrome X). The who is the person himself, who he really is, this unique human being with an identity of his own. The what can be expressed in explicit knowledge; the who can only be experienced in the personal relationship in which the other—his individuality—is acknowledged. The other, just like myself, is a subject with his own identity. Awareness of characteristics causes distance from the other; personal engagement with the uniqueness of the other brings us close to him. Equality in a relationship can only be achieved on the level of the who.

2.4.2 Equality in the Anthroposophical View of Caregiving

In anthroposophical care of the handicapped, the problem of nomenclature also exists. The founder of anthroposophy, Rudolf Steiner, even came up with an entirely new term for 'these children'. He called them *seelenpflege-bedürftig*—in English 'in need of soul care'. Steiner put the emphasis on the attention and care for the soul of the child, for its balanced psychic development, of course without neglecting physical care and treatment. Further it has been reported that Steiner found it important that handicapped adults be addressed with *Sie*, the polite form of address in German, with which he underlined the fact of their equality.

What did become a generally accepted anthroposophical term is the expression 'healthy in the core of his being'. The human being with a developmental disability is damaged in the way he functions, but in the core of his being, where he is spirit, he is as unscathed as anyone else. The who is thus allotted an explicit place in reality, namely the spiritual being.

The Threefold Human Being

In the anthroposophical conception of the human being the distinction between what and who is made explicit. To begin with, this view speaks of four kingdoms of nature: the kingdom of the lifeless substances, the kingdom of the living plants, the kingdom of the ensouled animals, and the kingdom of the individual human beings. Since the rise of Darwinism and the theory of evolution, distinctions between kingdoms, especially between those of the animals and human beings, have become less and less common. In the twentieth century the difference between man and animal has become increasingly blurred, because in modem science spirit and soul have no place.

Anthroposophy speaks of a threefold picture of the human being, which is also common in philosophical literature: the human being as a composite of body, soul and spirit. Classical Greek philosophers recognized besides the body (*soma*) also the soul (*psyche*), which could express itself in a variety of soul functions, for example, in anger. But connected with the soul there was also a higher principle, that of the spirit (*nous*). Through the spirit it was possible to reach the world of the gods, and spiritual laws could be known. The spirit was able to penetrate to eternal truth. The human capacity that was truly spiritual was described as the cognitive capacity that rests on thinking (*noein*). For Aristotle (384–322 BC) the highest bliss consisted in experiencing divine life as a human being, by uncoupling concentrated thinking activity from concrete things, and focusing this activity on itself.

One essential aspect of anthroposophy is its new foundation of the threefold nature of the human being as body, soul and spirit. In his basic books, Rudolf Steiner conscientiously described the results of his research, as well as the methods by which he obtained these results.[20] One of these results is that each principal part consists itself of smaller parts. However, the concept 'part' has to be philosophically understood, not spatially. The 'parts' consists of forces, not of places.

Body

Someone has a *body*. A body is a separately discernible amount of space of a particular world, and is separated from its environment by a boundary. The most concrete example is the physical body, which is delimited by a skin, and although it is fully permeated by the physical laws that also reign in the physical environment (such as gravity), yet forms its own inner space within that environment. When this physical body is not alive, it cannot hold fast to this inner space of its own. It is in fact also a second body, the *life body*, that maintains the physical body in its form. The human body is a living body, an organism.

In caregiving, attention to bodily functions and the body itself are of fundamental importance. Physical health is a primary objective. This health makes it possible to further and strengthen the life of the soul and the working of the spirit.

Soul

Besides a body, a person also has an inner life, a *soul life*, in which one's own emotions are experienced that arise in reaction to perceptions of the outside world. The most important reactions to those perceptions are, on the one hand, the pictures the soul makes for itself of the world—consciously, and unconsciously—on the basis of its interpretation (judgement) and, on the other hand, the feelings the soul connects with things by finding them attractive or repulsive. The manner in which a person forms pictures and feelings is strictly personal.

The way a caregiver handles a soul problem or need is by mediating between the inner life and the outwardly perceptible world. It is important to nourish the soul by the path of observation—of nature and through art and culture. Because human beings can think, judge and choose independently, their soul life will gradually develop an increasingly individual character. This is exactly what is lacking in an animal. An animal remains dependent on its instinctive reaction capacity, and will only through human intervention show human-like reactions.

Spirit

A person is a *spiritual being*. This being stirs when it says 'I' to itself, a word that can only be used and have meaning from within. This happens only in human beings, never in animals. The self-consciousness that is present in me when I stand awake in the world indicates the presence of this I. However, the I never appears before me as a thing. To experience it I have to activate myself as a spiritual being. This I-being, which I usually do not observe but which I am, wants to develop itself. Development is a fundamental characteristic of everything that is spiritual. Because in animals the spirit is not concretely and individually present, animals do not have this need. Human beings do.

You enter into a person's question of development in caregiving by discovering who the other is. How does this person want to develop, and which talents does he or she want to unfold in life?

Development

In many anthropological contemplations the who and what of the human being stand beside each other as a duality. They are then two aspects of an individual that do not touch each other. The anthroposophical view offers a conceptual framework to connect these two aspects with each other. The connecting link lies in the spiritual development of the human being. Because the term 'development' is of key importance for the spiritual-scientific conception of the human being of anthroposophy, it has to be briefly clarified. In daily parlance there is nothing that would not be able to develop. In most cases the term can be replaced by 'a non-arbitrary change'.

In its anthroposophical meaning an inner dynamic is added to the term develpment. In development an invisible essence is at work, a lasting spiritual lawfulness, that forms the changes and directs the entire developmental process. This essence expresses itself in our world of space and time (nature), and lets the consecutive stages of the developmental process appear in it. New manifestations then arise successively. We can speak of development if it is the same essence all the time, which lets a new stage appear and determines the successive process in such a way that the series of stages forms a whole.

Frank Teichmann shows that the spiritual concept of development is a young, Middle-European discovery. As a concept it was indeed a real discovery which, however, was never taken up by the modern sciences. The anthroposophical conception of the human being, however, follows this discovery.

> On the appearance side, we see how a thing continuously changes over the course of time, does not stay at any one point, and gradually undergoes transformation through various stages according to a system of laws. We can observe a plant, for example, how it pushes out the cotyledons from the seed, then spreads leaf after leaf along the stem, before opening its flower to the sunlight, setting fruit, and finally giving the seed once more to the soil.

> We should not forget that this whole process is the expression of a *being*, which we name with a particular name, and which is *present* at every moment of the development. Looked at as a being, we cannot speak of changes in time, for it is this being that encompasses and directs these changes according to its innate laws. We do not apply the name to a particular moment of the plant's unfolding, but to the period of its appearance as a whole. A rose is already a rose when it is just a shoot, and is also recognized as a rose when it is leafing or blossoming or forming fruit. The *being* lives at an extra-temporal and extra-spatial level; it works into our world and appears here in space and time.
>
> We can only speak of development when the connection between being and appearance is really present in our consciousness simultaneously. [...]
>
> So, if we wish to think in terms of development, there are two faculties we need to develop: the ability to follow movement consciously with our mind (to follow movement in our mental picturing), and the ability to think holistically, when at every moment we have an overview of the entire complex of relationships.[21]

What sets this (spiritual) idea of development apart is that it can only be fruitfully applied if human beings develop their own cognitive capacities.[22] From a cultural-historical perspective it is interesting that, as the idea of development arose in science, a noteworthy renewal also took place in literature with the *Bildungsroman*, the 'development novel'. In such a novel the principal character does not remain as he was; he comes into interaction with his surroundings which continually awakens new capacities in him that let him become more and more individual as he meets ever new situations in his life. The character develops himself phase after phase by becoming self-aware of who he is and has always been.

In the anthroposophical study of the human being this idea of development is worked out further by investigating the human biography as a path of development of an individual. This path of development runs according to a lawfulness that belongs to the human being who consists of body, soul and spirit, The biography consists of a physical development into adulthood, soul development into world citizen, and spiritual development into maturity and wisdom. Through it all runs the path of development which this unique human being goes, and which brings the individual being to development.

The anthroposophical caregiver will therefore look for the path of development all humans go, each in their own individual biography, no matter how disabled or handicapped they may be.

Karma and Reincarnation

In the same period when the idea of development arose, the idea of reincarnation was also rediscovered in Central Europe. The idea of reincarnation is the consequence of the idea of development. When we view the human being as a spiritual being that wants to develop, reincarnation is a logical consequence. In 1780 already German philosopher Lessing (1729-1781) pointed in a remarkable way to the plausibility of the idea of reincarnation. This logical necessity was also extensively elucidated by Rudolf Steiner, who described a method to arrive at empirical research on this subject with the aid of spiritual observation and cognitive capacities.[23]

Lessing wrote:

> Frequently, the dreamer sees very clearly how the future will be, only he is not able to wait for that future. He wants that future to break through as quickly as possible, and he wants that to be his work. The harvest for which nature takes its time for thousands of years has to ripen in the brief time of his life. For what good is it to him if the things of which he sees that they are better aren't achieved during his life? Will he come back? Does he believe that he will come back?
>
> Go your way, eternal providence, a way we are hardly aware of. But let me not fall into despair because of you, not even when it seems that you are going back in your steps. It is not true that the shortest line is always the straight one.
>
> There is so much you have to take with you on your eternal way; to make so many side steps. And how? And what if it were perfectly obvious that the great, slow wheel that brings humanity closer to perfection is put in motion by smaller, faster wheels, which all contribute to that?
>
> That way and no other way! The path along which humanity arrives at its perfection first has to be covered by everyone individually, one earlier, another later. It has to be covered in one and the same life? Can he have been a Jew and a Christian in one single life? Can he have left both behind in one single life?

> Certainly not! But why couldn't everyone have lived in this world more than once?
>
> Is the reason why this supposition is so ridiculous the fact that it is the oldest one? Because it arose in the human intellect immediately, before sophism and school had confused it and robbed it of its power?
>
> Why wouldn't I come back as often as I am able to gain new knowledge and new capacities? Do I acquire in one life so much that it is not worth the trouble to come back?
>
> Is that the reason? Or because I forget that I have been here before? It is a good thing that I forget it. The memory of the circumstances of a prior life would take away the possibility to make good use of the circumstances under which I am living now. And what I have to forget so that I can live now, have I forgotten that for all eternity?[24]

Every incarnation of a human individual can be understood as a form of manifestation. The human individuality as eternal entity connects itself with a physical substance (the foetus) and begins a human life to go through a development. Afterwards, the body of the person in question dies and the eternal individuality withdraws in order, at a later time and often in entirely different circumstances, to appear again by connecting with a new human foetus. A human spiritual being can manifest itself exclusively in a human body, and will therefore never re-embody as an animal, because no individual development can take place in an animal body.[25]

The relationship between the successive incarnations is maintained by the eternal individuality, which forms their unity. Just as the fruit comes only after the leaf is formed, one capacity follows after another. This process is governed by an intrinsic law that encompasses the total of our incarnations. This law is a law of development and its name is karma. Just as the fruit is the biological consequence in the development of a plant, similarly, and not arbitrarily but according to this law, karma brings consequences in the process of development of a human being with it. The fruit is not fate, not punishment, not revenge, but an organic consequence of the law of plant development. In the same way the course of a human life is to be viewed as a series of events and conditions that form the consequence of karmic law. This karmic law of development is intrinsically connected with the human spirit. This being does not undergo the consequences, they are part of its deepest essence.

Things look different for our everyday self-awareness. We usually observe our life circumstances and events without being able to view them in their mutual relationships, and most often without being able to interpret them as manifestations of karmic consequences. It happens not infrequently—and Tolstoy is an example—that when people at the end of their life look back, they can declare that everything went the way it had to. That is an indication that the course of life conceals a path of development that is governed by karmic consequences.

Karmic consequences may take the form of encounters we have with people, events that happen to us, and of the bodily constitution with which we go through life. They form our destiny, not things that arbitrarily happen—not coincidence therefore—but things that belong to us as spiritual beings, because they form part of our individual development.

In the light of the above, the equality of human beings means that all humans are spiritual entities who want to develop themselves, and all humans go through a path of development that encompasses many lives on earth, in which each life is a phase.

This concept of reality is critical for anthroposophical caregiving. The duality of who and what changes into a unity of being-and-manifestation, which forms the basis of the fundamental value of equality, and gives it its content.

2.5 Sense of Service

The insight that all human beings are equal in their deepest essence encourages a respectful feeling of being related to the other as a fellow human being. Because this equality in the anthroposophical view is connected with an individual path of development through many incarnations this relationship gets an extra dimension of being development oriented. We humans go side by side on the way toward self-realization. We are in the same boat because as part of humanity we have the same origin. We are in the same boat because we share in the destiny of humanity and that of each other. We are companions on one and the same way toward self-realization. This self-realization has the intrinsic goal of freedom of will (see also section 2.6).

Altruism

The insight that our path of development is connected with that of our fellow human beings offers a basis to give egoism a place. Egoism is an important driving force for people to take their own development in hand. It is therefore not reasonable to reject egoism as morally evil. But the question is whether egoism stimulates someone to self-realization or keeps him away from it. If egocentric persons can see themselves as spiritual and reincarnating beings, they will become able to put their lives here and now into a broader context. The larger that context is, the more they can recognize their fellow humans as part of their own life situation. They can then see that serving their own interests may coincide with serving the interests of others. In that way, a form of altruism comes into being out of a well-understood egoism.

Altruism, of course, may also lead to a situation where we keep others away from their self-realization. Patronizing people for their own sake is of no help to them. We can only serve the interests of others if we can help them out of their own perspective of (spiritual) development. Serving others presupposes an awareness of equality: both of us are spiritual beings with an individual path of development. Out of this awareness the relationship can be seen in the light of mutual service.

Meeting

In anthroposophical caregiving this value of service becomes visible in the striving to make the relationship between caregiver and care receiver into a personal meeting, the 'art of the meeting' as it is often called. I come upon you, you come upon me, and when we come together, a meeting occurs. This meeting as a coming together has in the modern sense of the word received the deeper significance of discovery. A real meeting is a dis-covering in which the truth of the other comes to light. In the meeting we feel secure, and behind all that hides and conceals us—such as being burdened with shortcomings—our true being can light up.

Now, with 'normally gifted' people it is already a real art to come to such a true meeting. With people with developmental disabilities it may sometimes be much more difficult. Yet, it may in such cases also be possible to discover them in their true being, sometimes by focusing especially on what they call up in us, or by looking at the way other people react in the vicinity of these persons.

Inner space

Another service aspect of caregiving is to give others space for their own views and to support them in their inner striving. People who have to be cared for or supported have their own cultural and religious background. They look for their own relationship with the values and norms of life. When adults with limitations orient themselves culturally or in their view of life, they deserve to be supported, not directed. Caregivers are then asked to let go of their own convictions, without denying those. Religious experiences, for example, can be extremely diverse, and need not be made uniform.

The Earth

Humanity is a part of Mother Earth; we belong to nature. In the anthroposophical view the earth is also a living organism. The three kingdoms of nature at the disposal of the human being—minerals, plants and animals—form an integral part of the evolution of humanity. These realms too have their origin in a spiritual world; these realms too have a future in a spiritual world. For that reason, the theological concept of 'stewardship'—the human being has to take good care of creation—is too limited. Not only does humanity have a responsibility for the well-being of flora and fauna now and for the sake of future generations, it also has a responsibility for the spiritual integration of these kingdoms in the distant future. For this reason it is of great importance that the human being in a spiritual-scientific way penetrates into nature in its inner cohesion, for example, by including the spiritual (Goethean) concept of development. Service to our fellow humans can in this way be enlarged to service to the earth and all its inhabitants.

Brotherhood

Service as a fundamental value in caregiving can also be viewed in the light of the ideal of brotherhood as this has of old been pursued in communities: sharing life with each other. Medieval monastic life was built on people's readiness to be of service to the whole of the community. In olden times, a new member was required to sacrifice himself for the brotherhood. In today's culture brotherhoods no longer exist on the basis of obedience and self-denial. Brotherhood can come into being by entering into a self-chosen and self-willed connection with other people based on an ideal. Then it is the ideal that is shared: you make a commitment toward the same mission.

In some caregiving organizations—for instance those inspired by Karl König or Jean Vanier[26]—a form of living community is pursued in which individuals with limitations are completely integrated. People live and work together, everyone counts and participates, and is there for the other. Service is practised by the readiness to share your own life completely with the others. Children with a limitation, for example, are completely taken into the family of the caregivers. This is often a striving out of the ideal of Christian neighbourly love. This radical form of brotherhood is not easy to maintain in our modern times. Parts of it, such as consciously chosen neighbours, spending leisure time together, or working together, are easier to keep up.

2.6 Spiritual Presence of Mind

Presence of mind is here presented as a value, but in its spiritual sense, as used by Rudolf Steiner in his book *How to Know Higher Worlds*.[27] What is meant is the spiritual presence of the human being in the here and now. The anthroposophical conception of the human being includes that on our path of development we can, to a progressively increasing degree, become spiritually 'awake'. This wakefulness stands as an Aristotelian virtue in the middle between two vices: sleepiness and obsession. Sleepy is a person who is 'not really with it', who is overwhelmed by fatigue, apathy, lack of interest, numbness, absent-mindedness. Obsessed is a person who is 'beside himself', because a certain capacity, a certain interest, a certain fixation takes possession of him. Awake are those who 'have a grip on themselves', who are and remain 'with it' and with themselves, who are grounded and rest in themselves. It is this form of conscious, attentive presence that is meant with 'spiritual presence of mind'. In the anthroposophical view of the human being this presence is seen as the consequence of an active, self-willed connection of the I with thinking. Thinking is the invisible capacity in human beings that enables them to observe, comprehend and know.

This spiritual presence expresses itself in the ability to form a sound judgement on the situation in which we find ourselves. We are not caught unawares in the situation and are not at its mercy. We stand in the situation with lucid judgement, and decide in true spiritual presence of mind what to do. When we are thus present, we are actively present as an I. When we have spiritual presence of mind we are 'right there', in the middle of the event, because we see through the event with our thinking and therefore act appropriately.

Reflection

How do I know that I am awake? How do I know how awake I am? I have to enter into a relationship with myself to become able to answer these questions. Reflection is more than literally looking in a mirror; it is the ability to contemplate ourselves in our inner world, to observe ourselves inwardly, and thereupon know ourselves. The human being is uniquely able to do this. We can focus our cognitive capacity on ourselves.[28] There has to be a capacity in me that raises me above myself.

In his *Philosophy of Freedom* Rudolf Steiner indicated that such a capacity does indeed exist and can be discovered when I analyse my cognitive capacities. When I know the world, conditions keep arising in my soul—conditions, for instance, like: wild, falling, crying, cause. The contents of such conditions have to become clear by bringing them into relationship with other conditions. A relationship, such as between cause and effect, cannot be perceived by the senses; you have to understand it. Understanding a relationship usually goes so quickly that it has escaped your attention before you know it. But you can try to deliberately direct your attention to it. You then discover a quick moment when you create connections between different contents. The capacity to create such connections may be called 'pure thinking in concepts'. The activity that is hereby referred to is dependent on my active attention and complete dedication of will. As soon as your attention flags, you no longer think the relationship between concepts purely; you then pass over to associative thinking based on habit.

We can direct this thinking activity, which is full of concepts, to outer observations, which can thus become known in their interrelationships (a wild child falls and begins to cry). We can also direct this thinking activity to our own inner world and come to know our own feelings and emotions in their interrelationships (concern, compassion, and guilt feeling made me rush to its aid). Thus with my thinking activity I possess a capacity to reflect on myself. In other words, in spiritual presence of mind reflection is possible; and without the (intuitive) capacity to think spiritual presence of mind is not possible.

Freedom

Thanks to thinking we human beings are able to create relationships with things and ourselves. This possibility of reflection gives us a realization of freedom. For we can disengage ourselves from all our bonds by reconsidering them. But freedom can not only consist of distancing ourselves from something. We would then withdraw from the world and remain caught in our subjectivity.[29] Human beings also want to be able to make connections with the world in freedom and change them. Can freedom also penetrate into action? That is only possible if human beings can integrate the thinking they have themselves accomplished into their actions. The freedom that then arises can be called freedom of will: we, thinking humans, determine ourselves the content of our actions.

However, our actions can be made unfree by many factors. We may be driven by many motives—ambition, greed, etc.—to achieve something we have thought about. In a free act the driving force—the will power that moves us to something—also has to be free. This is only possible if the driving force proceeds from free thinking activity itself. Rudolf Steiner named this driving force as the power of love that enables us in our thinking activity to completely dedicate ourselves to the contents of our thinking. This love is an integral part of the pure activity of thinking, and it is with this love that we perform our free deeds.[30]

The content of the free deed is determined out of thinking. Our own thought (a purely ideal content of a condition) becomes the foundation of our action ('first quiet the other children down'). If this thought also wants to become a factual deed, it must be connected with the world in which we live. We have to engage our imagination creatively to bring to realization what we will. A free deed is not characterized by loftiness (of content), but by the consciousness and definition with which we think our deed, see it before us, and perform it out of love for the goal of our action.

Intuition

Steiner used the term intuition for the freely thought thinking content. Intuition can be connected with observations in order to know them, or with our own will in order to act. Steiner's term is a technical term, and therefore means something quite different from what is usually understood as intuition. In common parlance the term refers to an idea one gets, or a spontaneous event. In such a case there is no freedom of will, but rather a (possibly meaningful) coincidence. We can later reflect on the ideas individually, and make ourselves conscious of what they contain. In that process of making things conscious, insight may arise into the deeper significance of the idea. Steiner's concept of intuition, however, differs from this idea because complete consciousness does not take place after the action, but before or during the action. For an intuition in Steiner's sense consists only of making a thought content that is not observable to the senses fully conscious in a loving way. Spiritual presence of mind is needed when we strive for the right action in a situation out of an intuition in the sense of the word meant here. Acting out of spiritual presence of mind presupposes a capacity of intuition. Freedom of will and spiritual presence of mind come together in the action in the situation.

In the Situation

An exceptional aspect of human beings—and certainly caregivers—is that, on the one hand, they form part of a situation and, on the other hand, want to purposefully change that situation. They can do this by making a consciously willed decision and let this decision control their actions. In their actions they must then bring their willed decision into harmony with the situation. Out of insight in the (unique) situation, they introduce an intuitively determined action into it that is closely bound up with only that situation. They do not execute what they had previously considered, but they decide in the moment which deed they now want to perform.

In caregiving, finding resourceful solutions to often difficult situations is a daily challenge and a great art. This art is not something that can simply be learned or handed on; it is a question of learning as we go along, a process of stumbling and getting up again. When we have the opportunity to change situations out of freedom, we practise developing spiritual presence of mind. Out of this presence of mind individuals can perform services for each other on their own personal path of development. The perspective of this service is the growth of the spiritual presence of mind in the other.

2.7 Consequences: Practising the Fundamental Values

2.7.1 Practical Effects of Equality

The awareness of fundamental equality makes it possible to show respect in the way we approach and treat each other; respect for individuals who are going their own paths of development as spiritual beings, and are in their current appearance, in this incarnation, in need of help.

Today respect for a person who needs care has become a self-evident requirement in the profession. Part of the professional ethics is respect for the person in question, irrespective of any particular properties. Out of respect for the person, professionals are expected to give him or her good information, carefully discuss the treatment ahead of time with them, etc. However, respect as a general norm of decency may in practice be a rather distant and legalistic content. Respect then degenerates into not much more than observing certain rules that prevent you from undervaluing the person. This formal kind of respect lacks human engagement.

Reverence

Out of the anthroposophical view of equality another dimension can be added to respect. Respect can grow to reverence for the spiritual individuality with whom we are dealing, and for their path of development, part of which we are permitted to witness. The word reverence is here used in a religious sense in that we stand in awe of the divine in the other. In order to achieve this form of reverence for a fellow human being we have to be able to develop a relationship to a spiritual (divine) world in general.

This search for a conscious relationship to the spiritual as the ground of (human) existence is a defining characteristic of anthroposophical caregiving. This actively sought connection with the supersensory world, which is to be based on personal experience, is a distinguishing hallmark. The mere search for this connection alone already supports the growth of reverence and works through into the professional caregiving relationship.

Respect and reverence can be fostered in a practical way by attending religious and also cultural activities. It is for this, and also for other reasons, that in anthroposophical caregiving organizations religious events, such as annual festivals or religious events, are felt to be important. They enrich the lives of the handicapped people and, in addition, offer the caregivers the possibility to strengthen their feelings of reverence (see also section 4.5.3).

> Each moment that we spend becoming aware of whatever derogatory, judgemental, and critical opinions still remain in our consciousness brings us closer to higher knowledge. We advance even more quickly if, in such moments, we fill our consciousness with admiration, respect, and reverence for the world and life. Anyone experienced in these things knows that such moments awaken forces in us that otherwise remain dormant.[31]

Modesty

In order to open ourselves to feelings of reverence it is important to practise modesty. From the point of view of natural science the human being is a minuscule piece of dust in an infinite universe. But this does not necessarily mean that the human being is worthless, if we can also conceive that our material multiplicity originates from a spiritual unity. Human beings not only form part of the earth, and therefore of the universe, but also of a spiritual world to which they belong. This realization that we are part of a great whole calls for modesty.

Acceptance

The striving to penetrate to our origin in the spiritual world may be strengthened by examining the course of our own life. If we manage to sit back and take a quiet look at the things we went through in life, without regrets and without pride, we might perhaps discover a red thread. That may be helpful to gradually better accept our own course of life. Modern people are used to thinking that they can make their own lives; they have lost the inclination to accept things as they are. The more we can take our lives the way they are, the better will we be able to develop a sense of gratitude. Such acceptance can help us deal with the presence of limitations.

Virtues

In the above we have named specific virtues that belong to equality. Modesty by knowing that we are part of an encompassing whole, reverence for the origin of humanity, and acceptance of life as it is. By developing those virtues we fulfil an important condition for giving good care.

2.7.2 Practical Effects of the Sense of Service

Intention

In the caregiving relationship with persons with developmental disabilities the sense of service as a fundamental value is needed to prevent the possibility that caregivers misuse their position of power. Service will base itself on the intention to do what is good for the other, with a view to that person's path of development as a fellow human being, to enhance his or her own spiritual presence of mind. Caregivers can easily manipulate persons with disabilities by making them believe that the world is other than it is. They can evoke feelings in them that point them in a certain direction. This may happen 'with the best of intentions'. But then the question arises: With what intentions exactly? The professional morality of the caregiver will therefore have to be based on the sense of service as a fundamental value in the above-described sense.

Sense of Community

One of the fundamental objectives of anthroposophical caregiving organizations is that they want to stimulate social abilities. Caregiving that focuses on development aims in the first instance on individualization, which completely depends on freeing the soul. As spiritual beings, we can gradually learn to direct and free ourselves. To learn this, however, we depend on encounters with other human beings. Our own development is connected with that of others. Having encounters and entering into human connections is therefore inextricably linked with our own individualization process.[32]

For this reason cultural life receives a lot of attention in anthroposophical caregiving organizations. Making music together or play-acting—also attending performances—stimulates the encounter. Art brings spiritual inspiration and material substance together, and opens space for our own human creativity. Cultural activities bring people together. In creativity individuals form a team together or become each other's opponents (see also sections 4.2.1 and 4.6).

In the organization of daily life caregivers also try to strengthen social abilities. For example, meals are arranged as a social process that begins and ends together.

Work

An everyday form of service, which is sometimes not recognized as such, is performing work or labour (see also section 4.6). Whereas in olden times work still served people to take care of themselves and keep themselves alive, in our time we all depend on the labour of others to take care of our own needs. Everything we take in as food, wear as clothing, use as appliances—it has all been produced and made available to us by others. As consumers we are anything but self-supporting. Performing labour or work, as physical and spiritual efforts of human beings, with the goal to put something (an economic value) into the world, can be considered as a form of service. The activity is intended directly for other people, and that is what gives it its value. This is equally true for unpaid as for paid work.

For adults performing work is an essential part of life. For people with developmental disabilities this is no less the case. You can mean something for others, also if you are in certain respects more dependent than others. Our feeling of self-worth comes from the meaning we have for other people. Creating economic value for others gives meaning to our lives.

Based on this vision, anthroposophical caregiving organizations discovered the significance of work and labour already in the 1950s. In the course of time, many different ways have been found to enable persons with disabilities to perform useful work. This practice of looking for ways to enable others to become service-oriented is a consequence of the sense of service as a fundamental value.

Landscape, Agriculture and Food

Service, in the religious, cultural, and economic sense, also includes care of nature. Without nature there is no culture. A sense of service to the earth and its inhabitants means caring effectively for a healthy earth, for a healthy life upon earth, for the flourishing of nature. Vice versa, a healthy earth also contributes to the well-being of humanity. The way the landscape in the immediate environment is arranged, for example, has an effect on the physical and psychic well-being of the people who live there. This is equally true for the arrangement of a built-up area. We can go even further. The way food is grown and prepared also has consequences for our physical and psychic well-being. In anthroposophical caregiving institutions the layout of the property, architecture, and food receive a lot of attention. They are carefully considered based on well-defined premises (organic architecture, anthroposophic principles of nourishment, colours—see also section 4.5.1).

Virtues

This leads us to the specific virtues that belong to the value of service. To be able to be of service to other persons, caregivers have to have the ability to deal with their own feelings and emotions in a sincere, unbiased manner. This ability can be developed by disciplining the three soul functions of thinking, feeling, and the will in a certain way. Our thoughts have to be taught to remain objective, the feelings have to be taught to stay in inner balance, and the will has to learn to stay steadfast and receptive. Rudolf Steiner gave six basic exercises that can help strengthen and harmonize the three soul functions.[33] If these functions are not harmonized it will have an impact on the interaction between people. The basic exercises make it possible to deal more freely with the feelings and emotions of other people. This in turn makes a more free unfolding of the soul functions in those individuals easier. Virtues we strengthen by means of these exercises are concentration, steadfastness, equanimity, tolerance, positivity, and open-mindedness.[34]

Another virtue that belongs to this is that of compassion. This virtue is in our time not much appreciated anymore; it is branded as rather unbusinesslike, sentimental, and misleading. The negative aspects of compassion do indeed show when it functions as the principal driving force of someone's actions. Whoever acts only out of compassion perhaps wants to deliver himself of his compassion. However, compassion can also be handled in a more objective manner as a form of observation. Then it receives the quality of empathy, the capacity to live into the other's world of experience. With the aid of this compassion we can better understand someone else's life situation. Strengthening this virtue enables us to better recognize what is going on in a situation.[35]

2.7.3 Practical Effects of Spiritual Presence of Mind

Meditation

An important help to increase spiritual presence of mind is the practice of meditation, in particular the anthroposophical way of meditating. Anthroposophy views meditation differently from many other spiritual streams. Both in word- and in image meditation, it begins with becoming conscious of the meaning of the words or images you take as meditation content. With your own spirit power you first try to make as clear as possible what exactly they contain. The words or images will work most effectively as meditation content if they are a reflection of a spiritual quality. Then they were formed by persons who were initiated and knew the spiritual world from their own experience.[36]

Your reverence of the spiritual world can then be directed toward the meditation content. You try to fill the process of becoming conscious of the words or images with reverence of their content. Thereupon the meditant tries to permeate himself with this content in complete attention and reverence, to the exclusion of any other content of consciousness. This does not ask for passivity, but total activity because the content is made present by myself. In this meditation situation, in which I find myself alone with a self-willed content, there is a continual battle for spiritual presence of mind. By meditating and engaging in this battle I can progressively become a better judge of my own level of concentration.

Knowing

In order to be able to act in a situation I have to know it, including myself. A prerequisite for achieving a cognitive process is spiritual presence of mind. It is needed to observe precisely and to discover how the observations are interrelated. Anthroposophy is based on a philosophical cognitive theory that investigates the relationship between observation and thinking. It goes beyond the purpose of this book to go into more detail on this cognitive theory.

In order to enhance the cognitive process I will have to train two capacities: my observation and my thinking. Good caregivers are almost always good observers. They see how someone is doing. Their observations are accompanied by clear judgement, which allows them out of their expertise to arrive quickly at conclusions. Building such expertise demands the schooling of both observation and thinking.

In anthroposophical training programmes special modules are often created for this. Observation can, for example, be practised on the world of plants, of painting, or of a case history. The thinking capacity is challenged by, for example, discussing illnesses in polarities (see also sections 3.4.2 and 7.2.2, and Appendix 1).

Knowing Another Person

Rudolf Steiner made a distinct difference in his theory of cognition between humanity as a generality and this human being as an individual in the here and now. The relationship to humanity as a generality is of a scientific nature and is focused on knowledge of the species as part of living and ensouled nature. The relationship to the human being as an individuality is of a different kind. The individual is not a specimen of the species. Specimens are interchangeable; human individuals are not. Steiner therefore sometimes called the individuality 'a species in itself'.

The individuality viewed as its own species can only be understood out of its own nature, by observation of the unique and specific properties of this individuality. A forming of concepts can therefore only proceed from the observation of this specific aspect. Knowledge of other individuals is insufficient to know another human being as a (spiritual) individuality. Whereas with knowledge of a particular syndrome we may already know a lot about another individual with this syndrome, with general knowledge of human characteristics we do not yet know anything about this one individual. For this individual we are dependent on all kinds of observations, including possibly supersensory observations. Especially in learning to know another human being we have to focus our thinking with an open mind on what we can observe in the encounter.

Openness to Critique

In caregiving it has become common practice to evaluate together, for instance in the form of a discussion about the way a person functions, or in team meetings. During the evaluation pronouncements are made about people. Of course, critique of someone's actions and attitudes will also be brought out in an evaluation. Caregivers have to learn to bear this critique, and learn to welcome it as an aid in their development. The flipside of the freedom to make instant decisions in a situation and take responsibility for these yourself, is the willingness to accept responsibility and the intention to take additional training.

What can help in this is to look back every evening on the course of the day with questions such as: What was working? When did I touch reality? Where did I function as an obstacle? It is a form of self-reflection during which we try to look objectively at our own behaviour. If we succeed in watching our own deeds without judgement, in a kind of quiet of soul, in equanimity, and with the courage to face our own failings with a cool head, or to remember our successes impassively, we create in ourselves an instrument to be objective, also vis-à-vis ourselves (see also section 6.8).

> Being able to look at our own experiences, joys, and sorrows as if they belonged to someone else is a good preparation for spiritual training. We can gradually acquire this ability to the necessary extent by taking time after our day's work is done to allow our experiences of the day to pass in front of us in the spirit. We should see ourselves in the images of these experiences; that is, we must look in on ourselves in our daily lives as if from outside.[37]

> As students of higher knowledge we must find the strength to view ourselves as we would view strangers. We must face ourselves with the inner tranquility of a judge. If we achieve this, our own experiences will reveal themselves in a new light. As long as we are still woven into our experiences, and stand within them, we will remain as attached to the non-essential as to the essential. But once we have attained the inner peace of the overview, the non-essential separates itself from the essential. Sorrow and joy, every thought, every decision will look different when we stand over against ourselves in this way.[38]

Purposefulness

Part of a development-oriented form of caregiving also has to be an explicit consciousness of the goals of caregiving. One of the tasks of anthroposophical caregiving is to support an individual path of development (which includes several incarnations). Knowledge of the conception of the human being and the world is required to be able to give this support a conscious direction. At the same time, the encounter with the other has to lead to insight into that person's own biographical development.

Out of the general view of the human being you can understand the importance of work for adult persons; but the next question is which trade, which profession belongs to this individual? Out of this biographical perspective a concrete purpose has to be determined. Even the small parts of the caregiving plan, such as the purpose of teaching someone to brush his teeth, require insight into the why—insight in the general purpose as well as insight in its importance for this one human being. The more consciously a purpose is handled, the more inventive can the way to it be (see also sections 4.2, 6.6, 6.7, and 8.2.2).

Virtues
Specific virtues in the realm of spiritual presence of mind can be called cognitive virtues. In classical philosophy already, including Aristotle, the cognitive capacities of the human being were seen as dependent on the acquisition of virtues, on strengthening certain personal characteristics. An important virtue that belongs to spiritual presence of mind is open-mindedness. Without it we are burdened by prejudice, preferences, and precepts. If we are full of prejudice we cannot observe with an open mind, we cannot know objectively and act freely. The ability to meet the factual situation in an unprejudiced way is an important prerequisite for judging the situation adequately, and for performing an intuitive deed in it in freedom. The same is true for people with preferences and partialities, because of which they will always appreciate one thing and turn down another. And if we let ourselves be guided by precepts we also do not meet the situation with an open mind.

Other virtues that particularly belong to a striving for knowledge and for inner freedom are those of patience and perseverance. Without patience and without perseverance you cannot make any progress on the way to insight and freedom. Exercising patience assumes the confidence that your active commitment will in the long term bear fruit. Human striving continually runs into things that undermine it, such as outer circumstances, inner distractions, personal vices. Every human striving requires a stubborn and imperturbable keeping-at-it against all obstacles that may arise. To keep going imperturbably and in all patience and confidence—this is essential if we want to reach our goal as human beings. In this regard, persons with visible functional disabilities such as a mental handicap or psychiatric disturbance are no different from persons who have no ostensible handicap.

2.8 Discussion: Professionalism between Ideal and Reality

2.8.1 Standards or Values?

In an ethically grounded organization such as sketched above the danger arises that the ideals become standards, and that the values are converted into precepts. In the twentieth century it happened not infrequently in anthroposophical caregiving organizations that co-workers became burned out because they considered themselves subservient to the interests of the organization, partly because people did indeed expect that of each other. As soon as an ideal functions as a standard and is not carried by one's own striving, the individual is weakened. That way the opposite is achieved from what is intended.

Therefore, the fundamental values must not be imposed as standards, but should be shown as ideals. It is the group of co-workers that keeps the ideals alive or lets them fade. Keeping the ideals alive presumes a strong connection with the view of reality from which the ideals originated. It is therefore extremely valuable for the co-workers to discuss the ideas and ideals with each other and make them as tangible as possible.

The three fundamental values or ideals that were described can also help to make those same ideals more concrete. There has to be equality between the ideals and myself, so that I am not sacrificed to the ideals, and the latter are not adapted to my wishes. There has to be a sense of service to the ideals in that I handle them as a perspective of the future; and the ideals also serve me in that they help me become conscious of the importance of my own development. There has to be spiritual presence of mind so that I can give the ideals a current content that matches the situation, and the ideals have to strengthen my spiritual presence of mind so that my freedom can grow.

In his *Philosophy of Freedom* Rudolf Steiner called ethics a descriptive science that investigates the motives and driving forces of human action. In his anthroposophical lectures, however, he continually seems to set standards for what anthroposophists would have to do. His texts are often interpreted as a form of regulation ethics that says what ought and what ought not. For Steiner himself his lectures did not contain standards he set, but conditions he named. His statements were hypothetical: one thing is necessary for the sake of another thing. Suppose we want to reach a specific goal, then we will have to develop such and such specific qualities or acquire this or that specific insight. In his lectures Steiner spoke to people many of whom he knew personally, and of whom he could expect that they wanted to reach certain goals. Now that these lectures have been published in the form of books, readers soon lose sight of this historical context. In the books Steiner wrote there are also no standards, but many descriptions of spiritual realities and exercises that can lead to more insight and capacities.

In Steiner's ethics the point is to become conscious of motives, and the idea of freedom is all important. In his anthroposophical science of the spirit Steiner gives us insights and exercises for the purpose of developing certain qualities (virtues) and capacities. These qualities enable us to progressively act in greater freedom. Ethics is freedom teaching; spiritual science offers a teaching of virtues in service of individual freedom. In caregiving the client's or patient's growth in freedom will be key. The presence of disabilities may make this growth in freedom difficult, but so can vices. The caregiving relationship offers opportunities to both the giver and the receiver of care to become more free.

2.8.2 Intuition or Protocol?

The increasing pressure to bind the practice of caregiving to written precepts creates a counterweight to the failings of people. At the same time, it lays a veil over the human experience in the encounter. This may lead to the circumstance that the other is no longer seen as a person, as a spiritual being which, in turn, may result in an objectivized form of service in which personal attention and the human encounter are no longer of prime importance. The emphasis shifts from the who to the what.

Because by personal shortcomings caregivers may neglect their tasks and not take their profession seriously enough, the tendency to create protocols is completely understandable. It is a way to ascertain that certain acts comply with certain demands. On the one hand, the emphasis on the formal side of caregiving helps avoid mistakes. On the other hand, this emphasis asks of the caregivers an extra effort to preserve the significance of personal engagement.

From an anthroposophical perspective the emphasis should actually be moved in another direction. To avoid 'mistakes' caregivers' acts should not be further 'protocolized', but the soul functions should be disciplined more strongly, by the persons themselves, in combination with others. Caregivers have to learn to reflect on their experiences, hold back their prejudices, control their emotions, master their vices. Thus they can get the space to act freely, intuitively, as demanded by the situation.

In anthroposophical and also in other literature efforts are made to give the striving toward protocols its proper place. Guidance and also treatment cannot be uniform if they would do justice to the individual person. A uniform approach presumes that humanity is but one animal species, in which each individual human being is a replaceable copy. Such an approach also means that caregivers would have to be readily exchangeable. The personal (and karmic) bond is then pushed to the background, whereas it is such an important ground for intuitions. However, as long as the professional has the possibility to reach his own diagnosis and make his own choice of the most adequate method for this particular person, protocols and classification systems can have their usefulness. But as the opportunity for an independent judgement (diagnosis and therapy, nature of the illness, and caregiving plan) disappears, the human aspect of the care will be at issue.

Anthroposophical health care tries to recognize each human individual as a species in itself that is in a process of development and brings its own conditions with it. General knowledge of general conditions does have a function within this vision of care; fever, aggressiveness, dementia, etc. are understood as general phenomena. One can in a general sense indicate ways of dealing with those. The manner in which individual persons go through these general phenomena depends, however, on their unique, individual biographies. The caregivers who accompany them on part of their way look for a method that is attuned to the individual in question, with the aid of their intuitive ability, based on their encounter with the patient or client. We can work with protocols; we cannot live by protocols.

The gap between precept and freedom should also not become absolute. Rules, standards, and precepts have both socially and psychologically an important role, because they offer a basis from which our freedom to act can be enhanced. Individual freedom is a final goal, not a natural possession. If freedom is the ethical principle of human action, both socially and psychologically organizations have to preserve sufficient opportunity and freedom to act out of one's own insight. However, this does not mean that rules and precepts have no more role to play.

2.8.3 Support or Direction?

The sense of service as it was described above fits in the modern support model. According to this model, caring for (especially adult) persons with disabilities consists of supporting them in the activities they themselves choose to engage in. The danger of the best-will principle—the principle that a person with a disability should, for his own good, absolutely not do one thing, and absolutely should do another—is avoided by the approach that the other directs and the caregiver merely supports. First and foremost the caregiver tries to follow the client's wishes. But what if someone with a disability chooses to get into trouble? How far does the responsibility of the caregiver reach?

A sense of service also encompasses the willingness to have a true meeting with the other. Offering support with the intention of directing a person as little as possible, and leaving him in his freedom as much as possible, is only an expression of real service if the one who gives support can relate to the other as a fellow human being. Treating the other as an object—client X with plan Y and choice Z—holds the danger of making a personal meeting impossible, and therefore of no longer being of service to the other as a spiritual being on a path of development. Out of a personal relationship and based on familiarity with a person's biography the support can be individualized to a great extent. The caregiver can then, in consultation with the social network of the person and with the team of co-workers, come to the conclusion that a particular experience is called for or not. The responsibility of the caregiver then has the signature of the sense of service as a fundamental value as described above. The support model is then not a standard ('follow the choice of the client') but an aspect of service.

2.8.4 Binding or Non-Binding?

The anthroposophical view can get people very excited, but can also paralyse them. People can become attached to an ideal and make themselves very unfree because of it. People will then judge others by the standard of the ideal and often find them lacking. This is part of the destiny of every community that builds on ideals. The other side of the coin is that the strict standard may flip to a seemingly tolerant openness. The organization then does not demand that the co-workers endorse particular premises, let alone practise certain exercises; it only demands affinity and a loyal attitude.

This is the weak spot of all communities and organizations that are based on an explicit and unusual mission. They often do not survive, because the mission does not live powerfully enough to convince new generations. The inner life of co-workers cannot be directed out of the organization. The co-workers justifiably demand to be left free in that regard. But if they do not take the mission of the organization seriously, which after all is the only shared standard, the organization risks becoming too loose.

Anthroposophical organizations will leave their co-workers free in their personal convictions, and at the same time try to win them for the common mission. That is only possible if they work hard at spiritual-scientific deepening, so that the terminology that is being used receives content. Words like equality, development, and freedom have after all in an anthroposophical context a comprehensive meaning, which may very easily fade from consciousness. In strict Christian caregiving organizations female co-workers are often supposed to wear skirts. Wouldn't it be conceivable for anthroposophical caregiving organizations to make specific (mission-bound) demands of their co-workers?

If the human and ethical premises in an organization are no longer shared, the methodology will more and more be determined by outer factors and will eventually be watered down. For this reason the determination of ethical premises is also part of the methodology (see also Chapter 7).

2.8.5 Positioning

The ethical premises described above differ from customary contemplations about professional morals in the care of disabled people, although in the practical application there are also concurrences. The difference comes from a particular view of reality. In ethical contemplations, authors not infrequently avoid making statements about reality. They mostly choose a 'neutral' position by not adopting a particular point of view and making no pronouncements on matter and spirit, death and the hereafter, etc. Rather, they prefer to place several conceivable views side by side, and possible considerations are presented and clarified.

In Rudolf Steiner's vision ethics without an explicit view of reality is meaningless. People who have no opinion of cognition, of freedom of will, of the individual, of life and death, of matter and spirit, may deem themselves living in the safety of neutrality, but they condemn their own ethics to vagueness. It is no coincidence that Steiner was an admirer of Friedrich Nietzsche (1844–1900). This man was quite ready to face consequences. If God is dead, if our knowledge reaches no farther than natural science and its materialistic views, if the human being forms no part of a reality that can be known and experienced, ethics is a parlour game for morality knights who keep each other amused. Everyone is then free to do what they want. Steiner subscribed to this view, but added to it that natural science can be supplemented by spiritual science, and that human beings, who go their own ways as individualities, can also draw their motives from the spiritual world in the form of intuitions.[39]

With the aid of the above-described three fundamental values many ethical positions can also find a home in the anthroposophical view of caregiving. The ethical positions take a certain principle as their basis on which they assess under which conditions actions can be called morally good.

Utilitarianism looks for a common goal that serves as a standard by which you can judge actions. Some people name pleasure as a goal. The most joy for the greatest number of people. Utilitarianism strives for 'the greatest possible happiness for as many people as possible'. In anthroposophy the common goal is a striving that is demonstrable in the human being, namely the striving for individual freedom (of will). The greatest possible freedom of will for as many people as possible is the highest goal for anthroposophical utilitarianism.

Regulation ethics, which tells you how you are supposed to act, uses strict standards to indicate to which rules we have to adhere as human beings in order not to go from bad to worse. This compelling approach does not occur in anthroposophy. In another way it can be identified in the form of necessary conditions if a person wants to bring certain ideals to realization. One's actions are therefore not regulated (you must meditate), but the person is placed before a conscious choice (Do I want to meditate or not?). Regulation ethics works in anthroposophy as a teaching of virtues that says that human self-realization is dependent on bringing certain virtues to realization. This realization of virtues is in its turn connected with performing certain inner exercises that specifically aim to develop the three soul functions of thinking, feeling, and the will.

In evolutionary ethics one views the demonstration of social behaviour as a strategy to survive as a species. The moral consciousness of human beings has its basis in the biological level of species-bound and group-bound tendencies. The basis of morality is anchored in the animal nature of humanity. This first, biologically determined layer of morality includes among other things the inclination to take care of offspring, horror at the death of other individuals of the species, and an inclination to collaborate.[40] In the anthroposophical view the life of instinct belongs to the unfree part of human beings, which they can transform in freedom. Anthroposophy sees social behaviour (sense of service) as a consequence of the evolutionary origin of humanity, and of the karmic bond among all human beings that is the ground of the idea of brotherhood. Rudolf Steiner views the continuing development of morality as an evolution of moral intuitions that succeed each other without being derived from each other.[41]

Finally, egoism as an ethical principle is accepted in anthroposophy as a premise. The egoist will evaluate his self-interest on the basis of his view of reality. If one's own pleasure is the only thing that is real, the egoist will pursue his own happiness (hedonism). If the egoist believes that he forms part of a development of the world as a whole, which includes karma and reincarnation as laws, well-understood self-interest will lead him to adjust his goals, and involve his fellow human beings in it.

2.9 What is Good Care?

2.9.1 The Good

We have named three moral values for providing care to persons with developmental disabilities. Equality is related to the anthroposophical view of the spiritual origin of humanity. Sense of service relates to the anthroposophical view of the connecting paths of development that people go together. Spiritual presence of mind relates to the anthroposophical view of the goal of the human being's development as a 'free spirit'.

In this broad perspective we speak of moral values, high ideals, and great development potential for the human being. These values and ideals are grounded in a vision of reality: spiritual reality is knowable, freedom of will can be experienced, the earth as a living organism can be observed. In this sense the anthroposophist can say that his ethics is true.

But can the anthroposophical caregiver also say that his care is good? In a philosophical sense, the good is the highest conceivable intrinsic quality something can have in the reality that is. People who say that neither quality nor reality are knowable, cannot place the good. For them the good is merely a word with a positive feeling content. That is the point of view of emotivism, which considers notions of value as expressions of emotion. Those who connect the good with a religion or faith will call good whatever is evaluated as such by that faith. And when does an anthroposophist declare that something is truly (ontologically) good?

In my opinion, anthroposophical caregivers will refrain from a final judgement regarding whether a deed was truly good or not. They will leave that judgement to the spiritual world, which will show the karmic consequence of the deed. This consequence, said Rudolf Steiner, serves to remediate disturbances that have occurred in the connections between things as a result of the deed.

Was not for the Greek philosopher Plato the Good the very highest that is the ground of all reality? Was not for the medieval philosopher Thomas Aquinas the general Good the One Being that is God? In this philosophical tradition good as predicate of a human deed means as much as divine. Who can say that his deed was 'divine' and precisely appropriate within the whole of all-encompassing reality?

In his philosophical works Rudolf Steiner gave minimal attention to the question of the good. For him a human deed is morally better according as it is individually freer. The more someone out of free will follows his idea (in the sense of intuition), the more evident the connection of this idea with other ideas can be. The more insight someone has into the connections between things, the better his intuition can be in harmony with those connections. Whether a deed is good will depend on the way in which the deed forms part of the whole of reality.

> If a man acts only because he accepts certain moral standards, his action is the outcome of the principles which compose his moral code. He merely carries out orders. He is a superior automaton. Inject some stimulus to action into his mind, and at once the clockwork of his moral principles will set itself in motion and run its prescribed course, so as to result in an action which is Christian, or humane, or seemingly unselfish, or calculated to promote the progress of civilization. Only when I follow my love for the objective is it I myself who act. I act, at this level of morality, not because I acknowledge a lord over me, or an external authority, or a so-called inner voice; I acknowledge no external principle for my action, because I have found in myself the ground for my action, namely, my love of the action. I do not work out mentally whether my action is good or bad; I carry it out because I love it. My action will be 'good' if my intuition, steeped in love, finds its right place within the intuitively experienceable world continuum; it will be 'bad' if this is not the case. Again, I do not ask myself: 'How would another man act in my position?'—but I act as I, this particular individuality, find I have occasion to do.[42]

This means that I do not go by external standards that purport to determine the good. I want to take personal responsibility for the deed I perform in freedom. Philosopher Dietz formulates it as follows:

> Ethical individualism is based on the premise that I form my concept of good and evil ever anew for myself, instead of adopting such a concept from other people, for otherwise it does not truly help me. I must myself

> take the responsibility that my concept of good and evil has the widest possible reach, therefore encompasses the greatest possible whole. [...] In the conception of *The Philosophy of Freedom*, the criterion for the good is: to be in cohesion with the whole. And this demands maximum effort and maximum concentration, and therefore: 'moral intuition'. [43]

Whether my deed was good or wrong, I want to take responsibility for it myself. Even if other people would want to help me, I cannot escape my own responsibility. I want to discover for myself how my deeds are connected with other things. The criterion of the good is something I will have to develop myself. This does presume that I want to know the reality in which I live and act. The connections in which I stand—the caregiving relationship, the department, the organization—I have to fathom them. Then, out of consciousness of the whole, I can make my own contribution. The flipside of freedom to act is insight into the connections of reality.

2.9.2 Good or Responsible?

The use of the term 'the good' in the general and higher (ontological) sense of the word does not contribute much to a better understanding of the expression 'good care'. But the word 'good' may be used when the intrinsic goal of a certain professional act has been reached. Someone can be good in his profession. An architect can make a good design; a physician can make a good diagnosis. In that sense a therapy can be well executed, a child well taught, a phobia well treated. 'Good' then means as much as effective, excellent. This requires not only professionalism but also an adequate concept of one's own profession and the ability to carefully observe the consequences of one's own deeds.

We can observe whether clients or patients feel themselves properly approached or treated, or whether they show themselves receptive to the chosen treatment. This an important aspect of caregiving: showing real interest in the consequences of what we do, and it is emphasized by so-called caregiving ethics.[44] It is a logical consequence of the view that caregiving first and foremost is based on the personal relationship. In this sense we can through observation determine that certain caregiving actions have been a 'success'. One has then succeeded in reaching what was set as a goal.

In everyday practice professional caregivers have to evaluate all the time whether things went well. In this evaluation a judgement has to be reached as to whether an action was 'good', and whether one has succeeded in reaching what one had in mind. The standard of measurement for this judgement lies in the first place in the human being who is being cared for. And this person will express in one way or another whether he or she is 'doing well' or not. This expression, however, will have to be observed and discovered in the encounter. This observation is an important condition for good care. But the receiver's receptivity should not show only at the level of the 'what' (the physical and psychic appearance), but also at the level of the 'who' (this individual human being). In observing receptivity, it is also necessary to note the perspective of the path of development of the other. Good care is therefore a human requirement with a spiritual yardstick.

A very different matter is the question of the good for a caregiving institution as a social organization. The management responsibility of a caregiving organization consists of guaranteeing responsible care here and now. This responsibility for what takes place in the institution is primarily a legal one. Quality control in fact boils down to observing external laws and regulations. The caregiving organization can, as an organization, guarantee that the care is provided in responsible ways, and is applied in conformity with the quality that is demanded in society. Responsible care is a demand of society with a legal yardstick.

For the leadership in a caregiving organization there also exists an ethical perspective. Leadership and management are a profession in itself, and have their own objectives. And someone's leadership may well be called 'good'. The principal objective of the leadership of a caregiving organization is to elucidate the mission, to anchor it in the organization, and to give it a position in society. Its tasks include to be responsible to society for what takes place in the organization, and for advancing the professionalism of the co-workers.

But first of all, the mission of a caregiving organization will have to be an extract of its conception of the human being. The mission shows the motive to which all co-workers want to conform, because it becomes their own motive. The mission must therefore be made recognizable, for example, by referring to the three fundamental values. These values contain a view of the human being and offer a moral orientation for acting in a professional manner. A shared awareness of values makes a joint orientation to 'good care' possible.

3 Spiritual-Psychological Aspects of Developmental Disabilities

Marijke Bijloo[45]

3.1 Introduction: The Incarnation-and Excarnation Processes in the Biography

To understand people with a disturbed development it is methodologically important to be familiar with the course of healthy human development. All the phenomena we see in people with developmental disabilities can also be observed in people without those disabilities, although in the latter they are present in more subtle and hidden ways.[46] Based on insight in the healthy course of development it can become clear which developmental steps and tasks were omitted, or were taken in a one-sided way, delayed, or accelerated.

The anthroposophical conception of the human being is based on the idea that before human beings are born on earth they have their origin in the spiritual world. Through their individuality which, unlike any other being, they call 'I', they first learn to live progressively better in their bodies, and learn to use their soul to live, learn, and work (the incarnation process). Their life experiences on earth enable them to mature in soul and spirit, and in the second half of life they slowly but surely withdraw from the body again (the excarnation process). After dying the individuality lives on in the spiritual world in order to process the life just ended, and prepare for a new incarnation.

The way the processes of incarnation and excarnation proceed depends on how individualities integrate the talents and shortcomings they have taken with them from the spiritual world with what comes to them from heredity and the environment (see Fig. 1).

From our pre-birth existence we bring forces with us that are uniquely ours (see vertical arrow). Among others, these are our strengths and weaknesses in the life of soul and spirit. But these forces also become visible in the way a child forms its body and makes it its own. Hereditary forces are handed on from one generation to the other (see horizontal arrow). Life circumstances and social-cultural influences we have to deal with come out of the environment. These come to us out of the circle, as it were (centripetal arrows).

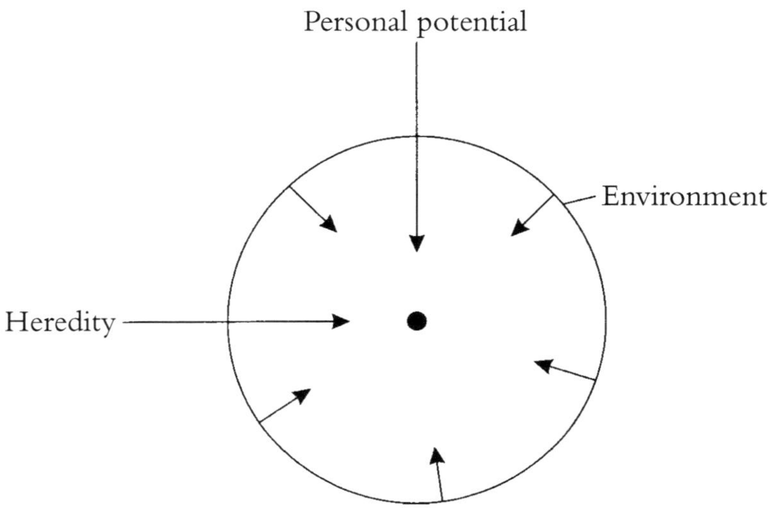

Fig. 1 Complex of forces that work into the individual.

In this chapter first of all the most important aspects of a healthy course of development are described in phases of 21 years of age,[47] for only in the perspective of the archetype of the healthy course of a human life can disabilities be understood and helpfully accompanied. These phases are the years of childhood and youth, young adulthood, the middle phases of life, and old age. The first phase is described in three periods of seven years because each of these periods presents important development tasks and challenges that form the foundation of the whole rest of life.

Next our vision on health, illness and developmental disabilities is described. In that connection the human being is described as a threefold being in whom processes play a role that are in balance with each other when a person is healthy. In illness this state of balance becomes disturbed. In case of developmental problems and disabilities the balance is also disturbed, but then as a consequence of incarnation problems that result in a different course of the phases of development.

Finally, issues that we often see with children in our time are described from the perspective of one-sided tendencies in our culture and phenomena of our current time. With this we offer a model to explain the increasing occurrence of these problems in our time.

3.2 Childhood and Youth

The process of development toward adulthood is a long one in human beings. During the first 21 years a series of physical and physiological up-building processes takes place. The final completion of all organs and organ systems—including the final hardening of the skeleton—takes some 28 years. This development process happens in phases, in a rhythm of seven-year periods. Physical and *soul* development are closely linked to each other. The basic picture in this phase is that, when an organ(system) has reached completion and maturity, a part of the up-building forces involved is freed and becomes available to the human soul and the I. Thus we see a dynamic picture of the way young people grow from the top down and from the periphery to the centre into their corporeality. Phase by phase, up-building forces are thus freed, and these create potential for the unfolding of corresponding soul capacities.

3.2.1 The First Seven-Year Period: Learning to Live

In this period the accent is on learning to live. The development task of learning to live lies in making one's body into one's home and making psychosocial and motoric steps in development. The central nervous system and the senses grow to maturity. The more the child is able in this first period to make the body its own and fully form it, the more solid ground it acquires in itself for its whole further life.

The etheric body connects more and more with the physical body in this period (see also Appendix 1). In the process, it engages in a struggle with the hereditary forces it has received from the parents, in order to transform these according to its needs. This struggle expresses itself, among other ways, in the occurrence of childhood illnesses. The degree to which the hereditary forces are transformed thus lays the basis of forces of health in later life.[48] This period is concluded when the child is ready to go to school around its seventh year. There will be a number of physical signs indicating this, such as the beginning of the change of teeth, the growth of the torso, arms and legs, and the development of the waist.

With its first breath and the cutting of the umbilical cord the child arrives on earth. It now has to learn to breathe in its own rhythm and, by extension, build its own day- and night rhythm in learning to sleep. In this first period, development takes place primarily from the head (also called the nerve-sense system, see Appendix 1), which is the most completely formed part at birth. The baby first lifts its head, only then it sits up, then it crawls, and finally learns to walk. In the first three years the great tasks for the child are learning to walk, speak, and think.

The first memory of a human being lies around the third year of life. What the child experiences in the years before conscious memory awakens at that time, is completely absorbed into the unconscious, and is reflected in the forming of the body down to the organs, muscles, and the still malleable brain structures. In this period basic trust is also acquired.

These first years of life are also determining for a healthy development of the four body-bound senses: the sense of touch, the sense of life, the sense of movement, and the sense of balance.[49] These so-called lower senses form the basis on which the higher senses can develop at a later age.

The sense of touch is strongly addressed for the first time during the delivery. This sense is important for the ability to experience ourselves within the boundary of the skin. In pre-birth existence in the spiritual world this boundary did not exist. A well-developed sense of touch lays the basis for the feeling of security and trust that the earth carries the human being (basic trust). The sense of life is nourished and strengthened by the feeling of comfort and contentment. If by a good 'mothering' the child is invited to devotion and fulfilment, the sense of life is strengthened and life processes are nourished (see also Chapter 6). The sense of movement is developed by experiencing and practising the child's own movements. If this sense is well developed it leads to a feeling of freedom and the ability to imitate. The sense of balance is developed by finding the right balance in the three directions of space: front and back, right and left, above and below. In the child's learning to walk we can distinctly observe the child's efforts to maintain its balance. At a later age a person with a well-developed sense of balance can transform this into an ability to make good choices.

In these first seven years a person learns everything by imitation, and it is therefore of the greatest importance that the child have good examples around it. The young child will thrive best when it experiences that the world is good, and it can be the way it is. The child then develops a natural sympathy for the good and antipathy for the bad. It does not yet possess a morally correct judgement; it does bring with it an innate affinity for the morally good, but this has to be awakened by good examples. The child does not yet have any defenses against negative influences from its environment, so that these too work deeply into its organism. The defense mechanisms the child will develop in the first three years to protect itself against lack of understanding, attention, and love, or in case of abuse (of power), grow into basic (defense) patterns in its behaviour. Thus each child develops its own safe or unsafe style of attachment. Physically safe or unsafe attachment is reflected in the extent to which the spirit and soul are anchored in its own body, in the abdomen down to the pelvis. The experiences the child has undergone are stored in the unconscious in the still malleable organ formation, down into the muscles and the brain structures.

Then comes the period when the child learns to play. By imitating what it sees, particularly from the important persons to whom it is attached, the child enters into connections with others and the world. Out of imitating others and exploring toys and household activities the child develops its own relationship to its environment. In the course of these years its play becomes more and more free. It grows from exploratory through the senses and motoric functions to the inwardly imaginative. The child enjoys playing and, without its being conscious of it, as it is playing the senses develop further. At this stage it also practises identification with and tuning into others (psychosocial development). Play also offers the possibility to become conscious of life experiences and process them.

3.2.2 The Second Seven-Year Period: Learning to Learn

In this period the accent is on learning to learn. The same up-building (etheric) forces that were used in the previous period to form the body, are partly freed in the second seven-year period for the processes of imagination, thinking, and memory.[50] If the preceding development has been healthy, the child will in this period be naturally eager to learn. Now only has the time come to tackle the more abstract learning processes of arithmetic and reading. If this learning content is given too early, namely before the child is school-ripe, (etheric) forces are called on too early for imagination and thinking. This means that they are then kept away from the healthy up-building of the body, which at a later age, when the etheric forces decline, may lead to health problems. For a healthy learning process, calling on the already present learning capacity at the right moment, and going through the first period in the right way, are prerequisites. Learning problems are often caused by disturbances that already occur in the first period, but are not always noticed. And it may also happen that a child needs more time to penetrate its body with an awake consciousness. This is a well-known phenomenon in children with a relatively large head; they tend to retain a dreaming consciousness longer.

This second period is especially characterized by the further development and forming of the middle area of the human being, also called the rhythmic system (see also Appendix 1). A distinctive aspect of respiration and heartbeat is that they move in their own rhythm by contracting and relaxing, which causes no fatigue. This forms the basis for social-emotional or feeling development. In this period the child likes rhythmical movement with exertion and relaxation in children's games such as jump-rope, ball games and other games, often accompanied by little songs.

In the ninth year of life a change happens in the consciousness of the child, that works down into its bodily processes. The child becomes aware that there is a separation between inner and outer world. Before that time, the world was perceived out of a 'dreaming' consciousness, as it were. Now the world openly shows itself, and the child realizes that it is its own person. But it has a definite effect on the soul of the child. The loss of the notion of being part of the whole may cause an irritated or melancholy mood. For instance, the child will observe its educators more acutely and make critical comments on them ('You have such a funny nose!') We may consider this as a further step in the incarnation through which the individuality connects itself more deeply with the body. When the child makes this step in itself and in the world, its I anchors itself physically in the abdominal area and becomes its own centre of warmth. This gives the child its own centre in its organism for the activity of its life processes (see also Appendix 1) so that it becomes less dependent on its parents for this.

In the time leading up to puberty the subject of belonging plays a role—the ability to make connections with kids of the same age.

In this phase rejection is extremely hurtful for their feeling of self-worth. Teasing happens especially to children who find it difficult to enter into social relationships and connect with the world around them. These children often have a tendency to withdraw into themselves. In this period the child has all kinds of judgements and opinions, but an independent judgement that is permeated by the I is not yet there. This is why children of this age are still so vulnerable and can easily be influenced by adults in their opinions and views. They are willing objects for the advertising industry and famous brands. It is also the age when the child wants to discover and challenge the world. It opens itself profusely to all the impressions it can get there. At this point it is primarily the senses that are bound to the soul that are further developed, namely the senses of smell, taste, sight, and temperature (see also Appendix 1).

In this period the child thrives best in an environment with sufficient examples from which it can develop respect and reverence for human beings and the world. This enables the child to develop veneration and religiosity.

3.2.3 The Third Seven-Year Period: Learning to Work

In this period puberty and adolescence succeed each other, and the transformation takes place from learning to learning to work. In puberty, from a physical point of view, the accent lies on the further development and individualization of the metabolism and the limbs (also called the metabolic-limb system—see also Appendix 1). In the life of the soul the person is developing individual judgement. Whereas younger children get to know the world mostly through playing and learning, young adolescents broaden their interest in the world also by getting to know work processes. They have their first work experiences in weekend- and vacation jobs. Adolescence is all about cutting ties and becoming an autonomous individual. In this phase, during and after professional training, the transition happens from learning to working. Learning to bear responsibility and facing the consequences of one's own deeds is a new element in this phase. Early in adolescence children get long limbs and the hormonal change begins that leads to gender characteristics and the development of the reproductive system. Rudolf Steiner has pointed out[51] that, after maturity has taken place in both the area of the nerve-sense system (first seven years) and the rhythmical system (second seven years), at this point it also develops in the area of the metabolic-limb system. In this phase the children can eat enormous amounts of food. The excess in metabolic processes often gives off an odour, and may become visible in pimples and a certain coarseness of the body. The changes in the body may happen with a certain fierceness, and puberty therefore puts young persons out of balance in the soul—mood swings from strong-willed and exuberant to indolent and depressed.

The difference between boys and girls becomes very distinct in this period. Boys incarnate deeper into their bodies at this time, which can be observed in the breaking of the voice and the growth of more hair. Physical strength, wanting to manifest themselves in the world, and demonstrating courage and aggression are important to boys. Girls incarnate less deeply into their bodies than boys. For them soul processes and social life are important. The group of girlfriends, attracting and repelling boys, and dealing with mutual jealousy are important themes for them.

Healthy adolescents want to make their own judgements, often in a black-and-white pattern, and want to judge or change the world according to their own ideas. They resist all judgements they experience as untrue or false, in order to arrive at their own opinion in the process. In the ground of their soul they are trying to get to know the human being and the world. They are looking for truth but, because of their still vulnerable I, they don't yet dare step out into the open. They explore and experiment, probing and breaking through boundaries. In that context the use of alcohol and drugs can take on huge proportions, often under the influence of a social group. In the area of sexuality falling in love and sex are usually experimental in nature. Later in adolescence love can develop a more inward colour.

How far adolescents take their experimental behaviour in this period often depends to a large extent on the degree of balance developed in the soul in the previous periods, as well as on their ability to deal with pressure from social groups. Adolescents thrive best in a mood in which they can themselves go in search of truth, thus to form their own judgements. But it is still necessary, and it gives them a sense of security, that their parents or other caregivers know in what circles they move. On the one hand, they need clear boundaries arrived at with their own cooperation, but on the other hand, they will be most open to advice from adults who, while interested in them but leaving them free, point them in certain directions out of their own individualized life experience.

Adolescents cut their ties to the milieu of home, and in the things they do they continually wrestle with underlying questions as to their own identity: Who am I? What do I want? What am I capable of? It is a search for the direction in life that is theirs. The extent to which they succeed in this also depends on the extent to which a fundamental sense of security and confidence in their own abilities were able to grow in the first years of life. The ability to connect with a life partner is also part of this.

The senses connected with the I (the spirit) which, based on the development of the lower senses, are growing in this phase are the sense of hearing, the sense of the word, the sense of thought, and the sense of I (see also Appendix 1). A good sense of hearing can, on the basis of the sense of touch, lead to the inner capacity of 'learning to listen', both in a spiritual sense and in being open to what the other is saying, even if it does not accord with one's own opinion. With a well-developed sense of word, based on the sense of life, the capacity can be developed to speak in such a way that words matter and put weight on the scale. With a well-developed sense of thought, based on the sense of movement, the capacity can be developed to think in accordance with the events, which enables a person to quickly understand and learn to 'see through' situations. With a well-developed sense of I, based on the sense of balance, the capacity can be developed to observe oneself and others as carriers of an I, which creates the ability to make good choices.

Not until adulthood can the I, which incarnates then only, give direction to our own life. Toward that time therefore we see stability and more balance growing in people's lives. In the first period of adulthood the search for our own direction in life, based on the sense of I, has an exploratory character. It may also be a lifelong search.

3.3 Adulthood

The capacities that grow in the first 21 years of life are as biographical material freely at the disposal of the then adult person. The task of the individual I in the subsequent seven-year periods is to transform this material into a rich palette, in order to put it to work in life, in social relationships, in self-deepening, and in our activity in the world. The earlier three phases serve in this as a biographical ground for all later developments, in which the ideal archetypal images of development are made possible by a warm 'nest', a culture of appreciation of our fellow human beings, and joy in life and a respectful environment.

In the practice of life we can observe in adulthood a natural psychological dynamic for the entry into a new phase:

- physical changes and needs arise;
- there is a certain saturation;
- there is a kind of crisis experience: the old no longer satisfies—the new is not yet.

This dynamic has its source in a deeply unconscious motive underlying our life that is directed by the I and stimulates us to further development.

3.3.1 Balance- and Achievement Phases from Age 21 to 42

The first phase runs from about age 21 to 28. In that period we are fully open to life impressions, and go through an extensive life orientation. We experience a need for expansion and for exploring social and global diversity, often accompanied by a need to discover the reach of our own inner world, of a sense of meaning and direction in life. The signature of this period is travelling, studying, experimenting, adventures, living in the now, exploring and crossing boundaries, not yet any lasting obligations. It is a pity when social tendencies distort this or hold it back, which happens if this exploration takes place in virtual and hardened worlds where value destruction plays a greater role than meaning and the search for values.

The next phase of age 28 to 35 announces itself by a kind of saturation, which may be accompanied by a mood of having lost one's course, a somberness, a lack of satisfaction, sometimes leading to a crisis period between ages 29 and 33. An awareness arises that the many changes in impressions and environment are in the end obstacles to self-development, that stabilization becomes a new life task. Indispensable to deepening and enlarging our capacities are a steady line in life, continuity in a relationship and/or family, and continuity in the challenges in work and home. Decisions need to be made that can determine the future for a longer period of time, such as a relationship and/or children, a home, a job and the need to show what we are worth, a career with perspective. The previous periods are evaluated and transformed into guidance and wisdom in life, and are integrated into the wisdom taken in at home long ago or, by contrast, may lead to a rejection of the old past and to an independent direction in this phase. If we succeed in this we will experience a period of relative balance, of development that takes place in a favourable social setting, in the awareness that a fruitful development is connected with our fellow human beings. Toward the end we may in our time observe a first feeling that our energy is not inexhaustible and that the energy we possess has to go to that which is really important.

Around the thirty-fifth year, when the effort to conquer a place in society has been important to us for a number of years, a different question creeps in. Am I not too much absorbed in my efforts to give form to my life? Who am I really? Then comes a search for the self and the purpose of life. On the one hand this asks for looking inward and building up one's own spiritual life. On the other hand, there is the realization that the connection with the outside world is of great importance, because it contains just as large a task as turning inward. Questions arise as to the deepest driving force, as to what is really important and necessary for us to use all our energy and capacities to put something of importance into the world. This phase is therefore also the most goal-oriented.

Reflections of Childhood and Youth in the Balance- and Achievement Phases

Initially, practically no parents realize how critical and far-reaching for later life the consequences are of their upbringing and environment. In many pedagogical and medical lectures Rudolf Steiner pointed out that the first 21 years of life only throw their—sweet or bitter—fruit in the later phases of human life. The basis of the phase between 35 and 42 years is rooted in the period between 0 and 7 years when, in the ideal case, warmth and affection were determining factors for the optimization of physical growth. A positive period from 0 to 7 years becomes a productive basis for ages 35-42; it gives a person the capacity to permeate his energy with qualities like warmth, interest, affection. In this phase we can also be original and creative, and fulfil great tasks. The counterimage is inhumanity, violence, cold.

The period of 28 to 35 unfolds on the basis of that of 7 to 14, when socializing, tuning into one another, and learning in school are all-important. The capabilities learned in this phase can now become fruitful by contributions to social initiatives and themes. But the period of 7 to 14 can then also turn out to be an obstacle. The power of habit from our own upbringing is difficult to recognize, but it certainly plays a big role and asks to be transformed into a more personal orientation.

Finally, the period of 21 to 28 years unfolds out of that of 14 to 21. Puberty and adolescence carry the signature of emotional ripening and the development of judgement, but they still have a strong compulsive character. In the period of 21 to 28 this is transformed into the ability to face the world with enthusiasm and/or indignation, and is deployed in service of one's own personally chosen development.

We are living in the cultural epoch of the dominance of the I, the self. The whole culture is permeated by consciousness, judgements, opinions, and of wanting to determine everything for ourselves. Because of this dominance in the culture, we can observe a general tendency to act without first developing a natural maturity and basis for judgement. If this begins at an early age, it leads to premature actions without observation of the right development-psychological sequence: first letting the physical basis come to maturity, only after which corresponding capabilities of feeling and judgement may be deployed.

3.3.2 Involution and Spiritualization Phases from Age 42 to 63 and Beyond

A brief sketch is given below of counter-movements of the human spirit in the light of physical decline. In the phase of 42 to 49 vital-vegetative forces come free out of the skeleton, the metabolism, and the reproductive organs (menopause). What at one time was built up for puberty now withdraws from the physical body. Everyone notices this decline of his forces because of the gradually developing physical problems such as sclerosis, rheumatism, psychosomatic ailments, and problems in the metabolism. At the soul level we notice a first and unexpected fear of growing old and becoming socially irrelevant. The devitalization in the reproductive system and metabolism calls on us to find out of our own initiative a new zest for life, a new idealism. We need to lead the ego-oriented soul to impulses and initiatives that transcend the ego: from soul to spirit. On the one hand, this leads to a capacity to have compassion and, on the other hand, to tapping new sources and initiatives.

In the 49–56 phase vital-vegetative forces become available out of the rhythmic system. We hear of complaints about breathing and blood circulation, such as shortness of breath, declining lung capacity, wrinkling, arteriosclerosis and stenosis, hyperventilation, heart issues. It is also the phase in which we see burnout and the fear of not being able to keep up 'if things go on this way'. The fear may grow of definitively becoming old and stiff, of no longer being pretty and loved, or tough and imposing.

However, new vital forces may arise from which we may draw when the I succeeds in transforming this process. This may be done, for instance, by the practice of a review of the day, by coming up with new ideas for social processes, by learning to 'breathe out' and taking time, by forgiving suffering and injustice. Then the I generates nourishment from inside for our own body, for the soul, and for the world.

In the phase of 56–63 vital-vegetative forces become available from the senses and the central nervous system. Hearing and sight diminish and memory is no longer exact and flexible. The fear of dementia or paranoia of old age is not unjustified when this occurs. The extent to which it does indeed happen also depends on a person's preceding way of life. When we have developed interest in the world and human warmth, and can admit new thoughts, the risk is less. When one occupies oneself with essential questions, such as what is spiritually relevant, what the archetypal images of life and death are, and what comes after death, one will grow new inner forces. In religious activity, inward beholding and creative thinking, new wisdom and inner light are awakened.

3.4 The Anthroposophical Concept of Health

So far the description of the phases of life were described from the perspective of a healthy development. The anthroposophical concept of health (see Appendix 1) is of importance to understand disabilities in development as incarnation disturbances, in which through one-sided tendencies the healthy balance in the middle is lost. This concept is treated in more detail in section 3.4.2 on the so-called threefold constitution of the human being.

3.4.1 What is Health?

The anthroposophical conception of the human being views health as the result of an active balance-creating process between opposite poles. This health-creating principle comes to expression in morphological processes, as well as in physiological, soul, and spirit processes. When we get out of balance, we are more susceptible to germs and other causes of illness, so that we fall ill more readily. Going through the illness completely, however, already contains the victory over the one-sidedness. After the illness we can therefore often become 'better' and more balanced. Also when a disease has a more chronic nature, or even if a person dies of it, the illness has enabled the person to deal with the one-sidedness it expressed, so that this does not need to be taken along into a subsequent life.

But difficult life experiences can also throw a person out of balance and cause one-sidedness. One might then start brooding and worrying and become listless and depressed, unable to act adequately. In this situation the forces of the head become dominant, which goes at the expense of the vital forces of the metabolism and limbs. But if it becomes possible to give the difficult life experiences their place and find a new relationship to them, in the course of time a new state of balance may develop.

In every case it is a question of finding the right middle point, the right balance between the processes of taking in impressions and digesting them, of building up and breaking down, but also of the balance between oneself and the surroundings, of breathing in and breathing out. In curative education and social therapy, the anthroposophical approach to illness always tries to build on healthy, self-regulating processes (see also salutogenesis in Appendix 1) that are present in the human being and, where possible, strengthen us. The guiding question is then how balance can be restored out of these health-bringing, self-regulating forces.

3.4.2 The Threefold Human Organism

The human organism shows a threefold nature (see also 2.4.2 and Appendix 1). For our purposes we will focus on the polar activity of the processes that are at work in the several members. The processes that are working in the head area are morphologically and physiologically, as well as psychologically and spiritually, opposites of the processes working in the limbs. The processes working in the middle area take a dynamic position between these. This holds true for all the qualities shown in the drawing below.

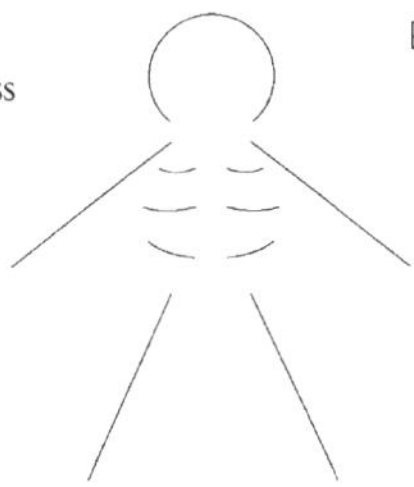

	Physical body	Etheric body	Astral body	Ego (I)
Thinking consciousness	round	cool	waking	self
Feeling	half-round	lukewarm	dreaming	self-experience
Willing	ray	warm	sleeping	self-realization

Fig. 2 Threefoldness as schematic outline of the human skeleton

From a morphological perspective the head is spherical, while the limbs tend to radiate out. The ribs between the two take on the characteristic forms of both poles, namely the upper ribs more round and the lower ones more radiating out. Physiologically, the limbs should be warm and the head cool, while the middle should be between the two, in order to function properly.

At the level of the soul, thinking takes place mainly in the head, willing in the form of acting, doing, takes place mostly in the limbs, and feeling has its place mainly in the middle area. Feeling happens based on respiration and heartbeat, which both react directly to every strong feeling.

At the level of the I, in the head the I makes use mostly of the processes of imagining and thinking (self-consciousness), in the middle area of feeling processes (self-experience), in the area of the metabolism and limbs mainly of processes of will (self-realization). At the level of the I we can be fully conscious of the thoughts we actively form in ourselves when we generate sufficient spiritual presence of mind. We do have to produce enough concentration for this. In the area of the limbs, however, our consciousness is asleep. Here the movement patterns, after they have been learned, have to become completely automatic (unconscious therefore), so that our conscious I is free to concentrate fully awake on the objective of the acts, which lies in the surroundings. For example, when we are driving, the movements needed to move the car have to be completely automatic if we want to be able to focus on the traffic around us and anticipate effectively. Another example of the way the I directs us through the limbs is the 'accidental' encounter in which our legs 'happen to bring us' to the place where we meet someone or something which will prove to be important to us. In the area of feeling our I-consciousness has a more dreaming nature, as it were. If we direct our attention to our feelings, we can become more conscious of them, but when we are focused on others we are usually less aware of our own feelings.

In this threefold nature of the human organism we can recognize how the several members of the human being are 'turned inside out' in the limbs as compared with the head. That which is working at the one pole on the outside, works on the inside at the other pole (see Fig. 3). Thus the bone formation of the skull is on the outside of the organism, and in the limbs it is on the inside.

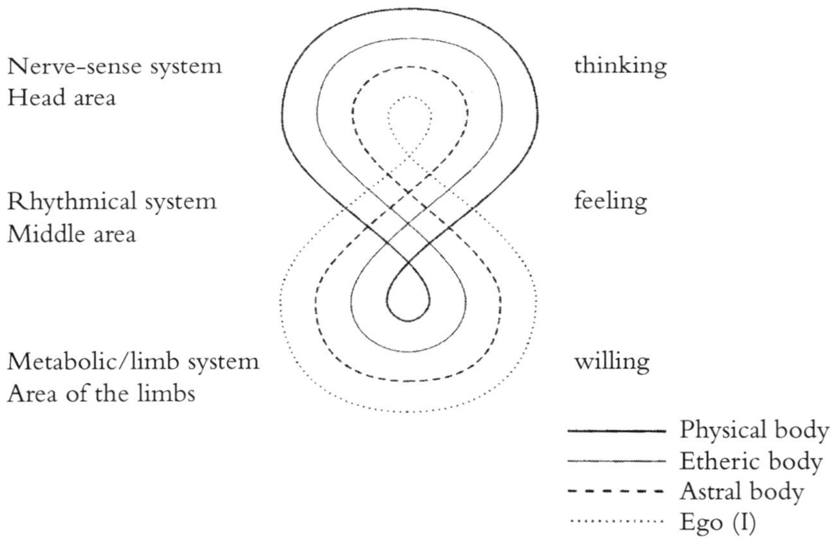

Fig. 3 Turned inside out

3.5 What Might Cause a Deviation in Development?

Based on the anthroposophical conception of the human being a disability in development can be understood as an incomplete incarnation of the soul and spirit into the body. In most cases of developmental problems and disabilities we can observe an innate lack of balance. Because the child still has to develop itself, this lack of balance penetrates into the growth of the areas of thinking, feeling and the will, and deviations grow as compared with a normal development. In this sense such a disturbance works pervasively into the developing organism and does not heal 'on its own' such as can be the case with a physical illness.

In addition, seriously disturbing life circumstances (see also 3.5.3) may do so much damage to an originally healthy organism that they also cause a developmental disability. Most developmental problems have to do with an insufficient anchoring in the area of the limbs (metabolic-limbs system).[52] Because of this, the soul and spirit are too loosely bound to the body and the earth, and can therefore work too freely in the surroundings. If the spirit and soul are not strongly enough attached to the body, the I does not have the free access it needs to the soul functions of thinking, feeling and willing. The spiritual core of every person's true being, however, remains unhurt, and therefore continues to lead life on earth from the spiritual world, also for people with developmental disabilities.

The following image may be helpful. A pianist (the I as spiritual being) can express himself in the sounding music (the soul as the sound) by playing the piano (the body as the instrument). The I as spiritual being cannot be disturbed or disabled. If, however, the instrument is insufficiently tuned or is missing some strings, the music does not sound right, irrespective of the proficiency of the I.

In case of developmental disabilities and problems, the development of a child deviates from the normal pattern. We then observe retardations, sometimes also accelerations and other one-sidednesses or deviations from normal development. Every child, however, develops differently as an individual, and it is important to pay close attention and observe which disturbances are taking place as compared with the normal pattern. Below follow descriptions of a few tendencies as examples.

Due to incarnation problems the four lower, body-bound senses—the senses of touch, life, movement, balance—are often poorly developed, and the child does not fully feel at home in its body. For instance, in children who have difficulty penetrating their limbs the feet are often cold and the legs have poor blood circulation. Because of an insufficient anchoring in the body it is difficult to be fully awake and open to impressions from the surroundings.

> A two-year-old girl in a curative educational daycare centre had brain damage and multiple handicaps. She was friendly and laughed easily, and liked to make contact with anyone who came close to her. She was soon tired and had many epileptic seizures during the day. A big problem was nutrition and therefore growth. She had trouble eating and suffered from constipation. Her feet and legs were regularly massaged with warming oil. This had a visible effect. She clearly felt more comfortable in her body and then also showed more interest in the toys.

Imitation may also be delayed or practically absent if the child is 'far away' and hardly penetrates its body. Because of this the capacity of connecting with people and the world will lag behind. The child is then also hardly able to play. This may happen because the child is not able to arrive at inner imaginations, and as a result, its playing remains limited to manipulating objects.

But the development of imagination and fantasy may also show one-sidednesses, with the result that the child lives too strongly in its own world of images and has trouble connecting with reality. In such one-sidednesses, therefore, the child's own constitution, but also factors of heredity and environment, may play a role (see Fig.1). It is often a situation of multiple factors that the individuality has to cope with in the form of the disturbance in his development in this life.

3.5.1 Influences from Earlier Generations and Heredity

Experience shows that capacities or problems in behaviour that played a role in earlier generations can become constitutional factors in a child. Research into attachment indicates strongly that the ability to give your child a safe basis (safe attachment) is carried over from one generation to the next, and is therefore strongly trans- and intergenerationally determined. Trans- and intergenerational problems can become anchored in heredity—down into genetic material—and can thus turn into constitutional factors. In recent years much research has been done into autism-related disabilities, which has shown that heredity is an important factor in this area.

In the one-sided tendencies in the constitution described below such factors from heredity and earlier generations may play a role. But there are also constitutional factors the individuality has himself brought with him from the spiritual world.

3.5.2 Influences from the Constitution

In *Curative Education* Rudolf Steiner describes six prototypical one-sided tendencies in the constitution of a child that may occur as a result of pervasive disturbances due to which the balance-creating principle of the middle area is lost (see also Appendix 1). We briefly show these six constitutional one-sidednesses in the schematic below.

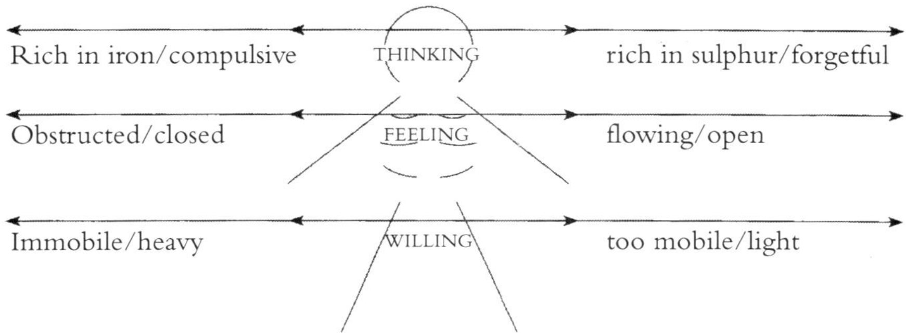

Fig. 4 Polar one-sided tendencies in the development of the child

In the area of thinking we may observe two polar tendencies that are in balance in normal development, namely the ability to forget and the ability to remember. When one-sided tendencies occur here the child cannot forget, let go of certain things and becomes compulsive; or on the other hand, it cannot take hold of memories and becomes forgetful. In the feeling area, in normal development the ability to be in itself rhythmically alternates with the ability to connect with the surroundings. When one-sided tendencies appear here the child becomes too much caught in itself (obstructed) or, alternatively, loses itself too much in the surroundings (flowing). In the will area, the area of doing, acting, one-sided tendencies of too much movement (light) or too little movement (heavy) may appear.

No one develops on these polar lines of development precisely in the middle. For instance, one person will have a better memory than another. However, within certain limits (the first arrows from the middle) that is part of normal development. But when a development one-sidedly crosses these boundaries, we may speak of the appearance of disabilities in the development.

As an example we will briefly sketch the problem of a child with an intellectual handicap (the child that is 'too heavy'), in whom we see a retarded and lagging cognitive, psychosocial and motoric development. This child reacts insufficiently or too slowly to incoming impressions and has to be awakened to its surroundings with great patience and by means of stronger impressions. Most likely, the physical and etheric bodies of this child are prematurely hardened or densified, due to which it experiences great resistance in the incarnation process and cannot permeate its body in a flexible way. In these children and adults there are obvious problems with the senses and perception, due to which they are often called mentally deficient. They frequently show impediments in posture because the form is insufficiently inhabited and illuminated by the soul, so that there is a lack of movement, both inwardly and outwardly. Around puberty, but also at later ages, this can become visible in the form because it becomes too heavy and the person has balance and posture disturbances.

3.5.3 Influences from the Surroundings

In addition, negative influences from the surroundings may throw up blockages or cause stagnation in the development. This happens to a serious degree in children that were neglected, or sexually or otherwise abused at an early age. This does serious damage to healthy living conditions. But other traumatic experiences may also throw up developmental blockages. Children with congenital handicaps or multiple handicaps often require repeated hospital treatments, and they are just the ones who have a diminished ability to understand what is happening. In the process, they become even more damaged in their feeling of security and develop traumas more readily. All these un-comprehended anxiety experiences are stored up in the organs and nerve-sense system as blockages, and raise the level of inner stress which is especially activated in situations that are experienced as insecure.

In curative pedagogy the objective is to create a healing climate in positive surroundings by acting and treating in a healing manner the process of education, as well as by fostering the growth of harmony in the constitution (see also sections 5.1.4 and 5.1.5). To the extent that one-sidedness and disturbances are anchored in multiple areas (the person's own constitution as well as heredity) harmonious intervention is more difficult to achieve.

3.6 Consequences of Developmental Disabilities for the Formation of the Personality

First of all we have to call to mind that living with a developmental disability or handicap is a life full of development potential. Learning and developing are always possible, both for the person with, and the person without developmental disabilities.

A noteworthy aspect in people with developmental disabilities is that they often have a fluctuating level of functioning. This is mostly the result of stagnations in development, due to which multiple stages in the development of the young person continue to play a role in the personality.[53] In areas that are less blocked or damaged their functioning lies at a higher level than in areas where stagnation has occurred.

In addition, we note that the bond between parent and child (or person needing care) often remains strong, symbiotically on a physiological level. This is a consequence of insufficient inner change. As a result, soul and spirit remain too free to work in the surroundings and too open to their moods and atmosphere. The dependence on the help and guidance by others is a central theme that has to be experienced and admitted time and again throughout life by the one needing care. It can be experienced as a repeating mourning process through the successive phases of life. People will often only realize when reaching adulthood, in part or in whole, what the consequences are of a life with their disabilities.

> A young woman related: 'I would so much like to become a nursery school teacher, but that is not possible because I am not good at reading and writing. I find that very hard to understand.' There followed a period of sadness and anger because of her limited potential. People around her supported her when she expressed these feelings, which helped her live with them better. When she then started looking for alternatives, it turned out that she could become an assistant in a children's daycare centre.

It is especially difficult for adolescents with less serious developmental disabilities and lightly intellectually disabled youths to accept their existence (destiny) when they get into the phase of detaching from the family and developing autonomy. They often want the same degree of independence as their brothers and sisters and do not fully recognize their own problems, which may then lead to overestimating their potential. The danger of abuse by third persons occurs regularly in such cases.

These adolescents are a target group for both curative pedagogy and social therapy. It is important that they be challenged by their caregivers to unfold their potential, but also to learn to become aware of their boundaries and develop an increasingly realistic self-image. Practising an individually achievable level of independence in the spheres of life and work in internships combined with job coaching, is helpful here, as is becoming part of social networks of people of the same age and with the same problems.

Especially in the transition to adulthood appears a heightened susceptibility to psychological disabilities. Psychosis and depression occur relatively frequently at this age in persons with developmental disabilities. But also in later life there are, relatively speaking, more often psychological disturbances. Unfortunately counselling and psychotherapy for people with developmental disabilities are not yet prevalent.

J. Sleigh[54] describes from his own experience that for many persons with a developmental disability there are two distinct turning points in the course of life; around the twenty-fifth and around the thirty-seventh year there are crucial moments in the biography. The turning point around the twenty-fifth year is most clearly visible in men with a developmental disability. For women this moment sometimes comes a number of years earlier; moreover, for women the passage of this point happens more in silence. The signs are restless behaviour, unhappiness with themselves, rejecting the handicap, wanting to be 'normal'. Provocative and brusque behaviour are recognizable expressions of discontent.

With good accompaniment this crisis moment in the biography can be transformed into a fruitful step on the path of self-acceptance and self-knowledge. Sleigh advises to observe a number of aspects in the accompaniment during this crisis. The first four follow below:

1. Intensify personal contact by having many conversations in which the young adult is encouraged to express his feelings, also the deeper ones.
2. In this process the co-workers themselves also need encouragement and support from others in order, in spite of his often provocative and often asocial behaviour, to continue to experience the one they are supporting with full regard and respect as an adult, and to keep meeting him in their contact.
3. It is important at this stage that the young adult learns to become aware of his boundaries as related to bearing his own responsibility, particularly through a firm work environment and through learning new skills.

4. Also in living together with others the young adult has to realize that he has development potential, instead of his having the feeling of being the last in line, without opportunities to get ahead. He has to be told that his problems are being heard, and that he can get help to find a way to work them through.

Finally, an accelerated ageing process in the last phase of life leads to reduced independence as a result of physical—and often also spiritual—decline. The need for guidance and care increases further and frequently the familiar living surroundings have to be replaced by a home that is specifically organized for care and nursing. This makes the person feel like a stranger, and eventually the bond with his or her own life also tends to disappear due to a fading memory capacity or the development of dementia. A thorough reorientation is needed regarding the manner in which ageing people are accompanied in the rhythm of their lives and the way they spend their days. Most of them find no satisfaction in work anymore, and they run the risk of missing the challenge of personal development. As regards daily living, we try to enable people to remain in their familiar environment as long as possible, preferably to the end of their life.

In this last phase of life, we can, together with the older person, actively look for a meaningful content of the day. It is important that particular attention is then given to a conscious working through of life experiences and to a review of their life (biographical consciousness).

3.7 Developmental Disabilities in Relation to One-Sided Tendencies and Current Developments in Society

This section contains a sketch of some one-sided cultural and social tendencies that aggravate developmental disabilities we bring with us into life or may be the cause of such disabilities. After brief descriptions of these tendencies (3.7.1) and disabilities (3.7.2) follows a call for the creation of a culture of the heart as counterweight against one-sided tendencies in our culture and society. In addition we describe the increasing phenomenon of 'children of our time' as a current contemporary development and the demands this poses for educators and caregivers (3.7.3).

3.7.1 One-Sided Tendencies in Culture and Society

Since the second half of the twentieth century, Western society has gone through great developments that have brought our culture much prosperity and progress. And the speed with which new discoveries are made appears to increase. In the field of scientific research, for instance, new developments and possibilities are being found that were originally thought to be achievable only in a much more distant future. In this acceleration of new developments computer technology plays an important role. Besides the blessings of progress, by this speed in development humanity is also increasingly confronted with questions regarding nature and the environment, and especially with questions of a moral nature. Should everything that is technically possible also necessarily have to be applied? Formerly, this was regulated by nature, without human intervention. These problems are particularly urgent in the case of life-extending interventions and the resulting quality of life.

As was described earlier, a healthy development is characterized by an active search for balance in new developments. This holds true not only for the human being, but also for the culture and society the human being creates. Due to the ever faster speed with which new developments appear, and the search for solutions out of a predominantly materialistic world view (the currently common scientific view), we run the risk of losing this balance and falling back into one-sided tendencies. If sufficient balance cannot be built into new developments, these can lead to illnesses in the culture and society. For example, in the West we have gathered great riches through trade, but this has happened at the expense of other parts of the world where people live in poverty. In the context of the description of developmental disabilities we will describe a few one-sided tendencies in our Western culture and show how these throw a shadow on the development of succeeding generations.

Stress

We are living in a time when stress, nervousness, and haste play a great role. We can point to many causes for the increase in stress, and want to mention just a few of them. Thus our enormous technological progress has not provided us with more time, as some had predicted, but has especially led to an acceleration of processes, both at work and at home, and also in our leisure time. In addition, in many families both partners spend much time and energy at work and in producing income. The combination of 'work and care tasks' often generates stress, especially for women. In turn, family life and the household can then come under pressure, which goes at the expense of a healthy and harmonious life rhythm in the family.

A frequently occurring source of stress are newly constituted families after a divorce, with a changing number of children through the week and in weekends. This demands a high degree of flexibility on the part of everyone involved, as well as an ability to deal with the loyalty problems that will then arise. On top of this, there is the increasing pressure on children of ever younger age to perform, which is a big stress factor for many of them. In Japan, this leads to a high percentage of depression and suicide among children and youths.

Materialistic World View

In our science and culture we can observe an overvaluation of materialism at the expense of spiritual life. The call for renewed discussions about norms and values is a result of this. For children there is the danger that, stimulated by advertising and promotion, they become spoiled by all kinds of possessions. Another example in which well-being and prosperity are confused with each other are the parents who feel guilty because they give so little attention to their children during the week, and try to compensate for it during weekends and vacations by all kinds of extras, for which they ask the children what they would like best. Such children don't get enough attention for ordinary things. Through compensation with matter (stuff) or all kinds of fun trips they do not sufficiently learn to limit their desires. They can thus become 'spoiled-neglected', resulting in great unease in their soul.

Intellect

Generally speaking, there is in our culture an overvaluation of the intellect, at the expense of the development of a harmonious feeling- and will life. The screen culture reinforces this one-sided stimulation of observation and thinking. When young children regularly 'play' in front of screens for longer periods of time, the wakeful senses and nerves in the brain get overstimulated at the expense of the four lower body-bound senses (see also Appendix 1). In addition to this, it becomes perfectly normal in realistic appearing virtual games to eliminate (murder) large numbers of opponents. Because of this, especially in children in which the functions of thinking, feeling, and willing are not sufficiently integrated, the feeling life then becomes extra disconnected.

Moving

From many sides we hear calls to let children move more. We want to do everything quickly and therefore rush to put the children into the car to bring them to school. If the children then also spend hours in front of a screen, they run the risk of moving insufficiently because the limbs hardly move at all. On the other hand, we are witnessing a culture of organized movement in clubs, mostly with pressure to perform, where kids may be trained to an extremely high level of performance. Although it is in principle healthy to move in the context of a club, it can also be exaggerated, so that it goes at the expense of the pleasure in normal movement and rhythmical children's games outside.

Eating

One of the biggest problems for the health of children in our culture is that of overweight. A lack of movement and of limits set on the children's life of desire because of over-indulgent parents are important factors in this regard. But in addition, feelings of unease, arising among other things by the above-mentioned one-sided tendencies, are seemingly briefly satisfied by eating (sweets, snacks, or binge eating). On the other hand, the same satisfaction may be sought in refusing to eat. In both cases the lack or the excess of movement will reinforce the overweight, respectively the underweight.

3.7.2 What Shadows Do These One-Sided Tendencies Throw on the Development of Children?

In this section we want to sketch principally the role of our culture and society as a strongly co-determining factor from the environment for the growth of developmental problems, besides the already mentioned influence of hereditary factors and a person's own constitution. We therefore describe first the most common developmental problems in children of our time. Then we ask in what ways the balance has been disturbed, and make a connection with the above-described one-sided tendencies in our culture and society.

The Most Frequently Occurring Developmental Problems

First of all we are struck by children who always seem to be in movement. They hardly ever sit still, and have trouble concentrating and controlling their impulses. They immediately pick up stress from their surroundings, look with their hands, have a lot of contacts, but don't often manage to have a real encounter because they always slip away again. In schools almost every class has some of those children. A number of them are classified as children with ADHD. In many ways they display an inability to hold back.

Another common problem is children who incline to pull back from contact. They do this in different ways, two of which are indicated below as examples.

There are children who withdraw into the security of the head, in rigid imagination and thinking. They become excessively intellectual, as it were; they want to know all the time how things are supposed to be, want to make everything predictable, are afraid to make spontaneous mistakes, and their need for control leads to compulsive and inflexible behaviour. As young children they generally make the impression of being older. They often like technology. After all, the button- and screen culture is predictable, controllable, and logical. Some of them therefore become excellent computer programmers. They are generally stiff in their movements and have a hypertonic muscle system. They tend to rigidity and the development of compulsions. It is as if the properties of the head penetrate their entire organism too strongly.

Another group is formed by children who have in a certain way shrunk back from existence on earth, and live behind glass or on a cloud, as it were. Their soul often lives in a young, still magical world, rich in pictures, in which the distinction between fantasy and reality is vague. They lack the I-force to deal with changes and transitions; they are not good at adapting to new situations. Many of them have a strong connection with nature and prefer contact with animals, which react much more reliably and predictably than humans. Especially the connection with their peers is problematic, because they cannot keep up with the twists and turns in games. In daily life they are easily disoriented and become overstimulated because of their overly open senses, and they flutter from one interest to another. They are afraid to connect more deeply with the earth and the world of human beings, and develop a young, flabby (hypotonic) muscle system.

Both of these groups of children who pull back from contact are often classified in one of the categories of the autism spectrum.

Then we have the many children with weight problems. The frequent occurrence of overweight in children has, besides a lack of movement, also to do with the way they are brought up. The eating disturbances, which usually begin around puberty, demonstrate how these children—often girls—deal with a life that generates so much stress for them. In cases of anorexia nervosa there is often a need to exercise control over themselves according to an idealized standard of a slender figure (with excessive movement), while they also shrink back from the consequences of an adult body. In bulimia nervosa we see a lack of holding back from eating, but in a broader sense there is often also a difficulty in controlling impulses. It may also happen that the need to control and the lack of holding back alternate. Usually, these girls do not succeed in finding their own appropriate connection with the challenges posed by life in school, family, girlfriends. They feel gloomy or depressed, and are often caught in dysfunctional, often unconscious notions about life which, besides previously mentioned personality factors and family culture, are also related to cultural views in society with which they grew up. They need help to find a new, more personal relationship to life.

The Influence of Materialism

What one-sided tendencies become visible in this category, and what do they tell us, besides the personal and hereditary influences already mentioned, about the way we function in our culture and society? First of all we want to recall a number of statements Rudolf Steiner made regarding future problems in children if the materialistic view of the world and the human being will continue. He points out that if the materialistic world view continues, this will lead to nervousness and that more and more children will be born 'trembling'.[55] Both in these lectures and in another series he emphasizes that especially for spiritually sensitive children a one-sided materialistic view of life may have harmful consequences. He stresses that these children do not find what they have come for on earth. Out of profound unease in themselves and their existence, they commit acts of violence, they lapse into feelings of hopelessness, depression, and suicide. Youth psychosis may also develop. Unfortunately, we have to admit that these problems are becoming more and more visible in our time.

One-sidedness in the Culture of the Heart

Striking in the above-mentioned one-sidednesses is that they all show a loss of balance in the human encounter, in making contact, on the one hand, by overshooting into the world or, on the other hand, pulling back into themselves (into the head), or even into a more cosmic existence by partially shrinking back from life on earth.

Fig. 5 Losing balance

It seems as if normal life with its everyday rhythm is slipping away from us. In the middle area of the human being the rhythmical movement of respiration and heartbeat take place. It is in this area, where being in ourselves and being in the world alternate in a natural rhythm in effort and relaxation, inbreathing and outbreathing. Life nourished by this middle area risks becoming lost in our hectic existence or in a society focused on security.

The question is whether, in our time, we dare to live sufficiently with our soul from the heart, and dare to feel what we experience. Do we dare let go of the perfectionism of the head and the haste of our limbs run wild? Only in the encounter of heart to heart can true contact take place that gives satisfaction. Our heart shows who we really are, even though we are vulnerable there, and not perfect. As a counterweight against the one-sided tendencies in our culture it is important to start working on the creation of a culture of the heart, in which we learn lovingly to accept the other and ourselves the way we are, including all our insecurities and vulnerabilities.

It is in meeting heart to heart that we can wake up to who we are ourselves and who the other is. It is in such meetings that people dare open themselves, step by step. It is in the voice of the heart that our conscience speaks. The heart is also the place where love resides that is not bound to earthly existence, but reaches across the threshold of death. In the heart-to-heart encounter with the other, the voice of universal love can be heard as a third power that works in a healing way.

In places where people work in curative education or social therapy they strive to create a culture of the heart, of healing encounters. In this context B. C. J. Lievegoed wrote the following verse for his co-workers in curative education, and it is recited every day to this day before they begin their work:

> We carry the children in our warm hearts,
> Thinking we seek for helping ways,
> Working we search for healing handholds.
>
> Christ's light illumine our serving thinking,
> Christ's force strengthen our healing will,
> Christ live in our young hearts.

3.7.3 The Time Spirit and Children of Our Time

The fact that we live in a time when everything is accelerating can also be observed in human development, when we realize that the seven-year phases have often become six-year phases. These days the toddler already goes to pre-school, and some schools offer learning material before the children are ripe for school. Many children have physically already reached puberty in their twelfth year, and by law we are adults at age 18. Even at birth we see a difference from some 50 or 60 years ago, when children kept their eyes closed for a few days after birth. Nowadays babies briefly open their eyes right away. In addition, we see that children develop more and more in individual ways, and that rules of behaviour do not have the same effect for all children. Upbringing and education also have to be increasingly attuned to the individual child.

This tendency to accelerate developments and go through them in an individual way is connected with a general law of development (see also section 2.4.2) through which human beings become more and more open to the spiritual world. Humanity is standing on the threshold of acknowledging our spiritual origin and destiny as individual human beings, and bringing them to continued development. We can see this, for example, in the greater openness that exists today to the spiritual, such as the idea of reincarnation.

A name often given to characterize our time is the term New Age. Children of our time have been called star children[56] and indigo children.[57] These names indicate children who bring with them great sensitivity or openness to the spiritual, and who have supersensory experiences.

In developing spiritual capacities, our children are showing us the way. More and more children are making statements about where they came from before they were born to their parents, or have other clair-feeling or clair-knowing capacities. For many of them these abilities disappear when they are ready to go to school, when adaptation to earthly reality is such an important step. If upbringing and education are open to a spiritual world as reality, we witness that in many of these children those capacities manifest themselves in a new manner from adolescence or young adulthood on. However, when spiritually sensitive children are brought up with materialistic pictures and ideas, problems may arise as described above with one-sided tendencies in our culture.

Children and adults with handicaps and developmental disabilities generally also bring with them a great openness to the spiritual world, precisely because they are less strongly connected with their bodies and live partially outside their bodies. It is important that they too be understood and accompanied when they speak of the dead, about voices they hear or about other super-sensory perceptions.

3.8 Meaning

All human beings have the task of deploying their innate abilities in life and to enlarge these. The meaning of life is not determined by the number of talents we bring with us at the beginning of life. What is important is that all individuals realize their own potential (their 'life assignment') and carry its fruits into the spiritual world at death. Many people go through an incarnation in which they cannot live autonomously, in order to learn what it is to be greatly dependent on others. We may view life as a place of schooling where, in each life, we can learn the lessons that we need to learn in that life. The meaning of life lies in the lessons we learn in earthly life, and in what we can mean for others in that process. Many people with developmental disabilities are less awake and less focused in their thinking, as a result of which they are by nature better able to understand the art of living from the heart. Besides the fact that they usually attach less value to material possessions, this is one of the things we can learn from them.

In addition, it is important to help people with developmental disabilities to inhabit their body more deeply, and to guide their interest to the earthly world. Every human being will gain new 'earth experiences' through interest in the earth with its mineral, plant, and animal kingdom; these experiences are needed in the life between death and a new birth to prepare a healthy physical body for the next life. The following law applies: 'What is outer world in earthly life is spiritual inner world in life beyond the earth.'[58]

Developing interest in the earthly world is also a topical theme in our current culture. It is of great importance for all children and adults who, through the computer and media culture, spend many hours per day in a virtual world instead of a real world. At the end of life all human beings will offer the talents they acquired on earth to the spiritual world. It is therefore important that these be talents that can be absorbed and digested by the spiritual world, so that humanity in collaboration with the spiritual world can continue to develop.[59]

4 The Core Elements of the Caregiving Practice

Willem de Koning and Marijke Bijloo

4.1 Introduction

In this chapter we will describe the most important elements of the practice of curative educational and social therapeutic caregiving. This will be based on experience and insight gained in the past almost 100 years in supporting people with developmental disabilities. The following aspects will be discussed:

- The goals striven for in curative education and social therapy (4.2).
- The means employed for this, namely the specific ways life is organized in caregiving, and how children and adults are supported and treated (4.3).
- The manner in which the learning process is organized and stimulated (4.4).
- The way elements from culture (4.5) and working (4.6) are used to foster and stimulate development.

4.2 Goals in Curative Education and Social Therapy

Curative education is focused on children and youths until adulthood. Social therapy focuses on supporting adults who need care or support until the end of their life. Curative education and social therapy overlap to some extent, such as in the fundamental approach underlying the way curative educators and social therapists offer care and support to children and adults. Also the culture and the therapeutic climate in which learning, living, and working take place are in many respects the same. But there is a striking distinction regarding the relationship of authority with which children and adults are supported. In the case of children there is a relationship of vertical authority; with adults a mostly horizontal approach to support.

The goals of curative education and social therapy can be briefly characterized as follows:

- to look for an individual path of development for the person needing help;
- to do justice to the universal equality of people in practical action and life;
- to awaken the health-bringing forces in both child and adult through education and the arrangement of the living, learning, and working environment, so that each person can develop and maintain him- or herself in a balanced way in body, soul and spirit;
- to form carrying social communities or networks, in which mutual human relationships make possible and stimulate the development of both the individual and the community.

In a different formulation: in curative education and social therapy social networks are created, within which people can learn, live, and work, and where they can develop themselves in accordance with their own possibilities and needs. These social networks are built on the power of the human encounter (4.2.1). The stimulation of development is given individual form out of a general care-, treatment-, and support framework on three levels, with specific goals on each level (4.2.2).

4.2.1 The Significance of the Encounter

The nature of the care for people with mental handicaps has gone through profound changes in the past 80 years. Normann[60] maintains that a fundamental change has taken place in caregiving organizations as a result of the emancipation of people who need care or support. Until the 1960s institutions mostly tried to assume the care as much as possible from the people needing it and, if possible, to take it out of their hands ('relieving'). In more recent decades this way of working has changed and was replaced by a striving to support people individually as much as possible by supporting them in ways specifically attuned to them. The goal was, and continues to be, to enable them to function as autonomously as possible and take care of their own needs ('enabling').

This social development—from care with a predominant orientation to medical care and support to care in which the accent lies on supporting individuals in their particular needs—has also changed the role of the caregivers. The new constellation involves the ones needing care as co-responsible persons in forming and organizing the support they need. An active, continuing dialogue between the persons needing care and their caretakers is in this process a guiding factor.

In anthroposophical care of children and adults the meeting of human being with human being, and the meeting of the human being with the surrounding learning, working, or living community are of central importance. In this connection, Denger[61] even called social therapy the 'art of the encounter'.

Out of encounters people come to individual and community development. The encounter is enacted in the free space between people. There are two influences that co-determine the free space in which people meet. These influences come from inside and outside the human being. From outside there are the impressions, circumstances, and conditions in which the meeting takes place. They give a certain colour to the meeting. From inside, the encounter is influenced by intentions, by memories, feelings, judgements and prejudices that may come up about the other. Creating a free meeting space demands of those involved to let go of all their 'certainties' (prejudices) about the other. If in our thinking we are able consciously to let go of old images, and learn to hold back judgements as we are observing, the encounter can become a wellspring of continuing mutual growth (see also sections 2.7.2, 5.1.3, 5.2.2, 6.3, 6.4, 6.5, and 7.2.3).

An active interest in the other and careful observation of what is expressed verbally and non-verbally must therefore be considered as one of the foremost competencies of the curative pedagogue and the social therapist (see also Chapter 5). An important professional skill is distinct, correct observation. We see such distinct, correct observation when the phenomena that present themselves are carefully considered before one arrives at an interpretation and judgement. The phenomena can then yield their essence. The content of the observations and experiences gathered concerning a person needing care forms the subject of periodical discussions in which the person stands in the centre (see also section 6.5.1).

4.2.2 Care, Support, and Treatment in Curative Education and Social Therapy

In the care, support, and treatment applied in curative education and social therapy we recognize different levels. We can distinguish three levels reflecting aspects of physical space and time, of the soul life within and between persons, and integrative aspects applying more to the individuality, the I. The therapeutic efficacy of social life, cultural life, and work life is reinforced by health-advancing therapies. In making a choice for the form of support the picture of building a house can be a help. Before the walls and rooms can appear, work has to be done on the soil and foundation, and only in the final phase the roof can be firmly anchored. When we are faced with a choice of a specific form of treatment, therefore, it is important to consider whether the basic conditions for the treatment have been satisfied.

The most important guidelines for the care and treatment are reviewed in the child or care team meeting (see also 6.5.1). If it is a child, it is important that the child, the parents, and the caregivers then be in tune with each other. Throughout the different levels this discussion is an integrating element, and is therefore always of essential importance for the success of the care and treatment.

In the following the three levels are discussed in detail for the curative treatment of children. In essence, however, they are also applicable in social therapeutic care, support, and treatment.

First Level

On the first level the basic conditions of the care and treatment have to be created and maintained, namely the creation of a *general health-fostering living climate.* This is the ground on which, to the extent achievable, further treatment and/or working through of specific individual disabilities or blockages can take place. The health-fostering climate is formed by observing the rhythms in the day, week, month, and year (see also 4.5.2), by creating healthy habits, and by tending to a safe environment and culture that nourish the senses and the soul in a healthy way. Taking care of life processes is also of primary importance (see Appendix 1). Diagnostic questions that may arise in this context are, for example:

- How is the balance between the elements of rigidity, order, and dissolution, and of exertion and relaxation?
- Does the day have a clear structure? Is this structure also evident to the child that is so badly anchored in its body that it is in a slight panic all day because it has no overview over the things that are about to happen while it is, because of this, extremely dependent on its environment and is continually surprised and overwhelmed by the events taking place, as a result of which it cannot find rest in itself?

It is important for the child to begin to feel its own body, and that spoken words or, if necessary, pictures be offered with what is happening, so that the child can begin to learn to know itself and the world by naming these. For example, the child can be asked if it can feel its feet standing on the ground, and its back against the backrest of its chair, so that it can feel itself defined in its body.

Great value is attached to the care given to the environment by making sure that it is whole, and that natural materials and pleasant, appropriate colours are used (see also 4.5.1). All of this serves to help the child connect with its surroundings through the body.

In addition, it is important that there be sufficient boundaries in the life situation. Relevant questions are for instance:

- Do the caregivers have the situation sufficiently in hand?
- Is the daily environment sufficiently safe? Or does, hidden below everything, trauma continue to be created because the child is belittled all the time or is beset by other children, so that it cannot develop a healthy sense of self-worth—which is anyway always a painful theme with all people with developmental disabilities?

If these aspects of life are not yet sufficiently mapped out or secure, this is a counter-indication for further specific therapies. For example, in individual therapy efforts may be made to diminish a child's defence mechanisms, whereas the child continues to need this mechanism in its life situation (at home or elsewhere) to protect itself. The result may then be that a child can get even more into distress because the most obvious problem still exists and is not recognized. A basic prerequisite for all following steps is therefore that all aspects of life be adequately known and be safe for the child. For this purpose help given to parents in a context of practical pedagogical family guidance is beneficial.

Subsequently, it is possible to explore which specific treatment possibilities exist for the child. This often takes place in a care team meeting together with all involved.

Second Level

Only when a healthy life situation has been created is the ground prepared on which the individual and social soul aspects of the emotional development of the child can be further worked through. Every time it is a treat to observe that if the first level has been sufficiently realized, a force becomes free in the child itself to develop further, whether it is in a short-term or long-term situation. It needs to be remembered by both parents and caregivers, however, that a new development will not happen along a straight upward line, but that in many cases after a slight fallback or brief arrest a bigger step forward can be made again. In learning to deal with adversity and resistance it is important to hold back all anxiety and scepticism regarding a fallback, out of the insight that it is part of the picture in any new development.

Based on the idea that children with developmental disabilities and handicaps are under the influence of one or several polar development tendencies (see also 3.5.2, 7.2.2, and Appendix 1), it is important on the second level to connect with the (one-sided) interests and possibilities of a child. A way must be found together with the child to take steps in the direction of the 'middle', and gradually to use even elements of the opposite pole in the treatment.

Example

A child that in its soul flows out too much into the surroundings always shows an anxious undertone, because it gets too far away from itself. It will then, for example in therapeutic painting, use light colours and a lot of water, because it does not dare express itself strongly. A therapeutic possibility is to let the child paint a story in which, out of being outside, an inner world begins to play a role. In that way a series of paintings can come into being, for example, about an animal that has all kinds of exciting and daunting adventures in the outside world, but in the end finds the way back to its safe burrow. Polarity: closed vs open.

Also on this level, the setting of the treatment should be agreed by all involved; in other words, both in an educational setting and in specific therapies there should be interdisciplinary collaboration. Besides therapies that are generally known, such as logopedics, play therapy, social skills training, and family therapy, therapies that were specifically developed out of the anthroposophical view of the human being are also used. The therapies most utilized are briefly described in the following.

In *logopedics* the method of 'total communication' is usually applied, so that also children who hardly understand spoken language or cannot speak themselves are supported by the most appropriate means of communication, such as pictures or otherwise.

In *play therapy* play is used as a means to go through blocked traumatic experiences from the past again with a safe person (the therapist) and in a safe place, and then let them go. In addition, *guided play* can be given to teach children to play. By learning to play in daily life, the children are offered a way to develop and process everyday experiences.

Other forms of individual psychotherapy, in which different forms of picture communication are used (imagination, making drawings of stories, playing roles) are especially applied in working through trauma. In addition, with *insight therapy* efforts are made to change impeding negative views of oneself and the world, in order thus to create new feeling experiences and active potential.

In *art therapy* work is done to bring about more balance and harmony in development through painting, drawing, sculpting in clay or wax, and/or working in wood or stone, as well as the corresponding elements of colour, black and white, straight and curved, wet and dry, hard and soft, concave and convex.

In *music therapy* we make use of the musical elements of melody, harmony, and rhythm, and the choice of instrument to bring about more balance into one-sidedness. Besides the old, existing instruments we frequently use instruments that were specifically designed for therapy, such as the CHOROI instruments that are made in social therapeutic workshops for this purpose all over the world.

In *eurythmy therapy*, a movement therapy based on the sounds of language and tones of music, by the purposeful and frequent practice of one or more sound gestures the power of the sound becomes therapeutically active, and one-sidedness can be balanced as much as possible.

In *anthroposophical physical therapy* there are, besides exercises, adjustments and resources, also external therapies such as rhythmical massage, baths, and compresses. These external therapies, which are non-verbal, work directly on the body through etheric oils and bring about more harmony, which has an effect on both body and soul after some time.

In *speech- and drama therapy*, by means of speech exercises, stories, texts, and dialogue in combination with movement exercises, the capacity to speak and express oneself are stimulated, which increases the confidence in one's own existence.

In *therapeutic storytelling* out of living into a child a story is made in which the child can recognize itself as the main character, who experiences all kinds of things that are related to the life story or problems of the child. The main character then finds a new way of dealing with the problems, which in the course of the story enters into the world of experience of the child unnoticed and is deeply absorbed there.

The *anthroposophical physician* works, in addition to regular medicine, also with remedies specifically developed to bring about harmony in the constitution of the child.

These therapies are usually employed alternately and in a rhythmic pattern to give the child the opportunity perhaps to embrace what is offered and to practise it in the actual situation.

Third Level

The third level consists of *integrating, further working through, and consolidating the newly acquired* in everyday life, and finding a *(re)new(ed) perspective* for the future. Depending on the development potential for independence and autonomy, the integrating process with other areas—school, home situation, peers—will take place to a greater or lesser extent. Sometimes this level consists of rounding off the treatment, and child and parents can proceed further on their own. Sometimes a new level of balance has been reached, and new steps need to be made outside the treatment situation, so that there too experience of success can be gained. On this level the unique individuality and nature of the child, with its specific gifts, talents, as well as limitations, will become evident.

Example of the Three Levels in a Treatment of Trauma of a Child

On the first level we are dealing with the question of whether the trauma-causing experience has ended, and life is safe in all respects. Together with the parents, we work to create a healthy living climate and a good school situation.

On the second level we can then work on the specific trauma of the child through an individual therapy. At first the child will repeat the trauma in (play) images, mostly without really accepting the therapist. After all, the situation was so unsafe that, as a survival mechanism, the child had to suppress or split off the trauma experiences in its unconscious soul life. The therapist helps the child in living through the trauma again, in order to come into contact, connection with the child. The anger, the pain, the sorrow are expressed again, but the child is now no longer alone.

On the third level the trauma has been integrated, the repressed or split off parts have rejoined and become part of everyday soul life again. Now the child will be open again to the other, also on the theme of the trauma. It then goes through a phase of great growth, inwardly and often also outwardly. It can concentrate again and improve its experience of competence and performance in school, and the feeling of self-worth and social contacts will also grow. Now that a new state of balance has been found, there will be regular problems with brothers and sisters who will feel that the parents are less burdened by the 'problem child'. Now only will they feel that they can claim what they possibly had to give up before. It is important to give attention also to this aspect.

The three theoretically distinguishable levels can in practice not always be clearly separated. They often flow into each other, and in crises a fallback to a lower level may be necessary; for instance the theme of offering security may then become all-important again. In childhood the progression in phases is clearly observable. At the onset of puberty, when also in healthy children disintegration takes place, in children with developmental disabilities an intensification of the problems often happens. The care and treatment of children with serious handicaps or disabilities in their development often alternates between the first and second levels. The third level is less important for this category because they mostly need continued intensive care and treatment.

4.3 Living

4.3.1 Quality

The concept of 'quality of life' has in the past few years received increasing attention. Questions are raised regarding the nature of life, whether it has meaning and is bearable, especially for people with a terminal condition, and for children who early in the pregnancy already were diagnosed with a serious abnormality or syndrome. The key question is then always that of the quality of life and the worth or dignity of life. What are the circumstances in which someone lives, and how do they relate to the personal will to live? When there is a dilemma, for instance through illness, a critical event, or a psychological change, the effort is made to find the answer to the question of the meaning of life with the aid of the concept of quality of life.

In this context there is also growing interest in the question regarding the quality of the circumstances in which people with handicaps live. For years already, parent organizations have worked for quality standards in order to evaluate the extent to which and the way in which a handicapped son's or daughter's need for care is responded to. This is in fact an emancipation movement. The group of people with mental handicaps has in the meantime been acknowledged in their right to their own identity, their own development, and living circumstances that are appropriate for them (see also 2.4.1).

In addition, from an economic point of view, the market, which has emphatically entered the caregiving and well-being sector in the last few decades, also exercises great influence. Competition, which formerly existed only in business, but has now also penetrated into the caregiving and well-being sector, often leads to a shaving off and undermining of existing care provisions. A lot of time is spent on the introduction of rules and regulations, for the maintenance of registration systems, protocols, and reports. All these requirements take time and means away from direct caregiving. Institutions are forced to work ever more 'efficiently'. In practice this often means more limited financial and human resources to employ in actual caregiving, and creates difficult situations for people working in caregiving. Under the influence of strict schedules and timelines the quality of care (attention, time) becomes subject to great stress, which has its immediate consequences for the living conditions of the people who need this care. Recent examples are problems with physical care in nursing homes because in daily practice there is not enough time to give the clients the care they need.

Also, for people in need of care the quality of life is to a large extent determined by the way in which they live and therefore are able, with the corresponding support, to arrange their lives. As has been demonstrated, leisure time too is mostly spent within the home. And yet, the quality of life and the feeling of well-being cannot exclusively be traced back to the outer influences caused by the way care, support, and home and work are made available. Human health is also nourished from an inner force.

4.3.2 Health

Human beings possess so-called *salutogenetic* capacities (see also 6.6.2 and Appendix 1), which have an influence on the way events and living conditions are experienced and dealt with. These inner capacities, which are (potentially) present in each human being, are awakened as much as possible already during our upbringing. In curative education and social therapy this inner source of strength is taken into account. The point is that the way living, working, learning, and leisure times are arranged can contribute to the stimulation and nourishment of people's physical, psychological and social health. Rhythm, structure, and an artistic environment have been proven to be effective elements in this regard. In addition, safety and familiarity with the living environment are also aspects that contribute to a sense of security.

The social therapeutic fields of activity of living, art, culture, and working are seemingly separate fields, each with its own function and content. Still, in mutual connection with each other, they can work more strongly than if each stood on its own. This is also true for curative education, where the healing effect of the arrangement of life and culture can be reinforced by intensive integration of the home, school and therapeutic treatment aspects. Out of these different areas, persons in need of care can then be addressed in the three soul functions of their being (in thinking, feeling, and the will). In all forms of living—intra-, semi-, and extramural—a connection of the areas of learning, working, art, culture, and specific therapies has fruitful results.

4.3.3 Social Practice

The health of social life is found when the whole community arises in the mirror of the soul, and when in the community lives the single soul's strength.

Rudolf Steiner, *Motto for the Social*

These days we often hear it said that we are living in the era of the I. People are primarily focused on themselves. Until the Enlightenment the Church or the State had a profound influence on people's personal sphere of life. Since then people have become more and more individualized. In our time the individual has become his own standard of measurement. On the one hand, this generates great self-consciousness and independence; on the other hand, it also brings about an anti-social development tendency.

Just as each individual human being is in development, humanity as a whole also goes through continued growth. Development is a ceaseless process of acquiring new capacities. The development human beings and humanity are going through has the goal of us all becoming as fully human as possible by transforming egocentric, anti-social behaviour that goes at the expense of our fellow humans (see 2.5). The purpose is, in the course of this development, to grow into a free and social human being, who not only focuses on himself but also on his fellow humans.

In curative pedagogical and social therapeutic communities this development is also worked on. In all places where networks come into being new social relationships can be practised. The efforts that are thus made can be considered as advance stages of future developments. Lievegoed indicated that this is 'practising being human', and 'striving for progress of humanity'. [62]

The most important step for the individual is that the focus on one's own ego is transformed into interest in the other. The fundamental attitude then changes from claiming for one's own benefit to giving for the benefit of the other. Through the mirror that people in a home or work setting can hold up to each other, growing self-knowledge can become the foundation for social community formation.

4.3.4 Integration and Community Formation

In connections with others personal forces can be exercised and skills developed. Integration—in the sense of forming part in an appropriate way of the environment in which one lives—can thus be realized. This comes to expression in a few passages in the integration document that was issued during the meeting of the Anthroposophic Council for Inclusive Social Development in Switzerland in 2003:

> Every human being has his own physical, soul, and spiritual needs. Living and learning are a lifelong process in which the human being brings his individual sources with him, and in which he depends on suitable circumstances and support.
>
> Community formation is a fundamental human need. Different forms of community and living together are urgently desired. Every human being has to be able to integrate into his own environment. Sometimes special provisions have to be made for this.

In the course of the 1950s Karl Kőnig founded a Camphill community on the North Yorkshire moors in Britain after the idea of a village community. This became Botton Village. Soon after, in 1960, Newton

Dee started, a village community near Aberdeen, Scotland. An important concept that lived in social therapy from the beginning was: to live and work as normally as possible. The village has always known a social order within which life together has its own order that is easy to oversee. Because of the relatively small scale people know each other and are strongly socially engaged with each other. The village offers opportunity for its own culture, in which customs and habits have grown that are strongly oriented to the people in need of care. There is often a differentiated work life in which every inhabitant can find a job.

> The community is the necessary basis for the provision of care. The community is formed in social life, in the school, or in work, and in cultural-religious life. The social network of which the community consists has a supportive function; care is individualized without making a person lonely. Integration of persons with developmental disabilities, who live and work autonomously as much as possible, is only successful when they can form part of the social network of the community; otherwise they run the risk of becoming lonely. The community participates actively in the social-economic network that shapes our society.
>
> Dutch Association for Curative Education 1999

4.3.5 The Individual and Community in Social Therapy

Anthroposophy is based on the premise that every human being is unique (see also 2.4.2). The differences between people give colour and dynamics to social life. Social therapeutic communities work with diversity and pluriformity within living and work relationships. They strive to create situations in which people who live or work together have something to offer each other. This means that people with diverse qualities and needs for support, with differing levels of functioning, speaking and not speaking, can constructively live together with each other. Besides situations in which four, six, or eight people live together in one house, in the course of years different forms of community have also come into being in various places.

The tension that inevitably arises between individual needs and the interests of the community has to be watched constantly, to prevent the sphere of life of the individual from being jeopardized by the general norms and customs employed by the community. It is also necessary to make sure that the social, carrying network of the community can continue to be active and effective, and is not splintered by one-sided tendencies to individualize. Three elements have to be brought into balance with each other:

1. the individual who wants to develop in freedom;
2. the community that has to offer basic justice and security to all who are part of that group;
3. the need of the individual to manifest also as a social being and to be concerned as a brother or sister about the individuals with whom he or she is living together.

Freedom, equality, and brotherhood are thus the three most important pillars of social life. The care of their own living environment, the house, the household, and the garden, is carried by those in need of care and the caregivers together. This is a principle which, if it is handled consciously, also has an influence on the overall situation of living together. By shouldering part of the care and maintenance tasks in and around the house, those in need of care can enter into a connection with the place where they live. Attention, order, and care of the environment work through at the same time as 'social hygiene'.

4.4 Learning

Curative education takes it for granted that education should be offered to all children, no matter how serious their developmental disability or handicap may be. This education is largely based on the curriculum that is used in the Waldorf schools. The curriculum is adapted to the age and level of development of the children. Besides developing cognitive skills, other important elements are artistic aspects and movement, to address the child as a full human being and to work toward harmony in its one-sided development. Direct experience through the child's own body forms the first condition for the learning process. Special attention is given to stimulating and supporting the lower four senses, the senses of touch, life, movement, and balance (see also 3.2.1 and Appendix 1). The education is strongly focused on the child's world of experience, in which household activities and arts and crafts are also important.

4.5 Culture

The cultural forms that are employed in anthroposophical caregiving are strongly based on the threefold nature of the human being, as this has been developed in the anthroposophical conception of the human being (see also 2.3, 3.4.2, 7.2.2, and Appendix 1). This shows that the human constitution is formed of three components, a physical part, a soul part, and a spiritual part. In the physical part we again see three parts, each with its own characteristics: thinking, feeling, and the will. Lievegoed shows this in the following schematic:

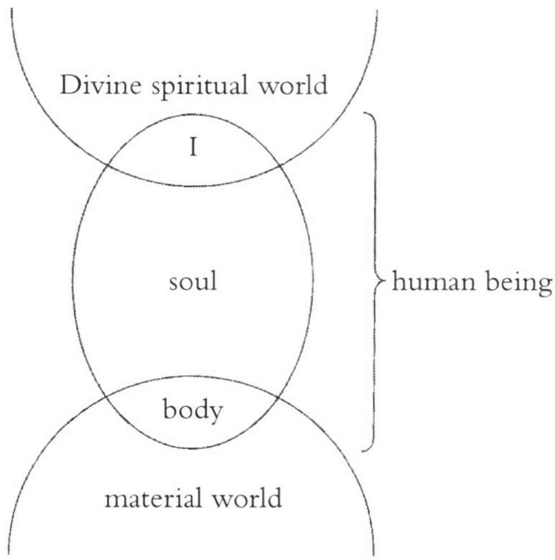

Fig. 6 The threefold human being

> The I, the deepest core of our being, reveals itself in our consciousness. In the soul the I is experienced as a reality. From the area of the body passions and desires rise up looking for satisfaction. They penetrate into the soul and are experienced there. The human soul thus receives its impulses and content from two worlds: from the physical world through desires and the senses, and from the spiritual world through the I. Spirit (I) and matter (body) meet in the middle area: the human soul.[63]

Thinking is localized in the head. Here lives clear consciousness. The will is bound to the limbs and the metabolism. The processes of breaking down and transforming food take their course in complete unconsciousness. Feeling takes place in the middle area of the human being and is closely connected with the heart, blood circulation, and respiration. A kind of semi-consciousness reigns there (see also

Appendix 1). Feelings and experiences come to realization out of the unconscious. For a person to function and unfold himself in a healthy manner it is necessary to address and educate all three elements of thinking, feeling and the will.

The cultural elements, as they are integrated in anthroposophical caregiving and support, primarily work into the feeling area. In this area a living balance has to be found between the impulses that work, on the one hand, from thinking and, on the other hand, from the life of will into the human constitution. When one of these two areas predominates, the balance is disturbed, which has consequences for the person's health. By taking in art and artistic forms in daily life a counterweight is offered against disturbing one-sidedness. Art, culture, and religion contribute to the moral and aesthetic growth of human beings. In this context, art can be viewed as a language that absorbs and expresses reality in its own way, so that it can then be experienced anew.

Culture means refinement, a step in development. In anthroposophical caregiving culture expresses itself in four different aspects:

1. in the way in which the living, learning, and work environment is artistically arranged;
2. in certain customs and habits that are rhythmically employed in daily practice;
3. in the way spiritual religious life is nurtured;
4. in the way cultural life is arranged.

4.5.1 The Integration of Artistic Elements

In anthroposophical caregiving organizations the artistic elements are not just an outer phenomenon. They strive to integrate the effect and significance of artistic elements into the living and work environment. The artistic forms can be considered as a carrying medium that wants to give form to the living space according to the laws of the true, the good, and the beautiful. For this purpose conscious use is made of materials, colours, and forms.

A concrete application of this can be found in the forms of organic architecture that is practised in a large number of curative educational and social therapeutic organizations. The objective in this form of construction is to create a meaningful, artistic connection between the needs of the clients/users, the function of the building, and the environment in which it is placed. The uniformity or endless repetition we see in many institutional structures is here broken through in a constructive manner. Each space receives a characteristic form and surface, which gives it an authentic uniqueness. In the choice of materials and colours the basic form and nature of the structure can be accentuated, and in the construction and finish natural materials are emphasized.

Research has shown that the well-being and physical health of people are directly influenced by the physical, built-up surroundings where they live. Medical and psychological research demonstrates that environmental elements have an effect on, for instance, health, recuperative powers, stress, and behaviour.

An initial important finding is that certain environments can increase people's level of stress. And as we know, an excess of stress can have negative consequences for people's health and well-being. Factors that influence people's level of stress are:

- the quantity of information and stimulation that comes at people (intensity);
- diversity and complexity (many different elements, little structure, a lot of chaos);
- newness (many elements that are new and unknown to the user; a lot of 'modernity');
- surprises: the extent to which expectation differs from experience;
- determinism: the extent to which people are 'directed' by the environment—no choice possible.

Research shows that the more factors are present, the more we see:

- cognitive fatigue;
- disorientation;
- lack of clarity, lack of understanding, feelings of insecurity due to loss of control.[64]

The fact that colours also have an important effect on the human soul has been known for a long time, but has in the meantime also been confirmed by research. By the conscious use of certain colours on the walls, a space can emanate a certain atmosphere. This is made use of in classrooms, therapy spaces, living rooms and bedrooms. For this purpose, a special technique, the veil method, has been developed to apply the colour. With this method the paint is applied in thin, transparent layers, as a result of which the space is not 'painted shut' with a thick layer of paint. The various layers on top of each other create the impression that the space is breathing, and that you can look through it. The pastel tints used in the veil method can enhance an environment with few stimulants.

The use of natural materials enables human beings to orient themselves adequately in the impressions they receive. Modern plastic technology through which, for instance, fibreboard can be made to look like beech wood, can be called misleading from a particular point of view. For instance, it might suggest that a table top consists of beech wood, but the weight, structure, and composition of the material do not correspond to this. In other words, the senses through which we orient ourselves in the three-dimensional world are led astray. The material is not what it appears to be, and that has an alienating effect on the human experience.

Persons with mental disabilities often have to make extra efforts to be able to orient themselves in the world of space and time. For them it is especially important that the impressions they take in be genuine. The appearance of things should correspond to what they actually are. This is particularly true for natural materials such as wood, stone, metal, wool, silk, cotton. The use of natural materials in the living and work environment has been shown in practice to evoke in the users the experience of well-being, security, and warmth.

4.5.2 Rhythm

Rhythm is an essential aspect of culture in curative educational and social therapeutic institutions and has great significance for the way life is organized (see 6.6.2). We meet rhythm everywhere in nature—in the waxing and waning moon, in the movements of high and low tide and, for instance, in the annual rings of trees. Rhythm is a dynamic principle that is inextricably connected with life.

Also in the human body we find in a certain respect expressions of rhythm. For example, the spinal column and the rib cage show how rhythm has helped form the human figure. During life, rhythm pulsates in the blood circulation, as well as in respiration and heartbeat, which are intimately connected with it. This life rhythm lies outside the domain of clear consciousness and carries all vital functions, carries life. The essence of this lifelong rhythm is that through its healthy, pulsating continuity it does not exhaust the human being. Rhythm forms the foundation of our health.

Anthroposophical pedagogy and also the arrangement of caregiving strive to make this life-carrying principle of rhythm the basis for all activities. This means a very conscious awareness of and living with the course of the day, the week, the seasons of the year.

The rhythm of the year offers a clear orientation potential to people who seem to lack consciousness of time. Just as after an inbreath an outbreath has to follow, activities also follow each other rhythmically. After exertion—and from a physical/psychic aspect that has to be viewed as a destructive tendency—follows a period of relaxation, within which the human organism can restore itself and build new forces. Of particular significance in this connection is the night. During the night the forces that were used up during the activities of the day are built up again and replenished.

Many people with developmental disabilities lack a natural, regulating feeling to maintain balance between exertion and relaxation. For them a rhythmical, 'breathing' daily schedule is a support that helps them to stay midway between overburden and underburden. Rhythm is also important in the customs that curative educational and social therapeutic organizations work with. It serves to anchor desired forms and habits, such as the close of day circle or afternoon rest, in daily life.

A good example of a rhythmically occurring activity is the morning assembly. Many organizations have, each in its own form, a joint morning assembly as the beginning of the school or work day. An example is the morning assembly of an institution in which a hundred adult people with developmental disabilities live and work together with support aides and other co-workers. Every morning they assemble to begin the work day together.

> At 8:25 am a bell sounds announcing that the morning assembly is about to begin. By that time many people have already assembled at the entrance of the great hall, those who live and work in the institution, the day-workers who need care, and also the co-workers in the office, management, kitchen, technical and household services. Everyone enters and is present at 8:30. The bell sounds again.
>
> As people enter there is music played by a small ensemble of co-workers. People stand in two large circles interspersed here and there with persons

> in wheelchairs. Most people are standing, because the morning assembly takes only ten minutes.
>
> In the middle of the circles stands a little table with a nice cover and a vase of flowers, if possible of the season. A candle standing next to the flowers is lit by a person needing care or a co-worker. Then a text is read that is interesting to hear and think about—a poem, verse, aphorism. This is followed by announcements regarding things that are important for everyone, such as special events that will take place that day. This creates order in the day, which has a supportive effect for people who have difficulty forming the overview, clarity and predictability they need to function properly. It may be the announcement of a group of guests who will be shown around; the fact that a certain workshop is making an excursion; or the happy news that someone has passed his driver's exam. People who are having their birthday are named and if they are present, Happy Birthday is sung to them.
>
> Finally, the assembly is closed with a song, everyone shakes hands and wishes each other Good Morning. The candle is snuffed out and music sounds again as everyone leaves the hall. The workday is now opened, and everyone goes to his workplace. In front of the hall there is still a kind of market situation for five minutes or so. Appointments are made, and important experiences can quickly be shared between caregivers. Around 8:45 everyone goes to work.
>
> (Morning assembly OlmenEs, Appelscha)

A similar form is also used to close the week, during which time the classes or workshops review the work of the week. Besides a clear beginning on Monday, the week thus also has a true end on Friday, which also marks the transition to the weekend.

The day is also consciously closed at a fixed time, individually or jointly by the persons who are living together. A verse or poem is then said to round off the day and prepare for the night. These moments work as thresholds and help a person experience that before the threshold there is a space in which we live with our day-consciousness, and after it a different space in which the unconscious night-consciousness reigns. The closing of the day and the transition thus begun to let go of day-consciousness receives an extra dimension when this transition, especially for children, is accompanied by (lyre) music or song.

4.5.3 The Religious Element

Just like the artistic element, the religious element also has a fundamental place in daily life. Anthroposophical organizations in the Western world are based on a general Christian conception that includes the view that the human being as a spiritual being forms part of a spiritual reality (see also 2.2). They view life on earth as a microcosm that is inextricably connected with a divine-spiritual world that envelops it as a macrocosm, and from which mankind and the world originate and to which they will return. The continuing development of the spiritual being of mankind, during the cycles of earth lives, is of great influence on the content of curative education and social therapy.

On the one hand, the idea of karma and reincarnation (see also 2.4.2) works through into all that curative caregivers and social therapists do. They can consciously live into the idea that the relationship that exists between them and the persons they support, has a connection both to the past and toward the future. This view of destiny connection is an important moral stimulus for caregivers, and can work through into their basic professionalism. On the other hand, out of the notion of the reincarnating human being grows the insight that the spiritual world is directly connected with life on earth, and with the experiences gained there.

Religious life helps build a bridge between the earth and the spiritual world. Curative educational and social therapeutic organizations look for forms that help people experience the content of the spiritual-religious element. This may be through the morning assemblies and closings, by celebrating the Christian festivals, and having religious gatherings such as Sunday celebrations.

In many schools, workshops, and institutions the Christian festivals are celebrated, but in many organizations the festivals of other world religions are also marked, especially when many of the people receiving care prove to have their roots in those religions.

4.5.4 Dealing with Dying and Death

More and more people in our time are making arrangements ahead of time for their burial or cremation. Funeral homes are often asked, instead of the standard ritual, to use an individual approach desired by the person in question. Also, in the case of people receiving care and their parents, attention is given to their wishes or ideas regarding the end of life and the way in which a leave-taking after dying can be given form. These wishes can be recorded in a special document or will, or become part of the plan of care. When the person dies the funeral is arranged in accordance with the wishes thus expressed.

When death approaches, it often evokes memories in people that go back further and further in time, and eventually take them back to their youth, to the very first experiences of their life. They are often under the impression that the events that thus rise up into consciousness happened only quite recently. For people with developmental disabilities too, such looking back over their life is important. When as partner, friend, or supporter we, together with the person, pay careful attention to these memories, we can help him or her to place experiences and events. Sometimes in such looking back over life, experiences can be 'harvested'. The process can be viewed as a becoming conscious of one's biography, and may develop individually in different ways.

> This becoming conscious of one's biography is a key concept here. It means to accompany the person receiving care in the thinking process of looking back on life. This seems important to us, because it is evidently a need all people have. [...] It is a process that needs to be accompanied with the greatest caution. We can call on the ability to reflect in many ways: by conversations about one's own life or that of others, by stimulating memory by means of observations through the senses—for instance a taste or smell that reminds a person of an experience of his youth—and artistic activities.[65]

In many anthroposophical caregiving organizations the manner of dealing with dying persons has a special place. Just like the transition between waking and sleeping, dying may be viewed as a threshold moment. Before and behind the threshold there are different spaces and states of consciousness.

Dying entails great, radical change. The physical form is let go and, for this earthly life, the individuality has to take definite leave of life on earth and the body in which it has manifested itself during life. In many people we can, already during the dying process, witness a change in consciousness which, after death has come, becomes definitive.

The transition process of the dying person is attentively accompanied by those with whom he or she has lived together and was connected.

For those who remain behind the ability to place and accept the death becomes greater if they can be close to the transition process of the dying person. For the dying one the attention of relatives and companions can help in the adaptation to the new form of being. The moment of dying and the thereby occurring new consciousness is described by Rudolf Steiner as one of the most important experiences of life. He spoke at length about what we experience after dying.[66]

The radical change the deceased go through immediately after passing through the gate of death initially also brings a feeling of loneliness. During the first three days after dying the so-called life panorama unfolds before the consciousness of the deceased. The memories of the life just ended appear in objective pictures that are watched by the deceased—experiences, encounters, events, in brief, all that passed through life. To assist the soul of the deceased during those first days after dying, if the person, parents, or representatives have so indicated, a wake is held. During the first three days and nights partner, parents, relatives, friends, and support aides can watch by the deceased. They too look back over the past life, with the light and shadow it contained, as the deceased also does across the threshold. The people participating in the wake can give the deceased their personal attention for instance by a story, a poem, a song, or prayer.

In the days until the funeral there may also be gatherings where teachers, friends, and caregivers share their experiences and memories of the deceased. The stories that are then told may show what the deceased has meant for his fellow humans and his surroundings. In such gatherings, and also at the funeral, the carrying community of which the deceased formed part can be experienced.

4.5.5 Leisure Time

A last important cultural aspect is the way leisure time is filled. Through participation in sports and cultural events, physical and spiritual health is nourished. A problem handicapped people run into in filling their leisure time is the fact that much fewer activities are offered that are accessible to them than to people without handicaps. Also sports for people with developmental disabilities to do together with non-handicapped people are not simple, and occur but rarely in practice.

Today the multimedia culture takes up a large part of our leisure time. On the one hand, through television and other media we obtain a connection with the reality of the world. On the other hand, there is also the diverse range of entertainment, games, and films that threaten to absorb ever larger parts of our time. Computer games call up a non-real, virtual reality that in the meantime is also raising social questions. Thus certain research is suggesting that the increase in violence in society may have to do with the disappearance of standards as a result of frequent watching and playing extremely violent games due to which the distinction between fiction and reality more and more disappears (see also 3.7.1).

A problem that also arises with frequent use of computers, smartphones, and television is that the physical condition declines in due course, that social contacts strongly decrease, and that this in an extreme case can lead to loneliness and isolation. As was stated before, maintaining and taking care of the social network is for people with a developmental disability of vital importance. It has also been demonstrated that the problem of overweight in many young people is immediately related to the long periods of time they spend sitting and snacking by the computer or phone.

Among people with disabilities both the need for and the use of virtual media is increasing. The modern media show us developments in the world, in science, leisure time, and the arts and music. It is therefore important to learn to use these media in a right manner. The amount, and also the proportion of time given to these media has to be in balance with the individual leisure time programmes. This regularly produces conflicts between the wish of the person receiving care to play with the computer frequently or even without limitation, and the considerations of the physician or parents regarding the person's physical and psychic well-being.

To break through this dilemma, efforts are made together with the persons involved, and taking their wishes and possibilities into account, to arrive at a good way to fill their leisure time in a way that allows different activities to alternate, such as appropriate sports or other physical activity like walking or bicycling. In addition many curative educational and social therapeutic institutions organize cultural activities such as concerts, theatre plays, storytelling, special courses, etc. A cultural influence thus emanates from the institution into the surroundings and people regularly come from outside to attend such activities.

4.6 *Work*

One of the three pillars in social therapy is the effect and meaning of the work process. Ways of working are sought that give everyone who forms part of a social therapeutic living and working community the opportunity to make a contribution to one of the many work processes. The village model mentioned earlier also formed a foundation for a large number of work processes. From the beginning working together in all kinds of workshops, in and around the houses and on the farm, was an important part of life within the social therapeutic village communities.

> From the beginning it was clear that village life was not strange or insufficient for the villagers [the co-workers and receivers of care]. It was their life, and the first persons needing care were determined to develop this life. Everywhere in the houses, in the stable, in the garden, the field, in workshops, church, and infirmary, they led their lives with a growing sense of responsibility and consciousness. Their sense of duty grew against all expectations, day by day. They helped the weaker ones as a matter of course, and carried and tolerated each other in a morally admirable manner.[67]

This is how Kartl Kőnig described the developments in Botton Village, England from 1955. His goal was:

> to create conditions in which the handicapped person can arrange the work- and living environment that suits him, and in which we do not from the start take it for granted that 'we' know better what he needs.[68]

With that the seed was sown for the development of workplaces, workshops, and work processes. In these, people with handicaps too would be able to work in a way that fits their individual possibilities. The concepts on the significance of work that were introduced by Kőnig in the early days of social therapy are closely related to the normalization criteria later formulated by Bank-Mikkelsen—among others, normal daily rhythm, normal activities.[69]

From a social and economic viewpoint, working has great significance. It is no coincidence that the preponderance of the instruction and training activities in schools, universities, and trade schools are focused on teaching people a profession. Working leads to change. By working, people take an active part in the process of change that is brought about by work, and through which a product comes into being. Through human work, original matter or existing processes are changed and put into a new form.

4.6.1 The Social-Economic Significance of Work

Work creates connections with the world and with people. The result of the work—a product, a service, or an idea—can be sold, which brings about a connection between the one who made the product and the one who needs it. By means of the product revenue is generated. Within social therapy working is viewed as a vital element, because work processes bring about encounters on three levels:

- On a *micro-level* an individual encounter with one's own person takes place. Through working people are confronted with themselves, with their talents and limitations. Through working they can be stimulated to unfold and develop their personal capacities. The work environment invites them to form their own identity further and experience it—'I am a gardener.' Producing motoric skill, attention, and concentration, learning to work together with others, and bearing responsibility are capacities that are challenged in the work and which, as appropriate in each situation, can be developed. And in the work gestures acquired in the process, the control the person has developed becomes especially visible, and because of this the handicap fades into the background.
- On a *middle-level*, out of the work an encounter takes place with the immediate surroundings. For a gardening team this means that the work is done in the direct living environment of 'clients', and that the efforts of this team thus contribute to giving this environment form and maintaining it. People who work in a kitchen at the preparation of meals can daily experience that through their work others are nourished.
- On a *macro-level*, there is an exchange and sale of products and services between the work community and society. In shops in town and in other places things like pottery, textiles, paper, printed matter, wood products, bread, dairy, and produce are sold. In service jobs people work, for example, in gardens, a cafeteria, a retirement home, or a neighbourhood centre.

Although working with people with developmental disabilities developed first in village communities and inside other institutions, there are also many social therapeutic workshops that exist on their own. In social therapy work is not in the first place or exclusively used out of economic motives. Through the work and its profit the persons performing the work also become visible as social beings. They want to mean something for others and contribute to the society of which they form part.

4.6.2 Meaningful Work and Valuable Products

In social therapy we look for work for everyone, in accordance with individual capacities and limitations, with or without payment. This means that we also look for fitting work for people with serious or multiple handicaps. It is important that the co-workers during their work can always have insight into the relationship between their own efforts and the joint work process, the product that comes into being out of it, and the destination of the product. The transparence with which the work process is arranged contributes to this insight, which enables the co-workers to connect with their work. Modern industrialization tends to reduce the efforts of a single person who may, for instance, work at an assembly line, to a replaceable little part of a complex machine. For many a loss of motivation and burnout are the consequences of this way of organizing the work. By getting co-workers involved in the total work process and the product it creates, motivation is implicitly awakened and there is visible pleasure and satisfaction in the work.

The wish to be able to offer work to anyone leads to the creation of diverse workplaces, which offer a broad range of work opportunities. Outside workplaces, such as farms, produce gardens, and work groups in forest and landscape management exist side by side with places like weaving, pottery and paper workshops. There are also basket weaving workshops, bakeries, dairy, metal, and woodworking places. Social therapeutic institutions try to make sure that the quality of their products and services lives up to generally accepted standards. The products from the workshop therefore have to be functionally and aesthetically up to par, and there has to be adequate demand for them.

4.6.3 Building Musical Instruments: CHOROI

A special place within the social therapeutic workshops is occupied by the activity of building musical instruments. Since the 1960s modern high quality instruments have been built by more than two hundred co-workers in nine international workshops. In the Netherlands, Norbert Visser and Bernard Lievegoed took the initiative for the later CHOROI movement (see also 7.2.1). They had two goals in mind. The first was renewing musical sound; the second, closely connected with it, bringing a social impulse within the curative educational movement (the term social therapy did not yet exist at the time). The social impulse would be realized by establishing productive workplaces for adults.

CHOROI is established in a number of countries in Europe and also in Brazil. The need for new instruments with unique sound qualities for the benefit of anthroposophical music therapy stimulated the development of the CHOROI instruments. For the purpose of building high quality musical instruments—wind, string, and percussion—teams were trained that consisted of experienced instrument builders, people with developmental disabilities, and people with social problems. With the aid of specially designed equipment and a good division of labour, it proved to be possible to arrive at qualitatively excellent end products.

In the CHOROI workshops the quiet and space exist that is needed for intensive handwork, in which many people with developmental disabilities participate. All the workshops work together without profit motive, and jointly build some twenty-five thousand instruments that are sold all over the world. For the builders of these instruments their work is not only an individual schooling and self-realization; in a direct sense they are also co-workers in a new music culture. This comes to expression in the fact that many of the workshops also have an orchestra in which the new instruments are played by the builders themselves.

It is interesting to hear how these instruments actually came into being out of concrete questions. For instance, the flute was developed pursuant to a question whether a wind instrument could be built to teach a person to use the stream of his breath and thus also help him learn to speak. Although the person in question never did learn to speak, since then thousands of flutes have found their way all over the world. For as it turned out, the new sound offers excellent potential for ensembles and in classes.

By the way, there is a general striving in the movement of social therapeutic workshops that they be led by experienced professionals. On the basis of their professionalism they arrange and offer the work in such a way that it fits in with the capacities of the co-workers who are in need of care.

4.6.4 Professional Training

Working means moving. Every trade has its own characteristic work movements. The movement is the carrying element for every work activity. Work and movement can be experienced in two different ways. On the one hand, through executing the work movements by self-acting; on the other hand, the movement made by a colleague can also be observed and experienced. This observation of the other as he was working played an important role in the guilds. Besides learning through exercise and acquiring experience in practice, watching the experienced workmen was also an important source of developing one's own skills.

In the guilds, the late medieval trade associations, the person who wanted to learn a particular trade began as an apprentice. He entered into a professional tradesman's service and had to do all kinds of simple chores. In addition, he watched how the more experienced workmen, the journeymen, performed the work. In due course an apprentice could become a journeyman. When he had worked himself up into a good tradesman and had gained sufficient experience, he could start working toward the master's test. He would build a masterpiece that would be judged by the masters of the guild. When it satisfied the necessary criteria the journeyman was promoted to master in the trade and was able to establish his own workshop.

In a certain respect, we see this path of development within a trade also in social therapy. One chooses a particular trade according to one's interest, constitution, and personal abilities. Then follows a training period that may last for years. One participates in the work as a farmer, woodworker, or baker. By watching and doing, one gets the hang of the specific work movements, and the arsenal of capacities and the familiarity with the way of working and technology can grow over time.

Also for people with serious disabilities and who cannot actually participate in the work process, observing it and experiencing it is an important link with a structure of the day that is as normal as possible. The ability to be present and experience the work in a bakery through the senses is an example of this. With the aid of adapted equipment, seriously handicapped people can participate in the essential work movements. This also creates a potential for collaboration. Where a seriously handicapped person can hardly or not at all work alone, with special means and the help of a colleague who cooperates in this, access to the work process becomes a possibility. Kistner, a workshop leader, stated on the basis of his twenty years of experience:

> Since people with serious handicaps can often work only with the help of a caregiver, the success of their work is highly dependent on the attitude and competence of the caregiver. When the caretaker acts only as helper, he effectively places the handicap in the foreground. When the caregiver acts as colleague and shows real interest in the joint process of creating the product or service, a fruitful social work relationship will arise.[70]

4.6.5 Work in Relation to the Need for Care

The choice of a certain kind of work or a particular working environment is in principle a choice for a longer period of time. After all, it takes time to develop a fruitful collaboration with colleagues, and to learn and handle the nature and technique of the work. The leader of the work should therefore not in the first place be viewed as a helper/support aide, but as the experienced colleague who works together with the different co-workers in the joint work process.

The choice of a particular kind of work, in which a certain work environment has a supportive effect, and in which specific materials are used, is as much as possible attuned to the person. In what environment will this person function best? What is he interested in? What capacities does he have or does he want to develop? With the aid of such questions we look, together with the disabled person, for an appropriate setting. Thus someone who tends to be cold will preferably not be put to work in a ceramics workshop, because the clay that is used there is cool and moist, and therefore draws warmth out of the body of the person working with it. Someone with great strength and coarse movements might be able to do good work in a forest maintenance team. Individuals who have trouble concentrating will function better in a clearly delimited space than in the openness of the meadow of a farm.

Positive experience has been gained by letting people with early traumas (sexual and other abuse) take care of animals.[71] In these persons basic trust in their fellow humans has been seriously damaged as a result of the traumatic events. They immediately experience people as unreliable, unpredictable and, most of all, as threatening. By letting such traumatized people work with animals, the social isolation in which they ended up because of their experiences can sometimes be broken through. An animal reacts predictably in accordance with its nature. When an animal is well treated it will gain confidence in the person taking care of it and more and more allow him or her to approach it. When an animal is badly treated it will reflect the behaviour of its caretaker and kick, scratch or bite. Both reactions of the animal are morally right. Therefore animals can work as examples for the person who takes care of them and contribute to a restoration of the person's own (self)confidence. This is an additional example of the way work can play a strongly supportive role to restore a person's disturbed state of balance. Work can thus make an important contribution to the process of becoming a human being.

5 The Professional Identity of the Professional Caregiver

Marijke Bijloo[72]

Clarity concerning the professional identity of the professional caregiver is of great importance. We understand professional identity as the totality of core concepts and ideas of professional educators in curative education and social therapy and their competencies, in other words the whole of the knowledge, insights, skills, and attitudes that belong to their profession. Explicitly formulated core concepts and competencies explain what are considered to be necessary requirements for good practice in the profession. For example, biodynamic farmers have the view that chemical fertilizer should not be used, and they consider their use as a lack of expertise. In addition, an explicit statement of competencies creates the possibility of purposefully focused training and of testing the practised care. In this way, a specifically directed striving becomes possible for a practice that is viewed as 'good' in the profession.

Competency means the totality of knowledge, insight, capacities, attitudes, and personal characteristics, through which adequate results can be reached in the context of the profession. Competencies are individual capacities. They have to be viewed within a specific context, which determines what is adequate. Whether a professional in caregiving to the handicapped indeed achieves adequate results depends not only on the person, but also on the possibilities of his or her environment. And vice versa; good organizational conditions or a favourable learning environment may stimulate a person to show competency. It may also happen that a particular environment or situation makes only a limited appeal to a professional's competency.

In this chapter the professional identity, in other words, the core concepts and competencies of professional caregivers are described. It is built on the foundation of the fundamental values described in Chapter 2, which underlie all anthroposophical care for people with developmental disabilities: equality, sense of service, and spiritual presence of mind. First of all the central core concepts of the professional identity are discussed (5.1), the fundamental attitudes in the profession (5.2), and the most important training subjects on the basis of these core concepts and attitudes (5.3). Then follows a description of why the core concepts and attitudes are also important for collaboration within the team of caregivers (5.4). Finally, in order to further emphasize the professional identity of the caregiver, we discuss the similarities and differences in position between the professional caregiver and the parents and family.

5.1 Core Concepts

Professional caregivers have five core concepts, which co-determine their actions. They relate to the driving forces in the human being, the fundamental values underlying caregiving, the person of the caregiver, the process of caregiving, and the manner in which education and treatment are provided.

5.1.1 The Universal Human Driving Force to Develop

The first core concept is that human beings, in their deepest essence fully worthy and whole, try to bring to realization during their lives on earth as many of the intentions and motives living in the core of their being as possible.[73] *As a result of this, human beings live out of a deeply anchored driving force toward development.* To look for the wish and will to develop the persons who need care is a fundamental task in curative education and social therapy. They want to offer personally focused support in this development, which means that they offer support and treatment attuned to the persons' individual desires to develop (see also 6.2 and 6.5.2).

5.1.2 Three Fundamental Values for Caregiving

The second core concept is that *there are three fundamental values for caregiving* (see also 2.2): *equality, sense of service, and spiritual presence of mind.* This section contains a sketch of what significance these values have and how they are worked with in curative education and social therapy.

Equality

In curative education and social therapy the emphasis is on the idea that people with developmental disabilities and their caregivers are on a journey together. Getting to know and dealing with one's own strong and weak points and, connected with this, the self-education of one's own person is constantly in the foreground, both for people with developmental disabilities and their caregivers (see also 5.3). In practice, efforts are made to create living conditions and learning- and work circumstances that make progressive development possible for both parties. In this way, the person with developmental disabilities and the caregiver share the same reality as equals.

The person of the curative pedagogue or social therapist is during their work the most important instrument. This means for them, on the one hand, great responsibility, on the other hand, also a problem. The problem that has to be solved all the time is the fact that professional caregivers are, on the one hand, fellows of the persons with developmental disabilities, which means that, on the level of the essential core of their being, they are equal to the ones they support. On the other hand, however, professional caregivers are also directors, when the persons they support are not sufficiently able to make responsible choices. Then the caregivers determine out of a sense of service to the disabled persons what can best be done. The way these two very different roles are handled ultimately determines the quality of the support.

Sense of Service

The will to help, to do something about the vulnerability or dependence of the other, is for people who work in professional education or caregiving what leads them to act. Through these deeds, which are in service of the development of the person with developmental disabilities, a relationship develops between the person who receives help and the one who gives the help. A bond grows from this.

Ever and again careful consideration has to be given to the question of whether the support is based on the sense of service to the true essence of the human being one is supporting. If such a sense of service is indeed the active motive, caregivers will undertake the responsibility of making choices for and on behalf of the persons receiving care—choices these persons cannot make for themselves. The danger of patronizing or even abuse of power is then always lurking around the corner. In this context, morality and integrity, which can be practised through self-reflection and interchange with colleagues, are important beacons to guide the actions of the curative educator and social therapist (see also 5.3). A sense of being in service to the other then leads to greater consciousness of one's own person, and to experiencing one's own strong and weak points.

Taking responsibility is a form of service whereby people perform their deeds on behalf of others, and thus enter into a relationship with them. Being able to bear responsibility can be considered as a moral foundation of human action. What occurs when someone takes or receives responsibility can well be described with the concept of 'moral technique' that Lievegoed introduced.[74] In moral technique the nature of the situation and the circumstances indicate who, in the given circumstances, can meaningfully and effectively bear responsibility. This responsibility can be given to different people, depending on the situation. In this context Lievegoed speaks of 'situational leadership'. Whereas traditionally leadership has been connected with power, social status, or education, in situational leadership the nature of the situation determines more and more who is best able to give leadership in it. This may lead to changes and alternations in leadership based on the specific competencies of the people involved.

This principle is also observed in curative education and social therapy. It is important that younger and adult people with developmental disabilities also be enabled and encouraged to take (co)responsibility, in accordance with their ability to bear it. This may contribute to their personal growth and will increase their feeling of self-worth and self-respect. Depending on the situation and capacities, responsibility is shared by the person receiving care and the caregiver.

> Ella's (a person receiving care) task as chief baker is justified, because her sense of responsibility comes from her insights into social aspects. As leader of the workshop I try to use her capacities to form policy. What is feasible for her, namely baking bread for the entire institution, becomes the task of the whole bakery. In this way the mission of the whole workshop is found. Her social capacities indicate a natural ability to lead. I then identify that leadership becomes her explicit task, and I test this identification for its correctness in meetings about the work.[75]

Spiritual Presence of Mind

At a time when protocols and regulations more and more determine and limit the space for personal action, and prescribed procedures have to be followed, anthroposophical caregiving also works based on intuition (see also 2.8.2 and 6.7.1). Acting out of intuition is characterized by Blomaard (see 2.6) as 'spiritual presence of mind', and by Fischer as:

> The courage to go in new and unusual directions, and to trust in the biographical strength and potential of the person one supports.[76]

In acting out of intuition the caregiver always has to try, out of active interest, to get better and better 'in conversation' with the being of the other. In this approach the effort is made to support people in need of care out of deeply experienced character insight. For this type of support, the caregiver tries to live as deeply as possible into the potential and situation of the person needing care. Such intuitive action seeks to be attuned to the other's will to develop, and cannot be fixed in a protocol ahead of time. This approach demands patience and social courage. It is also a creative process in which new findings can be made based on careful, unprejudiced observation (see also 7.5.2: the virtue of *phronesis*).

> Thus it becomes possible that caregivers perform their work not according to guidelines and rules, but fully awake out of their own responsibility and inner engagement. One thing that is of great significance in this is trust, for they have to enter into an open process with an unknown outcome. Trust in what is still unknown is necessary for free support, focused on the well-being of the supported individual, to exist. At a time when distrust reigns, and when one wants to know ahead of time the result of what has not yet been done, this is a huge challenge.[77]

5.1.3 The Person as the Most Important Instrument

A third core concept of the professional caregiver is that *you as a person are yourself the most important instrument in caregiving, support and treatment.* Therefore, the training not only consists of acquiring knowledge, insight, and skills, but self-education and inner schooling of the personality of the caregiver are of key importance.

To explain why the person of the educator is so important for the success of the support and treatment we first quote from Rudolf Steiner's *Curative Education*:

> For you have no idea how unimportant is all that the teacher says or does not say on the surface, and how important what he himself is, as teacher.

Steiner refers here to the task of caregivers to learn to attune themselves purely to the persons in need of care, with the result that their professional actions are ever more in service of the needs of the others. The core question here is whether the person of the educator is sufficiently 'tuned' to be able to act truly in service of the other (see also 2.2.2), or whether self-interest is predominant. This is also important in connection with the increased risk of abuse of vulnerable, dependent people needing care. Another reason why the tuning of the person as instrument is important is that children with developmental disabilities are so poorly anchored in their bodies (see also 3.6) and are therefore more finely attuned to their environment and more dependent on their caregivers. They often react less to spoken words but much more to intention, authenticity, and the underlying emotional charge.

The fact that the person of the educator has such a strong influence is not only true for children but for all situations where help is given, also to adults. Research into the effect of psychotherapy has shown that 30% of the result depends on the therapeutic relationship, in which the person of the therapist is all-important; only 15% depends on the methodology used.[78]

5.1.4 The Healing Effect of the Relationship and the Caregiving and Treatment Process

A fourth core concept, which is especially meaningful in curative education, is that *a healing (curative) effect can result from the educator's relationship with the child.* Of course, every educational relationship is intentional in the sense that the pedagogue wants to teach the child to adapt and really enter into life to further develop the talents it has brought with it and has acquired. In many areas, however, curative education has to mediate or correct, so as to be able to intervene in a healing way into one-sidedness or deficiencies in the constitution of the child, as was described before (see 3.1). Because of one-sided tendencies in the constitution a conscious effort is then made toward a more balanced, and therefore healthier, position in the middle (see 3.5.2, 7.2.2, and Appendix 1).

This requires that professional educators dare connect themselves with the destiny situations of the children The educational process itself then emanates a healing effect because as many hindrances as possible in the incarnation process are overcome (see also 3.1).

In addition, there is the concept that *the arrangement and form of the caregiving and treatment process has a healing effect* by the creation of a healing pedagogical or social climate. The effective elements of this climate were discussed in 4.2.2.

The healing effect that can result from both the relationship and the caregiving and treatment process can be understood from the principle of the pedagogical law that is described in 5.1.5.

Sjoukes & Wessels[79] describe how a two-and-a-half year old hydrocephalic boy, paralysed on one side, is admitted into a curative educational institution. The prognosis of regular medicine gave the child only a few weeks to live, and it would never be able to sit and stand, nor ever develop intellectually. Thanks to the curative educational care and the treatments with various anthroposophical therapies, and also his own strong commitment, he literally and figuratively grew past these predictions in the first three years of his life. One of the premises on which the treatment was based was the view that, because of the one-sided growth of his head, sense impressions had to be kept to a minimum. Because of this, initially he was often only approached with soft sense impressions in a poorly lighted room. In the book, the authors describe the boy as a young adolescent who follows special education.

5.1.5 A Pedagogical Law as Guideline for Education and Treatment

The last core concept is that *education and treatment proceed according to a pedagogical law*. In his lecture cycle *Curative Education* Rudolf Steiner describes based on the anthroposophical conception of the human being a generally applicable law, which he calls a pedagogical law. It mentions four elements, each of which has an effect on the element below it:

1. from the community or social context;
2. from the I;
3. from the emotional and feeling life;
4. from the life of habit with the rhythmical, vital processes.[80]

The core of the law is that out of a higher element a person can work in a healing way on the element below it in another person.

Educator/Caregiver		*Child/Person needing care*
Social context	→	I
I	→	feeling life
Feeling life	→	life of habit
Life of habit	→	physical body

The Law on the First Level

When a child is having *problems in the realm of the I*, it is necessary to intervene out of the social context. Problems in the realm of the I we see, for instance, in people whose functions are poorly integrated such as in autism, or by neglect in their early years, and by serious traumas. With such problems the help you can give will fall short if as parent or caregiver you have to face it by yourself. Our own I has insufficient potential to offer the weak I of, for example, a person with a serious trauma a sufficiently broad range of security and helpful possibilities. The better everyone involved (within a multi-disciplinary community) can arrive at good collaboration in service of the person needing their care, the more positive will the healing effect be. The principle of the therapeutic community is based on this healing potential. What has fallen asunder can there become a unity again through the working of the surpassing whole—the whole is more than the sum of the parts. Psychologist Bloom uses in this connection the concept of 'creating sanctuary', in which both the aspect of the safe harbour, and the healing working of the spirit are aptly indicated.

Rudolf Steiner described how the spirit self works through such a community of people, especially through the spoken language, whether or not they are conscious of it. It therefore depends, at least in part, on the spoken language what kind of spiritual influence we attract, and whether this will have a healing or ill effect on the I of the person receiving care. Because of this, words in which respect sounds for the fellow human being and the world are of such great significance. In curative educational and social therapeutic living- and work communities, therefore, the spiritual world is asked for its healing working through a verse, meditation, or prayer. In social therapy taking care of the community, and therefore furthering the healing power of the first level, is all-important. For when a person is an adult, the possibility to work into the constitution in a healing way is mostly no longer there.

The Law on the Second Level
When a child or adult is primarily having *problems in the realm of the emotional and feeling life (problems living in the soul)*, the educator/caregiver can give help from the I. For example, when a child has a tantrum, it does not help also to start yelling. Educators/caregivers must not be shaken out of their balance and must be able to give a reaction that fits their own I. This may be a consciously spoken and very clearly authoritative sentence like: 'Now stop it!' It has to be an appropriate reaction of the I of the caregiver in the moment. In the confrontation with the voice of the strong I of the other, the unchecked emotion allows itself to be guided and the child can come to itself.

The Law on the Third Level
Out of the feeling life we can *work in a healing way on the constitution when the feeling life is handled objectively*. Usually the feeling life alternates between positive and negative feelings, with the result that we naturally approve or more or less disapprove of what the child or adult is doing. In this regard it is important, however, to distinguish between the behaviour and the person, which makes it possible to reject the behaviour while preserving the loving acceptance of the person. If we have good contact with our own feeling life and accept it the way it is, the risk of projecting our own unprocessed feelings and emotions on the other is not as great.

When someone feels judged through an unfree emotional pattern he will inwardly arm himself. This is also true when the judgement is too positive (You are my darling), because then the person in need of care will do his best to keep it that way or even better. The caregiver's critical self-reflection and sincerity have a positive effect. The person needing care then has no need to arm himself, and can just be himself.

Undeserved judgements call up strong emotional defensive reactions and disturb the balance in the soul life, which in the long run has a weakening effect and may cause illness. Striving for sincerity and objectivity regarding oneself as well as the person needing care has a health-fostering and stimulating effect. It awakens the ability to be forgiving. In such a climate the life of habit can also work fruitfully because it is not disturbed by subjective emotions.

The Law on the Fourth Level
Rhythms in the course of the day, week, and year that form part of the life of habit work positively into the physical body. Rhythm creates the basis for a healthy life (see also 4.5.2 and 6.6.2). Chaos causes breakdown, collapse; order in healthy habits—which are not up for discussion with a young child—bring rest and strength. Especially for children who come in just for the day, creating a healthy life of habits takes much time and energy, because around the child with developmental problems conflicts and stress often cause many unhealthy habits.

> Every night Sven wants a light and a little bottle, from which he then does not drink. He only wants to be carried through the house in a particular way, and instructs his mother in what ritual the light switches have to be thrown.
>
> Irene insists that her mother take her out of her bed every night at exactly 1.20 am. She then has to sit cross-legged (and not differently!) humming (not singing!) a specific lullaby, and this forced ritual is only over when her mother turns her wedding ring on her pinkie, every night anew.

In a full-time setting a healthy atmosphere can have a healing effect. For example, parents expressed their surprise about the fact that their child, that always refused to eat, was eating normally a month after its admittance. To their question of what had been done, the answer can simply be 'nothing special'. The child lets itself be taken long in the rhythmical, habitual pattern around eating and sleeping; there is rest and quiet, and physical health increases. In this way a healthy life of habit lays the *basis for physical health.*

5.2 The Role of Attitude in the Profession

There are two aspects that form the basis for the fundamental attitude of the professional caregiver: the attitude of loving acceptance, and the attitude of openminded, inward listening as the basis for the caregiver's actions.

5.2.1 Loving Acceptance

A good professional attitude includes first of all the *loving acceptance* of the child or adult needing care. This loving acceptance goes a step further than the now obvious respectful treatment of a person. In *Curative Education*

Rudolf Steiner points out that we can develop this loving acceptance by practising *increased interest in the being different* of the other, in what deviates from 'normal' development.

Truly increased interest requires the capacity of *'objective' observation*, in other words, to distinguish observation from judgement. Factual observation says something about the other, the judgement of this usually says something about yourself. The point is to become conscious of these often half-conscious judgements. Especially people with developmental disabilities have strong reactions to our unconscious or half-conscious judgements, emotions, and feelings, precisely because they are so open, dependent, and sensitive to atmosphere. A well-known example is the caregiver who, after a tense meeting with colleagues, walks in a black mood into a room. Not long afterward a child with autism has a tantrum, and the mood of the caregiver changes from frustration to anger without him realizing the connection between his mood and the tantrum of the child.

The next step involves not only the observation of the other through the physical senses (among others the senses of touch, vision, hearing, and smell), but *using one's own soul as an instrument for observing the other.* When the noise and unrest in myself have been silenced, I can become observant of what the other evokes in me, via my living into the other in my observation (see also 6.3). This loving and interested living into the other can, on the one hand, have a liberating effect on the soul movements and blockages of a person with developmental disabilities. Sellin, an autistic adolescent who cannot speak but has learned to type wrote in his book:

> One single word spoken with love can heal countless wounds, and a loving gaze has an enormous effect without words … but many looks are so difficult to bear and lead to incomparable suffering.[81]

On the other hand, when you thus make your own soul into an instrument of observation of the other, you acquire more and more essential knowledge, insight, and understanding for and of the other. By schooling observation it is possible to gather objective knowledge of the other, through which conditions are created to also better attune our actions to the other. In this way *loving acceptance* becomes a *cognitive instrument*.

5.2.2 Acting out of an Inwardly Listening and Openminded Attitude

In order to perform a deed that is attuned to the individual in a particular situation, the professional caregiver has to develop an attitude with which he or she can from the heart inwardly ask questions of the person in need of care. In his book *Is It Worth It?*, Meininger describes how the German pedagogue Karlheinz Kleinbach makes a distinction between the pedagogy of malleability and of 'being touched'. He quotes:

> But … I am addressed in the encounter, no one else. I am looked at, I am meant, I am called, I cannot hide behind anything. I am responsible for my answer. In the other human being I meet a 'once-only', a uniqueness that transcends all sociological, psychological, or historical definitions. This is the pedagogy of being touched. […] looking for a world to live in together, that is the challenge! That requires us to look differently and anew.[82]

By your effort and will to help, the being of the other will feel known and heard, and will answer. Such question may be regarded as asking the Parsifal question.

> When Parsifal, grown old and wise, at the end of his long wanderings comes for the second time, but now consciously, to the Grail Castle (read: spiritual world), he asks out of the bottom of his heart, and with sincere interest, the question of the suffering of the old, mortally ill Fisher King Amfortas. This compassion has a liberating effect, and the old sick king can finally die. It is Easter, and the Grail Cup appears showing on its edge the name of Parsifal as the new Grail King. After eating and drinking the substances of bread and wine, Parsifal is filled with new (eternal) life. The compassion and asking the right question made him king.[83]

By asking the right questions the old (Amfortas in us) can be let go, and the new (Parsifal in us) can be born. Goethe spoke in this context of *stirb und werde*—die and become. The Parsifal story represents the process of a long search (through many lives) for the spirit. In paintings this is often represented by a white dove that descends onto the Grail. It is the spirit (the spirit self, the Holy Spirit) that helps the I to transform the knots of destiny, so that the lower ego can die and the higher I can be born in the human being. The Parsifal story also shows that in an encounter not all opportunities are used. Parsifal comes to the Grail Castle for the first time as a young man out of curiosity and by coincidence, but he neglects to ask the question about the destiny of the sick king out of a living concern in his heart. However, if we have the courage to ask the right questions and to listen to the answers, healing can be found.

For people with developmental disabilities it is the 'helping/healing' caregivers (the circle of people around them, including the parents) who can ask the question of the destiny of this person, and can learn to listen to the answers that come to meet them. When in children with developmental disabilities there is still a constitution that can be positively influenced, it is the educators' task to intervene in a healing way, in service to the further development of the child, in order to diminish the seriousness of the disability to the extent possible, and strengthen the quality of life and the will to live.

To avoid misunderstanding, it has to be said that a 'healing education' does not mean that, for example, a child with Down Syndrome needs to be cured of this syndrome. Apart from the fact that this cannot be done, in such cases of inborn syndromes the point is to develop a loving acceptance of this singularity. Especially children with Down Syndrome live strongly in the imitation of their surroundings, and this means that their education largely contributes to their later ability to fit harmoniously in life. In this way the specific capacities that belong to the syndrome and the individuality of the child can come to development, with respect for the limitations the syndrome brings with it.

5.3 Schooling

The core concepts and attitudes of the professional identity have led to specific forms of schooling, which also connect up with the fundamental values of equality, sense of service, and spiritual presence of mind.

5.3.1 Schooling in Sense of Service

The aim of the schooling in sense of service is particularly the development of two capacities: making yourself into an instrument, and practising loving acceptance.

Schooling to Make Yourself into an Instrument

If your personality is the most important instrument it is extremely important that you learn to tune this instrument, in order to come into harmony with the child or adult in need of care instead of sounding in disharmony together. What methods are there for tuning the personality?

Self-knowledge is of prime importance for this. For in the first instance we are all inclined to project our shortcomings and one-sidedness onto others. Getting yourself in view, not treating your own past and your own upbringing as an obvious standard, and recognizing and letting go of your own projections—these things are part of the professional training. In the learning process, working with personal goals is an important means. In addition, working together with others is a means to get to know yourself better, and by working on self-knowledge this working together can grow from a field full of pitfalls into a source of enrichment (see also 5.4).

In the training for therapeutic caregiver in curative education and social therapy the so-called *Triale Method* is used.[84] This method consists, first of all, of acquiring knowledge and insight into the anthroposophical conception of the human being, regular orthopedagogy, care of the developmentally handicapped, and child and youth psychiatry. In addition, it also encompasses the sharing of experiences that have been gained in the past 100 years in curative education and later also in social therapy. The training also works on the schooling of the person's own soul through artistic subjects. The objective of this artistic schooling is not the art in itself, but to become inwardly mobile and learn to tune yourself in head, heart, and hands. During these artistic activities—painting, sculpting and moulding, working in wood or stone, singing, making music, stage acting, eurythmy—one-sided tendencies and inner blockages become conscious and can be worked through into new insights. This inner mobility and learning to tune into the other and yourself is a prerequisite for dealing with children and adults with developmental disabilities. If caregivers are too stuck in their own track they will not sufficiently succeed in living into and tuning into what is needed.

Schooling in Loving Acceptance

The schooling in loving acceptance includes developing interest in a person's being different, learning to observe objectively, and learning to observe with one's own soul (empathetic observation).

You learn to *become observant of what happens differently* in the person with a developmental disability as compared with a person with a healthy development. Acquiring knowledge of the course of normal development, and learning to recognize deviations from this, are therefore of prime importance (see also 3.1). In practising heightened interest in being different, you also run into yourself. Are you able to generate sufficient inner quiet, silence your own inner voice, to open yourself to the other?

In the different ways in which people observe, some people live more out of their head and tend to keep a distance. Others are doers and fail to hold back. And others again react out of their feelings and tend to lose themselves in others. In this respect, self-knowledge is important in order to learn to find a *balanced middle point* between the extremes of excessive distance and failure to hold back, withdrawing and being carried along. Through it all, humour—without sarcasm, self-mockery, or ridiculing the other—is an important relativizing means for dealing dynamically and respectfully with what you have discovered through self-knowledge.

In learning *objective observation* it is important to ask yourself in self-reflection where your own experiences and judgements come from. Is your mood saying something about what you have experienced somewhere else and is still hanging there, or about something that reminds you (unconsciously) of an earlier event, as a result of which you project the feelings and judgements of that moment onto the current situation? You meet feelings of sympathy and antipathy which, by recognizing and acknowledging them, you can let go as not forming part of this human being in this situation. This practice has a strong educational effect on your own soul life.[85]

Schooling in empathetic observation takes different forms. Two variants are described below of the methodology of imitation from an attitude of acceptance. It is their purpose to develop knowledge of and insight into the person with developmental disabilities out of the experience of living into their situation.

The anthroposophical view of the human being describes that all learning begins with imitation. This learning principle is most strongly present in the period to the change of teeth. The high point in the imitation period lies in the third year of life, when the child consciously or unconsciously imitates everything that happens in its surroundings. The 'knowledge' acquired through imitation is stored in conscious and unconscious soul life in the organs and muscle systems of the body. This imitation method can also be consciously applied at a later age by imitating the *outer gestures* of someone else with your own body, and then tracking what you experience and what it tells you when, for instance, you move the way the other moves. You can also do this by literally imitating the movements of a person receiving care. It may lead to recognition and a form of contact that was previously not possible.

Another possibility is to project yourself into the condition of soul of the person receiving care, and *inwardly imitating this in your own soul*, with the question of what you then experience. You might, for instance, try to live into a 'too open child or adult' (see also 6.3 and 7.2.2) and to follow what this does to your thinking, breathing, your ability to react to a situation. Subsequently, you might wonder how, in that condition, you might want to be approached, or what would be helpful. It is important that this exercise be done under the supervision of a teacher, who afterwards helps you to come back 'into your own soul' and to the reality of the day.

These projection exercises are practised in the professional training and have proven to be a rich source of insight and ability to provide appropriate help. Moreover, the knowledge acquired in this way proves to be quite lasting.

5.3.2 Schooling in Spiritual Presence of Mind

Schooling in spiritual presence of mind encompasses the application of a specific meditation for the profession, learning to act well in a situation by asking questions, and developing the ability to (self)reflect.

The Meditation for the Profession

In *Curative Education* Rudolf Steiner not only indicates a way to tune one's own soul, but also a way to strengthen the working of the spirit, and to learn to trust in one's own ability in collaboration with the spiritual world (see also 2.2.3 and 2.6).

To this end, the *meditation for the profession* is described, which can be performed as follows. Caregivers inwardly imagine a blue circle with a yellow point, and thereafter a yellow circle with a blue point. They then imagine how the blue circle becomes a point and the yellow circle appears and, the other way around, how the yellow point becomes a circle in which the blue appears as a point. In the process they check which inner movements they have to make to bring this about.

In this way the principle of the inversion of 'the outside becomes the inside and the reverse' can be discovered. Steiner pointed in this connection to the relationship of this meditation with the dynamic shown by the I respectively in the head and in the limbs (see also 3.4.2, Fig. 2). The I is awake during the day in observing and thinking in the head. It takes concentration and quiet to think clearly, to focus inwardly (to become a point), whereas in the limbs the I, in all its doings, connects with everything that happens around it (to become a circle).

In the realm between the head and the limbs, the middle area where the heart and lungs are, constant inversions are taking place. There the inside becomes outside, and the outside inside. For example, we breathe in air from the surroundings and then breathe it out again into the surroundings. Also the heart shows in its working the dynamic of alternately becoming a circle and a point, namely in the heartbeat of the systole (contracting/point) and diastole (relaxing/circle). In the soul life, this rhythmical movement can be recognized in the social process between people. In the outbreath we live into the other, and in the inbreath we connect again with our own feeling life (see also 3.4.2, Fig. 3).

When we sleep at night the working of the I is reversed as compared with the day when we are awake. At night the limbs are at rest, and the spiritual world is, unconsciously to us, working on the regeneration, the building up of the body (point). The I, which during the day works consciously in the head, is at night in deep sleep in the spiritual world, its actual home (circle), of which human beings have no conscious memory.

By practising this meditation we can experience how the spiritual world works in the human being in reverse during the day and at night. In the morning we imagine the yellow circle as the working of the spiritual world, with the I as the blue point; this can awaken the awareness: 'I am in God or in the divine or spiritual world.' In the evening we reverse the picture and imagine how the yellow circle becomes the point in us and then how our I turns from blue point into blue circle evoking the awareness: 'In me is God or the spiritual world.' The next morning we again make the reverse movement: the yellow point becomes a circle and the blue circle becomes a blue point in the awareness: 'I am in God or in the divine or spiritual world,' et cetera.

The point is not only to think this content, but also to feel and will it, so that it is not only working in the head, but permeates the whole person. Practising this meditation strengthens our inner trust in the working of the spiritual world. In this way, we can directly work on strengthening *spiritual presence of mind* in the practice of our profession. It helps to overcome our own anxieties, rationalizations, or self-satisfaction, and strengthen inner courage in care and support relationships.

In the same lecture, Rudolf Steiner also points out how important it is that in the consciousness of the caregiver there always is an inner and sincere mood of: 'I can do this.' Because of this, inner resistance, for instance, avoiding something out of fear to act, can be overcome, and we can act adequately in the situation. It is the true, higher I in action. In a real encounter the spiritual world can work together with us as a third power.

At the same time, however, we are made aware of the pitfalls of our lower I (or ego), such as vanity, assertiveness, self-overestimation, and the danger of floating up into abstractions when speaking of grand missions. An eloquent picture of this is the myth of Icarus who rose up so high that his waxen wings melted in the sun. What helps is to go back down every time to the concrete situation and focus our attention on the concrete person who needs help. The principle to observe in this process is *attention to the little things*. It is in the little things, in the smallest detail (point) that the great working (circle) expresses itself. We can practise attention to little things, for instance, by inwardly imagining a child or adult. Attention to little things means observing details with heightened interest. Heightened interest together with objective, empathetic observation leads to loving acceptance.

In the (self-)schooling of the caregiver, the point is that you have to dare *connect* yourself with the other person so as to be able to act in a helpful way out of the context in which this person lives. As long as caregivers shrink back from the problems of the other or reject these, they cannot help or arrive at loving acceptance. Especially for helping people who were neglected or abused in early childhood this fear is totally realistic and understandable. Then it takes work to let go of expectations and hope of success. This calls for great inner courage. Practising the meditation for the profession may strengthen the confidence that the invisible reality is present and helps in this process.

Learning to Act Well in a Situation by Asking Questions

It always requires an encounter to learn to act well in a situation, but this encounter can also take place inwardly by asking questions. The efficacy of asking and living with a question lies in our active interest and courage to want to connect with the person asking for help.

A valuable exercise is to find a spot in the evening or in a quiet moment during the day, where you are not disturbed, in order to call up the outer appearance of the person needing care as a memory picture (see also 6.3 and 7.2.2). The picture must be filled in with as many details as possible, such as the colour and form of the eyes, nose, ears, and the clothing that was worn. The picture should be as complete and accurate as you can make it. The person in the picture can then be truthfully moved and observed. Unknown details can be filled in to the best of your capacity, and checked the next day to see if they were truthful or need adjustment. If it is difficult to call up the whole picture, you can start just with the head. The whole thing should not be given more than five to ten minutes.

The person can then be *inwardly asked a question*, such as: 'Can you indicate to me how you want to be helped?' or 'Can you show me what is the matter with you?' Any question is good as long as it is asked in service of the person's further development and care. Next, the picture is erased, is actively let go, and you listen to what wants to express itself in the inner space you have created. What answer will come is unpredictable. Some people receive an inner picture right away, others hear nothing. Often nothing happens in the moment itself, but someone wakes up the next morning with a picture or thought that is important. To an actively living question an answer may come during sleep. Sometimes the answer does not come in the form of a picture, thought, or in words, but you find, when you have done this exercise three times or so, that when you next meet the person you suddenly know what you have to do. It may feel as if it happened all by itself and came as a spontaneous brainwave. The answer comes in through the portal that is most accessible for the person to gain knowledge from the invisible, objective world. It may be the portal of *imagination* (picture), *inspiration* (word, feeling), or *intuition* (deed).

When this empathetic, listening attitude has been developed, it is possible in the concrete encounter with the person asking for care to inwardly ask questions, and to 'listen' how the answer comes back in direct statements or from the environment. The following is an example.

> During the examination in a clinic for child- and youth psychiatry the child was asked to inwardly picture a tree. Then he was asked to make the picture as detailed as possible, also the area around the tree. Before the person told his story of the tree, the staff member inwardly addressed the being of the person in need of care and asked him the inner question of why he had come and what was the matter. In this way remarkable life stories are told, in which the person shows in the symbolism of the picture how he stands in life. In the dynamic of the story inner blockages and other problems the person has with his environment become visible. Besides other results of the examination, these pictures are of great value to understand the person in his or her social context and how to offer help.

Thus we can all, in our own ways and in our specific specialties, make use of learning to ask inner questions in essential moments, and become sensitive to the answers that stream to us out of the inner being of the child and the spiritual worlds. However, because of the pressure of work, hectic circumstances, and limited alertness in the moment (spiritual presence of mind), many answers are lost. The trick is to develop a sense organ for what is really essential in the encounter with the person in need of care. Particularly in little details significant answers come to meet us.

The Development of Reflective Capacities

Self-observation is one of the most important instruments caregivers have at their disposal in their professional and personal development. Their actions can continually be tested through their own reflections on their expertise as well as their professional engagement. This is an unceasing, methodical work with the ancient mystery words: 'Know Yourself.' It asks an attitude on the part of caregivers of critically looking at their own actions, of being willing to adjust and relativize opinions and interpretations, and of receiving and giving critical feedback. The development of reflective capacities requires schooling.

Some examples of forms of self-reflection that can be schooled are:

- *The review.* In the review a person actively makes an inner picture of an event of the past day, days, or weeks. As indicated before, in doing this we should strive for precision and clarity as we build this inner picture.

The point is not to be caught in the feelings that spontaneously arose at the time of the event. The event should be observed impartially, as if by a spectator and as if you were looking at something done by someone else. Rudolf Steiner mentioned this form of review in several of his books and lectures as an exercise on the path of schooling. Such a review of our own actions opens the possibility to face our successes and failings with equanimity.

- *Reflexive professionalism.* In action and treatment we can distinguish three qualities. The first quality is technical professionalism, through which we master the trade in order to be able to act expertly and according to agreements. The second quality is personal engagement. Entering into direct interaction with the person with whom we are working demands objective and subjective qualities. The third quality is reflexive professionalism. It connects the first two with each other and lays the basis for individual intuitive action. Reflexive systematic professionalism can also be practised in a group of people, for instance, by describing an 'unexpectedly successful (or failed) action', looking back on it together, and examining what proved to be effective.
- *Individual supervision and 'inter-vision' in a group of colleagues.* Supervision is a competence-furthering method aimed at teaching one to function (more) autonomously in the practice of the profession. The supervisor guides others in actively reflecting on their thinking, feeling, and will to create as much integration as possible in their own soul life, as well as between them as persons, their profession, and their work situation. Usually, personal teaching goals are used to practise new capacities. Besides this, inter-vision is also of great importance to exchange experiences among colleagues and learn from each other. It is a way of working among colleagues without having to be concerned about hierarchical, service-oriented, or personal relationships, so that work experiences can be discussed among equals. All these forms of support can only be effective if one feels secure and therefore dares to show vulnerability and a desire to learn. In this sense, another important aspect of this form is that it can also bring needed security.

5.4 Working Together

The core concepts and attitudes of the professional identity described above do not only play a role in dealing with people in need of help. They are just as important for the cooperation among colleagues.

In working together with others we regularly run into our own incapacities and shortcomings or those of colleagues, perhaps projected onto others. Here it is a real art to regard the weaknesses of yourself and colleagues with the same mildness and heightened interest we generate when dealing with a person in need of care. The same principle holds sway: as long as you reject these weaknesses or fight them and refuse to own them, you remain trapped in them. Acknowledging them and gradually accepting them make it possible to take new steps to patiently transform these weaknesses.

We witness a tendency in curative education and social therapy to make the treatment as short and specific as possible, and therefore centres offering ambulatory care and help at home have been rapidly growing. Although in itself this is a positive trend, the consequence is that people who qualify for full-time admission and treatment are mostly showing complex problems. It is especially in this target group that the interactions among people in need of care and group support demand a high degree of awareness and spiritual presence of mind. Fruitful collaboration is then no obvious given.

What is true in the relationship between a single child and a professional educator, namely that the child can further develop provided the professional educator him- or herself is in movement and development, is also true for a group of children and a team. The critical point is always the inner readiness to further develop self-knowledge and continue one's schooling; and the point is not that you aren't allowed to make mistakes, or that things have to be perfect. If such a fruitful cooperation does not come about, the situation of the people in need of care will not improve.

On the contrary, the danger then exists in the case of complex problems, that these pass over, as it were, into behavioural patterns of the group caregivers, and can even have an unhealthy effect. That is called a parallel process. The pedagogical law indicates that in case of problems on the level of the I (such as in cases of neglect and abuse), one single I is not able to work in a healing way, but that good working together in a community (group) can emanate a healing effect. The circle then radiates strength onto the point (see 5.3.2).

A significant help can in such situations be given in the form of team counselling. An experienced team counsellor, who is not part of the existing team, can advance upbuilding processes and challenge undermining processes.

5.5 Similarities and Differences in the Positions of the Professional Caregiver as Compared with the Parents/Family

The professional identity of the professional caregiver is further defined when we compare it with the position of the parents and other family members. Besides similarities there are great differences in their positions. The emotional engagement with the person in need of care is much stronger with the parents and family, and the bond is deep because of the blood relationship. In many cases the parents first have the shock of the discovery of having a child with a developmental disability. Then there may come a long time before the parents know what is the matter with their child, sometimes after a period of disagreement among experts. This period is most often one of much inner anxiety and tension. Then come inner distress and pain, the people around them who often do not understand it or play it down, and the process of letting go of normal expectations of the future. This process is often repeated through the different phases of development. The ability to go through this mourning process and to find good support for it is of great significance for the parents and family; it colours the quality of the relationship with the future professional caregivers. When this mourning process is insufficiently lived through, the danger exists that the professional caregiver is experienced as a competitor.

Every parent with a child with a developmental disability experiences that the process of bonding and detaching proceeds differently. The child that goes through a normal development will, in its third year, when in its rebellious phase it begins to say no and consciously says I, more and more detach itself from the parents and stand more on its own two feet. Characteristic for the relationship between parent and child with a developmental disability is that the symbiosis (the bond on the etheric level) continues to exist much longer, sometimes forever (see also 3.6). A striking aspect is that the bond with the mother (the principal caregiver), on the one hand, is remarkably intense while, on the other hand, there are almost always strong ambivalences and irritations. The ambivalences come from the fact that on the physical level a loosening is indeed taking place, but the child also continues to need the parent. The child that has to cope with its limitations feels the resistance of its disability and wants more help. It finds that the parent is not supportively present every moment, becomes frustrated, and may start showing headstrong behaviour. The parent offers extra help out of a strong bond, but over time this may go too far and become overprotective and suffocating.

With the professional caregiver the person in need of care often also tries to create such a symbiotic relationship, but because of the emotionally more neutral connection and the professional training this connection usually does not reach quite as far. On the other hand, the relationship with a human being with a developmental disability can be a source of further growth and development for everyone. Learning to handle the underlying symbiosis objectively contains, both for parents and professional caregivers, individual challenges. Whereas for the professional caregiver there is the challenge to dare to connect more with the destiny of the child, the parents, and especially the mother, face the challenge of engagement with sufficient distance, so that the child, to the extent possible, can function more autonomously.

Isarin[86] describes and examines the experiences of mothers with handicapped children with all their ambiguities and peculiarities. Isarin, herself a mother of a handicapped child, points out that we do the most justice to the experience of the parents by using a both-and approach. The parent often experiences both love for and rejection of the child, acceptance and resistance, shame and pride, estrangement and recognition. In addition, the parents often have known their child longer than the professional caregiver, and feel burdened with the lifelong duty to care to the child and with many questions of how it will all go in the future.

Another important difference is that the professional caregiver is surrounded by a team of 'experts', and the caregiving process is realized and carried by this multi-disciplinary team. Add to this that the professional caregivers after their shift can let go of the situation and come back fresh to their next shift, whereas the parents can never take any distance and can thus become overburdened. With the development of ambulatory treatment centres and daycare there is fortunately much more potential to support parents and family. Also for the people in need of care themselves there are all kinds of ambulatory care and help available.

6 The Caregiving Process from a Methodological Perspective

Martin Niemeyer

In this chapter methodological aspects of the caregiving process are described, as these are practised in anthroposophical caregiving for people with developmental disabilities and for youths and children with psychiatric problems. These methodological aspects create conditions needed for providing good care, including support and treatment. The inspiration for this methodology comes from anthroposophical spiritual science and its conception of the human being.

Based on anthroposophical spiritual science, the human being is to be considered a unique being, which has its origin and future in a spiritual reality, the spiritual world. In their biography the development is manifested that each individual goes through. Development is a characteristic of being human. In the realization of their developmental tasks individuals work together with others in mutual dependence (see also 2.2). This concept becomes the basis for the way caregiving to individuals with developmental disabilities is approached. They are respected in their inherent (equal) worth as human beings, and have their own responsibility for the choices they make. Their capacities determine the extent to which they can bear this responsibility, as well as the measure of care and support they need.

Each person possesses development potential and abilities to restore inner balance and health, and take charge of themselves. Anthroposophically inspired care is in its support and treatment first of all oriented toward supporting and making use of these abilities. This general premise is individualized in anthroposophical caregiving based on the particular need of the client. This holds true for children and adults, to whom support is offered from a broad range of forms of care, from out-patient to full-time forms of anthroposophical caregiving. The word client is used here as a general term that includes adults as well as children in need of or receiving care.

The different phases of the care- and support process are successively discussed in this chapter: the *need* of the client (6.2), the *observation* (6.3) and *image forming* (6.4) that result in the *diagnosis* (6.5) and the *care plan* (6.6), the *treatment* (6.7) and the *evaluation* (6.8). The model described by A. H. Bos to arrive at forming a dynamic judgement is helpful in creating cohesion in this process, and is therefore described first.[87]

6.1 Dynamic Judgement-Forming

The provision of care takes place, based on the need of the person who asks for it, in his or her encounter with the caregiver(s). In many cases, this need and the response thereto only gradually become concrete. In this process situations continually arise in which choices have to be made. These choices are made on the basis of judgements. For example, judgements have to be formed in the process of reaching a diagnosis for the evaluation of the need and the response thereto. Even an every-day support situation like resolving a quarrel among children asks for forming a judgement.

The need guides the caregiving process: the steps in the diagnostic process and the response to the need. Dynamic judgement-forming creates a way of working based on the anthroposophical conception of the human being for responding to the need for care, as well as a model for the individualization of the care.

Dynamic judgement-forming is based on questions. Questions rooted in engagement and interest determine the process of dynamically forming judgements. Generally speaking two types of questions can be distinguished: a cognitive question to understand the world or a situation, and questions of choice about how to change a situation. These questions form the starting point and a guiding impulse for both the cognitive and the choice process. The strength of this impulse will be the stronger as the need is more important to the client and the caregiver is more interested and engaged in the case. In the cognitive phase appears an insight (an image and/or diagnosis) as a cognitive judgement; in the choice phase, choice judgements are applied in the concrete practice of caregiving. In daily practice, both types of questions most often arise at the same time. A support worker who helps resolve a conflict between two children will in the cognitive phase try to understand what is going on, and immediately want to act adequately in the choice phase.

Each of these two phases is characterized by a specific dynamic. In the cognitive phase there is a constant alternation between observations and concepts through which the observations can be explained and ordered. This process is rounded off when through the right concepts the observations lead to an insight in the form of an image or diagnosis. In a comparable manner, in the choice phase a coordination occurs between the objectives for taking action and the ways and means through which these objectives can be realized. The objective of supporting someone so that he can live on his own can only be realized if the ways and means are available that are attuned to the person and the situation.

The process of dynamic judgement-forming described here can be represented in the form of the lemniscate, a form in which the dynamic of mobility comes to expression. The loop on the left refers to the cognitive phase and leads along observing and thinking to insight into what has become out of the past. The loop on the right shows the phase of choice and leads to realizing the objectives into the future. In between, at the crossing, stands the question that arises out of interest and engagement, which guides the judgement-forming process in the present.

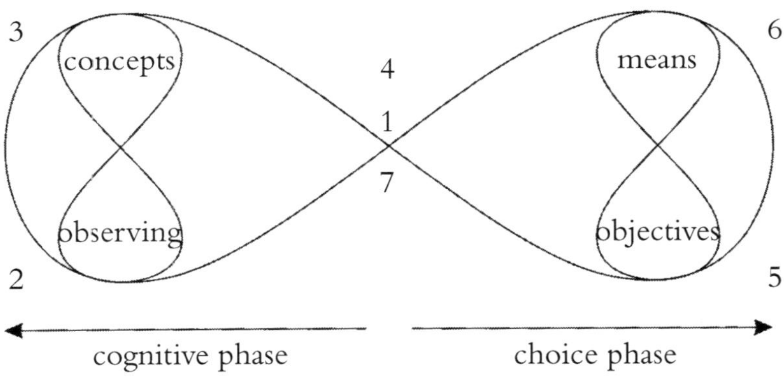

1 question
2 observation
3 picture
4 diagnosis
5 care plan
6 treatment
7 evaluation

Fig. 7 Cognitive phase and choice phase

6.2 The Question of the Need

In the encounter between the provider(s) of care and the person with a developmental disability, getting to know the need of the client is of primary importance. As described above, this question determines the course of the caregiving process.

We can distinguish different kinds of questions. Questions may primarily lie in the cognitive process. Their purpose is to understand whatever is not clear or can hardly be comprehended. In this way, a regularly returning question during the early phase of caregiving may be: 'We want to know what is the matter with Nancy?' Another question may relate to a lack of understanding of a stagnation in development: 'Why is Josh not yet potty-trained?' Such questions have the purpose of getting to know more about the cause. In addition, there are the questions that are more oriented toward action and the future; these belong primarily to the phase of choice.

In caregiving, many development-oriented questions are asked, such as: 'How can Tom learn to get himself dressed?' or 'How can Kate learn not to start hitting others when she is mad?' and 'What work would be right for John?' In most cases the problem of what care is needed does not remain limited to one question, but there will be a whole chain of knowledge- and action-oriented questions. The original question can be adjusted in every phase of the dynamic process of forming a judgement. For caregiving, this is important because the question gives expression to the wishes and expectations of the client. Dealing correctly with the question of what care is needed is a prerequisite for the client's ability to develop further.

Another aspect of the question is the factor of time. If the situation is urgent because the person is suffering in body or soul, an acute answer is needed for the caregiving process. Questions may also have a longer term perspective: 'What do I need to be able to live on my own?'

In situations of long-term care, the awareness of the question may fade to the background, and a kind of automatism may become predominant in the given care. Therefore, it is desirable to give regular attention in client reviews and discussions to the question of the need of the client, and shine new light on it. It is a call to explore what the development question asked by the client is: to arrive at an insight into what the question and the perspective of the client are, where does his will lead him, what resistances will he try to overcome, and what talents does he want to unfold?

Responding to the need of the client may lead to questions the caregiver asks himself: 'How can I help find an answer to this question of the client, and how can I help him fulfil his wishes? What does this ask of me, and what do I have to bring to development in myself to be able to do this? Do I have enough access to possibilities of support for this? How do I bring that about in the relationship and encounter with this human being?' The encounter with client and his need for care helps the caregiver become conscious of these questions. In this way, a task awaits both the person in need of care and the caregiver, and both search for answers to their development questions.

In the model of dynamic judgement-forming this can be indicated with an extra lemniscate in the crossing point of the question:

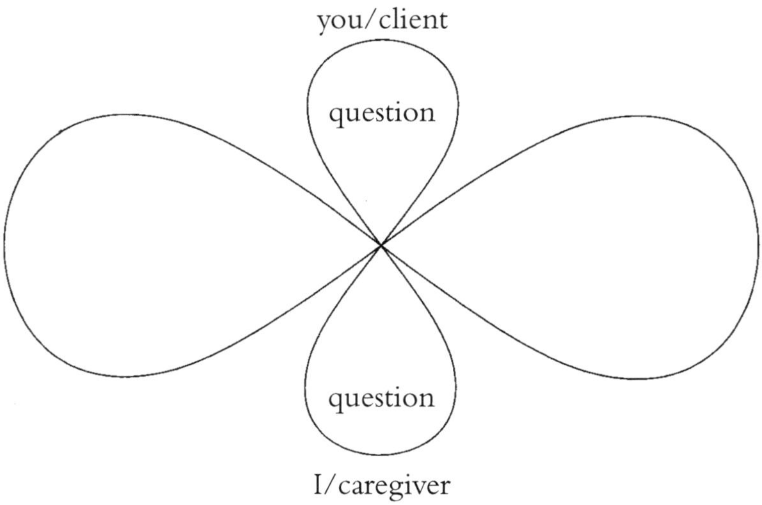

Fig. 8 Dynamic judgement-forming

6.3 Observation

A first step toward answering the question of the need for care is watching and observing. Every caregiver has a particular way of looking at a client and, depending on this, more or less definite areas he or she observes based on personal qualities and specific expertise. A support worker will in his observation of a client primarily look at events in daily life, the way daily life proceeds. A teacher and a work boss primarily watch the client from the perspective of learning and working. Similarly, a physician, psychologist, ortho-pedagogue, and therapist each have their own specific areas of observation. Together they form as complete a picture of the client as possible. Depending on the need this may include:

- The client as a person:
  - the physical and external appearance;
  - the life functions: the course of the day with sleeping, eating, metabolism, excretion, vitality, health;
  - the soul functions: cognitive development with observation and thinking, social-emotional development with feeling and experiencing, the will and action;
  - the biography, particular interests and hobbies and critical events; expectations, wishes and plans the client expresses.
- The client in relation to others: social functioning, the client's network and his place in it.
- If necessary, observations of specialists regarding the client's physical, soul, and social functioning, the level of his mental capacities, et cetera.

In the cognitive phase a difference has to be made between observation as such and thinking about what was observed, between observation of phenomena and the concepts that can be connected with them in thinking. This has an influence on the quality of the judgement that will be formed. The difference becomes evident when someone does not (yet) possess concepts to apply to what was observed. For instance, someone who does not know what epilepsy is will describe a seizure in a completely different way from someone who is familiar with the relative concept.

It is important that the process of observation and concept formation be conducted methodically. In observation, therefore, we distinguish two successive steps. The first step is the factual and exact observation of the client and his situation. The second step is empathetic observation, a living into the client. The first step produces through the senses, for example, an observation of a pale and unhealthy seeming person who looks startled and afraid as he watches a broken dish he has just dropped in front of him. In the second step the observation is turned inward through empathy and imitation, and the observer can in himself experience a resonance of the insecurity and helplessness of the man who dropped the dish (see also 5.2).

In empathetic observation in addition to the senses, soul capacities are also used to arrive at knowledge. Generally speaking, observation by unschooled observers is coloured by their specific interests and prejudices. However, it is the task of the caregiver to become conscious of these things, and learn to deal with them. The capacities to be used for this have been derived from Goethean phenomenology.

Goethean phenomenology offers a systematic method to attain knowledge and insight through observation. The basis for this method was laid by Goethe[88] and further developed by Rudolf Steiner.[89] It describes the practice and intensification of observation, and the resulting confidence in one's own observation. The method is here described in three steps:

1. The first step is exact observation during which attention is given to the whole and the details in it. It is repeated as often as needed for the picture one has formed from the observation to be in conformity with the observed as much as reasonably possible. What is important at this stage is attentiveness and interest in the phenomena as they present themselves. The object is to allow the phenomena to show themselves and to become conscious of one's own judgements, which should be held back as much as possible. When these are held back we develop a receptivity for what is being observed. As a result, memory pictures arise of the observed phenomena. The capacities through which the memory picture is later brought back to consciousness again is called 'fantasy' by Goethe. The building up of a memory picture that is true to nature is then called 'exact sensory fantasy'.
2. The second step is inner imitation and empathetic observation. Living into a person or situation happens with the forces of imitation (see also 5.2). Imitation is something natural, indispensable to the child in its development. In later life the forces of imitation can be transformed into a capacity that can be used in the cognitive process, as empathy. Empathy makes possible the capacities of projecting oneself into, and inwardly imitating, the phenomena that are being observed. Do not right away try to explain observed phenomena, for wonder and holding back give expression to a phenomenological attitude. Out of a subjective experience in empathetic observation, feeling is developed into a means of experiencing the dynamic in the object of observation.

3. The third step is when the phenomena express themselves and make themselves known; via the steps of observation and empathy this leads to insight. The object of the observation shows itself, expresses itself, as it were, in what it 'wants' or 'wants to be'. According to Goethean phenomenology insights thus obtained are to be considered as 'sign language' which characterizes the observed object.

There are different methods to intensify observation on the cognitive path. In *Curative Education* Rudolf Steiner mentioned the importance of this intensification as 'loving dedication' to the curative educational way of arriving at a diagnosis. The following are some of these methods:

- expand the observation by applying more senses to it; use besides viewing, for example, also listening, smelling, tasting, touching;
- don't stop after one observation, but repeat it at different times and in different situations;
- make notes or a drawing from the direct observation and from memory;
- at self-chosen times build up a memory picture, notice imperfections, and correct these after a new observation;
- call up a memory picture repeatedly and improve it by means of further observations.

Also for the second step, the imitation and empathetic observation, different methods can be used (see also 5.2). The beginning is in principle always the same: at a self-chosen moment a picture of the client is called up from memory. The memory picture is formed as lively and exact as possible, through 'exact fantasy'. What does the observed person look like, how is his posture, how does he move, speak? The memory picture can be enlivened by recalling several encounters with the client. In a few minutes the picture can reach a certain completeness and precision:

- by living into the posture and movement of the client, for instance, by actually imitating them;
- by living into what the client is going through;
- by examining feelings and experiences that arise then. These can be feelings of the client himself, the way he experiences himself and his surroundings, but also the feelings that arise in you as caregiver.

Another way to live into the client is by examining the memory picture through your body-bound senses. Through the *sense of touch* you can get an impression of the boundaries and consistency of his figure. Through the *sense of life* you can experience something of his vitality and mood. Through the *sense of movement* you can observe dynamic and direction in both the physical-motoric movements and the soul movements. And through the *sense of balance* you get an impression of balance and lack of balance; the degree of harmony.

In the third step of Goethean phenomenology empathetic observation leads to insight into the being of the person. As was mentioned above it may, as it were, make itself known, express itself. Such insights may differ in nature, depending on the concepts used to explain the observations. These different concepts are discussed in the sections about image forming and reaching a diagnosis.

6.4 Image Forming

In everyday life images play an important role. An image refers to something, brings something to expression. We see it in advertising, but also in art. The visual arts, a piece of music, a poem, a painting or sculpture—they abound in forms of expression. With the images called forth by the arts, a bridge can be created between the invisible spiritual world and the world perceived through the senses which, so to say, is lifted to a higher plane. Imagery is helpful to attain spiritual insights on the basis of observable phenomena.

When we intensively call forth a memory picture of a client this can evoke an image in us. Such an image may originate from the creative power of what Goethe called exact sensory fantasy. It will correspond with reality when we have observed with precision and the memory picture is realized as exactly as possible. To the extent that these images relate to and are expressions of a spiritual reality, Rudolf Steiner calls them 'imagination'. [90]

In anthroposophical caregiving images are an aid in the step toward the diagnosis and the care plan. Images can portray the true being of the client in another guise. The observations made in inner imitation and empathetic observation may be described in words, but they can also be presented in imagery. Useful in this process are images that are derived, for instance, from a landscape, a plant or tree, an animal, a symbol like a tower or castle, or a trade (hunter, postman, salesman, etc.). You can 'invite' images to appear, for example, in a landscape as an expression of the developmental dynamic of the client. An image of leaves flying around in the wind on a sunny day might represent a frail child that is excessively lively and has trouble focusing its attention, whereas an image of dark clouds above a forest at dusk has a completely different dynamic.

In working with images we discover that they can be obtained in different ways. In analogue thinking we look in precisely built-up memory pictures for underlying gestures or sign language. This makes it possible to build up a memory picture of a client in a process of active imagination, and then 'translate' it into the dynamic of, for example, a landscape.

Another way is the meditative method. The memory picture that was built up as exactly as possible is then actively let go; the picture is erased, as it were. What is then left is a still, empty space in which an image may 'echo' and light up. This is often a new visual image, with a certain dynamic in relation to the client, but it may also be a melody or another sensation, such as a sound, a certain taste or smell.

To conclude this section a word about how images may influence caregiving. Concepts and insights that arise in image forming can work in two ways to lead to action.[91] The first way is that of the daily practice of caregiving; observation and image forming can give intuitions for action in a direct way. For example, the image that is evoked by observing a quarrel between children demands quick insight, presence in the situation. It leads to action in the situation in spiritual presence of mind. The other way is a longer one and leads to caregiving through the process of reaching a diagnosis as this is practised in the review and discussion about the client. This methodological form is explained in the next section.

6.5 Reaching a Diagnosis

In the lemniscate of dynamic judgement-forming the diagnosis marks the crossing point of the cognitive phase and the phase of choice. The connection of these two phases in the diagnostic process shows that a true insight also forms the basis for providing good care.

Above it has been shown that image forming can work into caregiving in two ways. In the first way, the diagnosis is reached by being present in the moment when a situation has to be assessed and action has to follow practically immediately. In the following discussion of the diagnostic process this way will be left out of consideration; we will return to it in the discussion about providing care in section 6.7. Here we continue with the care team meeting in which the entire caregiving process is reviewed, from identifying the need to evaluating the care (to be) given.

6.5.1 The Care Team Meeting

The provision of care comes about in the encounter between the person in need of care and the caregiver(s). In most cases several caregivers are involved and coordination is needed. The entire caregiving process is reviewed and discussed following the model of dynamic judgement formation. The actual need for care is formulated, the cognitive phase and phase of choice are followed, a diagnosis is made, and agreement reached on the beginning of the caregiving process. And in similar meetings the given care is also evaluated.

The client as a human being with his need for care stands in the centre in the care team meeting. Caregivers and others involved try to give answers to the question this person is asking, or which the parents or a caregiver is asking on his or her behalf. The participants in the meeting are professionally involved persons and, depending on prior agreements, also the client himself and/or his parents or legal representatives.

The care team meeting is to be regarded as a workshop for the social art.[92] Each participant brings in knowledge, skills, and experience in service of the client and his need for care. The meeting among people who live with this question of need and look for answers creates a circle around the client where, in engagement with the person of the client, shared insights can arise. Engagement and interest, equality and mutual trust are prerequisites for its success.

There are differences between institutions and forms of care as regards the form and frequency in which client discussions take place. The frequency varies from every three months in treatment-oriented groups in child- and youth psychiatry to every three years in forms of care for adults with a developmental disability. The meetings are carefully prepared beforehand and evaluated afterwards. More importantly, in several institutions the meetings are held in two parts over several days. In the first part, the accent lies on discussing the collected information and identifying characteristics; in the second part follow the diagnosis, care planning, and/or treatment. The time between the two parts gives the participants the opportunity for (meditative) reflection regarding the steps to the diagnosis, support, and treatment.

The care team meeting is preceded by preparation by the participants. Everyone gathers and looks back on experiences in encounters with the client as was described in 6.3. The past is viewed on the cognitive path out of the present.

In the first part of the care team meeting the participants bring their observations. The three steps in Goethean observation described earlier provide a method for this. A separate contribution may be a biographical description, especially of developments that took place after the last discussion. Ideally the observations together will give a complete picture of the life of the person or, at least, a sufficient picture to arrive at answers to existing questions. A second part of the discussion is devoted to identifying characteristics, phenomena that are typical for this client because they have been named by several participants or because they are conspicuous. The discussion is concluded with a question: What expresses itself in these characteristics, and what kind of care is therefore called for?

In the second part of the care team meeting the diagnosis is reviewed in detail and a step is made toward the care plan. What this entails follows below in a description of the diagnostic process on three levels. In section 6.6 the care plan, as preparation for the future in the phase of choice, is described in detail.

6.5.2 The Diagnostic Process at Multiple Levels

In *Curative Education* Rudolf Steiner presents a beginning toward a diagnostic process at multiple levels for developmental disabilities. He speaks about symptoms and a complex of symptoms in relation to the 'substantive nature' of the developmental disability. Such a complex is to be regarded as a specific pattern or complex of symptoms that can be classified as, for instance, Down Syndrome, autism, or epilepsy. The 'substantive nature' refers to the underlying dynamic, the configuration of the four members of the person according to the anthroposophical conception of the human being. A third part of the diagnostic process is ascertaining the perspective of the client.

The diagnostic process takes place on three levels:

1. the diagnosis based on the *constitution* and its four members, physical, etheric, and astral bodies, and ego;
2. the *classification* of the developmental disability;
3. the *perspective* viewed from the will of the client.

1 Diagnosis Based on the Constitution

In the anthroposophical conception of the human being we find diagnostic concepts to characterize the 'substantive nature' of the developmental disability. These concepts are based on the concept of the human being in his three and four members, and on different typologies. A distinctive element in these diagnostic concepts is that through these the developmental dynamic, with its variations and one-sidedness, can be characterized.

In the second part of the care team meeting the participants speak of the images they have obtained of the person. Initially these images speak for themselves and just stand there. In the course of the discussion they are compared with each other, in order thus to recognize the distinctive phenomena, as well as the imbalances and particular gestures of the client. It can thus be discovered that, for instance, the landscape images of several participants contain elements of a threatening thunderstorm or an ominous atmosphere. By the mutual exchange and analysis of the images, the participants become less invested in their own image and experience, and a new, shared image can arise.

In the diagnostic process based on the constitution the developmental dynamic of the client comes to expression. Important parts of this way of arriving at a diagnosis are balance disorders such as one-sidedness and accelerated or delayed development (see also 3.7.1). The identification of this developmental dynamic takes place with the aid of the above-mentioned concepts from the anthroposophical conception of the human being in its three and four members, and of the typologies such as those of the constitutional images.[93]

Connections for a care plan are found by asking the question of what the relative image 'wants' or 'needs' to become more unified and balanced. In the planning phase for the actual care a translation is made to make the diagnosis based on the constitution more concrete in care, support, and treatment.

2 Classification

Identifying the developmental disability and the concomitant limitations, but also the possibilities of the client, is an indispensable part of the diagnostic process. In anthroposophical care this has as important a place as in general caregiving. Knowing that someone has a particular syndrome or disability, or that he has more or less serious limitations in his intellectual capacities, is important to be able to give this person appropriate support and treatment. Classification is therefore a meaningful contribution in the diagnostic process because it is part of the basis for the care and support the client needs. Knowing that someone is a bearer of Down Syndrome helps to recognize its related physical and psycho-social problems in a timely manner.

To arrive at such a diagnosis, diagnostic classification systems have been developed, such as the International Classification of Diseases (ICD X) and the Diagnostic Statistical Manual (DSM IV). In classification the focus is primarily on the disability and the limitations of the client. In addition, especially for the care of people with intellectual limitations models have been developed, such as that of the American Association on Mental Retardation (AAMR). In this model the ability of people with intellectual disabilities to function is represented in several dimensions, so that the disabilities and limitations, but also the strong points, of the person can be clearly mapped out.

Establishing the classification or the functional profile demands specific expertise. The remedial educator and psychologist focus on the identification of the seriousness of the intellectual disability. Together with the physician (or psychiatrist) they identify the developmental problem or disability, and the way the person functions in the family or social environment.

3 The Perspective Viewed from the Will of the Client

All human beings on earth seek to recognize their individual developmental task and bring it to realization. We all give our will a particular direction and have our own perspective on life, with possibilities and limitations for bringing these to realization. This path becomes visible in the self-realization of the person, in the steps we make on the path of development, as we go through our life history (see also Chapter 2).

The perspective includes a description of life as the client pictures and wishes it, and of what the parents and caregivers indicate about this, given the possibilities and limitations of the client and his surroundings. To this end, caregivers and support workers listen intensively to wishes and expectations as the client expresses these himself, or as they are indicated by parents or supporters, and/or as they are gleaned from the client; not every person with a developmental disability will be able to express that himself. The perspective describes the wishes and expectations the client has of his life and wants to bring to realization. This means that it is to be regarded as a development question for care and support asked by the client of his environment. The task of the caregivers is to integrate this question with the expectations that they and the parents have of the development of the client. This jointly formulated perspective can usually only be realized step by step over a longer period of time. In the care plan the means are sought to implement the goal formulated in the perspective.

The three levels of this process of reaching a diagnosis mark the point where the cognitive phase and the choice phase cross. In the diagnosis based on the constitution the developmental dynamic is characterized that is working in humanity in our time. In the classification the developmental disability that results from the past development to the present is defined. The perspective points to what wants to become in the future. In the care plan, each of these three levels is elaborated into goals and means for support and treatment.

6.6 The Care Plan in the Choice Phase

The care plan identifies what care, support, and treatment are able to respond to the need of the client, and how the perspective can be realized. The diagnosis indicates the direction for the formulation of the goals that will be striven for. The perspective formulated in the diagnosis represents the wishes and expectations of the client and his representatives and caregivers. These are modified by the conditions of imbalance and one-sidedness revealed by the diagnosis based on the constitution, and by the limitations identified in the classification. It demands resourcefulness and a moral approach to bring to realization appropriate and effective answers in the care given to the client. The 'pedagogical law' (see *Curative Education* by Rudolf Steiner) gives general truth in this regard, that can be applied in the caregiving.

For the realization of the goals formulated in the care plan, the necessary ways and means have to be created. In the following we will first indicate which general principles regarding the goals and means underlie this process, based on the anthroposophical conception of the human being. Subsequently we will go into the question of the individualization of the care, adapted to the need of the client.

6.6.1 Goals of the Care

We distinguish three generally valid goals of care:

1. supporting the development of the client;
2. minimizing the consequences of the developmental disability;
3. realizing the perspective and the client's will as he expressed it.

The primary goal of the given care is, in response to the client and the expressed need for care:

a. to realize the perspective that has become visible for the client;
b. to create conditions favourable to his further development;
c. in case of balance disturbances and one-sidedness in the development, to bring these back into balance to the extent possible.

When a developmental disability becomes chronic and develops into a handicap, complete recovery is no longer possible. In that case the task becomes to help the person deal with his limitations and, where possible, compensate for them.

6.6.2 The Means

The care given out of the anthroposophical conception of the human being makes use of medical-therapeutic and pedagogical means to support and strengthen health-bringing and harmonizing forces in the human being. This is based on the principles of healthy development (see Chapter 3) and self-healing capacities.

Making Use of Self-Healing Capacities

Human beings possess forces of health, growth and recovery, and development. We have access to sources from which we can draw for our physical, soul, and spiritual health (see also 4.5.2). In caregiving, means drawn from these sources are applied. Two concepts that refer to these sources are 'hygiogenesis' [94] and 'salutogenesis'. [95] Hygiogenesis points to the sources of physical health and recovery from illness. These sources are working in processes in nature. Especially the rhythmical processes in nature, which can be witnessed in sprouting, growing, blossoming, and decaying, contain forces for health and recovery from illness. Salutogenesis points to sources of soul health (see 3.4). The 'sense of coherence' postulated by Antonovsky refers to the feeling of coherence, the measure to which we experience a connection with the world in which we live. There are three pillars that uphold this sense of coherence:

1. *comprehensibility*: the person understands the situation he is in and what is going on around him;
2. *manageability*: the client has the confidence, with the help of others, to handle the situation so as not to be overcome by it;
3. *meaningfulness*: the client experiences that what is happening and what he does has meaning and significance.

A strong sense of coherence lays the foundation for health and the ability to face life experiences positively. The sense of coherence is strengthened by offering people an environment they understand and can handle, of which they can recognize the meaning and significance.

A contrasting principle is 'pathogenesis', identifying the source of suffering, of disability. Acting out of pathogenetic insight has the objective of fighting the cause of the illness. Hygio- and salutogenesis on the one hand, and pathogenesis on the other are complementary; both are needed. The point is to apply the right aspect of each at the right moment. Take for instance a chronic infection; treatment based on pathogenetic principles means that you repeatedly have to administer the antibiotic that has to neutralize the bacteria. Treatment based on hygiogenetic principles means strengthening the defence mechanism and immune system in order to gain the upper hand over the infection in that way. Also in cases of soul problems, for example of psychotic decompensation,* salutogenetic and pathogenetic interventions may be effective at the same time.

---

* 'Decompensation' is a term used by mental health professionals to refer to episodes during which a person's existing mental-health or psychiatric disorder deteriorates, for a time, to include symptoms that are unusually severe (*Wikipedia*).

The health-promoting forces can be the better used as these pillars are more solidly anchored in the person. For the response to the need for care of the client there are three sources from which inspirations can be drawn for physical, soul, and spiritual health and development: nature, art and culture, and spirituality.[96]

Nature as a Source of Physical Health and Development: Creating a Healthy Living Climate

All human beings bear forces in themselves to become and remain physically healthy, to recover from illness, and for optimal vitality. When these forces fall short in a person, there are sources from which we can draw to support and strengthen them. These sources are to be found in nature. Nature incorporates laws of life: of sprouting and being born, of growth and blossoming, and of dying. Rhythm is characteristic for life in nature, in the alternation of day and night, and in the course of the seasons (see also 4.5.2). A reflection of these processes in the human being are the life processes (see also Appendix 1).

Core concepts for care are: naturalness and rhythm. The objective of the care is to bring about a safe living climate and to take care of the life processes; these form the basis of an optimally healthy development. Care on this level means that we are working with natural laws of space and time. This can be translated into creating a safe environment and using natural materials in the living space. The same goes for the material used in clothing and for the origin and preparation of food. In addition to these general elements of care, an individual rhythmical order of the day and week can also be arranged, with a healthy balance between exertion and relaxation. For clients who need it, space and time can be more strictly structured.

Therapies have also been developed that, via the care of physical processes, support the experience of the body as one's own safe home, as well as one's overall development and self-healing ability. These encompass external therapies, such as massages, wraps, and baths; rhythmical massage which is part of the work of physical therapy; food and anthroposophic remedies. These remedies are made from substances obtained from mineral, plant, and animal nature. The way these remedies are prepared is such that they effectively support and strengthen our own health-restoring forces.

This natural approach in the given care does not exclude that in certain situations allopathic medicines are used that work much more compellingly. The same is true for situations in which additional means are needed to impose the structuring of space and time from outside, in a compelling way. These means may especially be used when it proves to be too difficult or impossible to minimize the consequences of the developmental disability for the client.

Art as a Source of Health and Development of the Soul

When the gifts from the source of nature are nurtured, the foundation is laid on which psychological and social-emotional forces can come to development. It is a recurring experience that in a human being forces emerge for further development, when the living climate is sufficiently secure and looked after. Sources of psycho-social health and development can be found in the encounter with other people and in art and culture. 'The art of the encounter' (see also 4.2.1) asks of the caregiver a proficiency in making contact and entering into a relationship with a client. Encounters and conversation, doing or making something together take place in a creative process of listening and attuning to each other, appreciating each other's talents, and respecting each other's limitations. In anthroposophical caregiving 'the art of the encounter' is practised in this sense.

The arts and crafts encompass a broad range of forms: architecture, sculpture, drawing and painting in the visual arts, music, movement, speech, and the dramatic and social arts. In each of these arts specific means are used. In painting these are the paintbrush and paint; in speech the human voice. Each art is characterized by its own creative process and results in its own typical forms of artworks such as a sculpture, music, a poem, or a drama. The creativity that works in each of these arts, works also in the human soul, especially sculpture, painting, music, speech, movement and theatre.

Interest and motivation are key concepts in the use of artistic sources for the growth and development of the soul. Offerings of activities in arts and crafts support the client in the development of the soul. For young clients therapeutic artistic curricula have been developed grounded in the curriculum of the Waldorf School. For adults there are programmes of work and other activities in arts and crafts (see also 4.5.1).

In artistic processes forces are working through which you create connection and coherence. In every art form that works in its own way. In artistic creativity the artist works on the material in such a way that inwardly he moves with that which is arising under his hands. In this sense, artistic work creates a coherent balance between head, heart, and hands—in observation and thinking, in feeling, and in the will and action. If soul development is in danger of stagnating and developing one-sidedness, sources are available in the arts from which we can draw to support soul development and bring possible one-sidedness back into harmony.

Inspired by the anthroposophical conception of the human being therapies have been developed that are specifically aimed at soul development, such as artistic, eurythmy, music, and drama therapies.[97] Therapies that have been developed in more recent decades and contribute equally to fostering healthy soul development include system therapy, (social) skills training, play therapy and garden therapy. The artistic process is also effective in school learning and working in trades.

Pathogenetic approaches may be necessary on a supplemental basis when the social-emotional development is disturbed and the consequences of this interfere with the development of the client or the people with whom he is living. This may require medicaments to prevent a further disturbance of the development as much as possible.

Spirituality as a Source of Gaining or Regaining Individuation

In all human beings an individuality is active that wants to develop in this life and strives to bring its own individual perspective to realization. Based on experiences from prior lives, we bear talents in us that we want to bring to development. The way in which this can be realized is not always clear. Human encounters may help us wake up to our own life plan. They are also a means of gaining insight into the sense and meaning of events and of a life afflicted by problems or limitations. The engagement and interest of others is helpful for the client to become conscious of his own path of development and how he wants to flourish in this life. Hope and nourishing expectations are general preconditions that can lead to a view of the future. Religious and spiritual activities are means of arriving at a more intense connection with the actual core of existence, the higher I. For many people this is a help to gain more insight into their own development task.

In this process the social environment can also play a therapeutic role. Insights may be gained for this from ideas about group formation and therapeutic communities. A group of people, parents and educators, can form a circle around the child within which it finds a stimulus and can develop itself. A prerequisite for arriving at a health-bringing collaboration in a circle is the will again and again to inwardly correct the picture of the other that you have in you. The positive effect depends on everyone's ability to emphasize each other's best qualities and compensate for each other's weaknesses.

In caregiving the task of the support aide is to stand beside the client, to oversee the field of possibilities and limitations, and to give support. The basic elements of this perspective include living, learning and working, daytime activities, and the social context within which living, learning, working, and leisure time take place. It may be a battleground where the client, falling and getting up again, through doubts, aggression, and depression, finds his way. It may also be, such as in case of a client with a serious intellectual handicap who has difficulty communicating his wishes, that these have to be gleaned from his moods and bodily reactions.

From the point of view of the human constitution, this process makes an appeal to the I, to the striving for self-realization. It is a task of the caregiver to show respect for the person of the client, and offer support when he makes choices in his development. Regarding the development of the I, insights into individuation and self-regulation are guiding elements. All human beings carry seeds for the development of an individual perspective in them, with ideals and wishes they want to realize. All of us have the ability to give direction to our lives in freedom. We can find sources of inspiration for this when out of our own forces we seek a connection with objective spiritual reality.

Therapies that can foster the ripening of the personality and autonomy are speech-, eurythmy-, and psychotherapy; biographical counselling, and group counselling.

6.6.3 The Outcomes of the Care Planning Process

The outcomes of the care planning process are recorded in the individual care- and treatment plan. The diagnosis marks the transition from insight to action, from the cognitive phase to the phase of choice. It indicates the direction of the care plan. In the care- and treatment plan goals are formulated as well as the means by which these can be reached. Depending on the choices made by the care team, the care plan may include the following elements:

- a picture of the person, a description of personal characteristics;
- the diagnosis on three levels:
  - the constitution;
  - the classification;
  - the perspective;
- the principal goals of the care;
- the concrete working goals derived from the principal goals;
- the ways and means to be employed in working toward the goals—the action plan;
- the care and support style in the intercourse with the client.

The care plan is written down, and presented and explained to the person in need of the care and/or his representative(s), and after mutual agreement it is adopted and undersigned.

6.7 Providing the Care, Support, and Treatment

Caregivers have to know the care plan of the client and work with it. When the content of the care plan—specifically the image that emerged in the diagnostic phase—is regularly reviewed and discussed among the caregivers, the quality of the care and treatment will benefit. For then it offers a firm ground and promotes a shared approach and style by the members of the support team in their daily intercourse with the client. However, this more structural approach to the care process is not sufficient, because the daily practice of living and working with the client is full of unexpected situations. These demand creativity and spiritual presence of mind in the actions of the caregivers, a being present in the situation.[98] That is the reason why authentic and intuitive actions play a role in the encounter with the client.

6.7.1 Intuitive Action Based on Individual Judgement

In the context of quality control the way care is provided is more and more fixed in protocols. The positive side of this is that it gives the client clarity regarding what he can expect of the caregiver, and what they can appeal to each other for. Protocols are important for recording agreements on responsibilities and time limits. For instance: how long does it take for me to get answers to my request for help? When do I get the report of an examination? Who is responsible and who do I go to when I have questions?

Things become different when protocols impose the content of the caregiving. Some protocols prescribe the treatment that must be followed upon a specific diagnosis. This seriously infringes on the freedom of both the giver and the receiver of care. Protocols fall short in unique situations and needs. Caregivers then have to rely on their own judgement. In this process of judgement-forming two sources can be very helpful, namely guidelines and the images that were formed during the diagnostic phase. Guidelines are based on experiences of experts and on research; they indicate general directions for making choices for the treatment. The same is true for images. Caregivers can use these guidelines and images as general sources of inspiration for their actions in order to form an individual judgement on that basis, in other words, to perform a specific action that flows out of the general direction and is attuned to the need of this particular client in this particular situation at this particular time.

6.7.2 Coherence and Coordination in Support and Treatment

The effects of a pedagogical approach, a therapy, and a prescribed medication ideally are in harmony with each other and are compatible with the support and other advice. Concrete, practical things can be arranged through the care plan. But how do you achieve structural coherence and coordination in caregiving? This requires coordinating the ideas and views of the various caregivers with each other. The outcomes, the processes of image forming and diagnostics are helpful for this.

At first, an image may not look like a solid foundation, but if you nourish the image together, it comes to life and starts to work. When you look at a painting or tree, or listen to a piece of music only once, you soon forget it. This changes when you look at it or listen to it more often, and call your image back into memory regularly. You then get a connection with it, and experiences are deepened into insights into the painting, the tree, or the music, which lead you to look, listen, and act differently. A regular recalling of the memory image of a client and his situation, together with other caregivers, has the same effect. It creates coherence and coordination and thus reinforces the solid ground of the caregiving. When you succeed together to support a client out of a jointly carried image, a new inspiring quality can come about that gives direction to the caregiving (see also 5.3).

Earlier it was shown that the client's need for care also leads to questions the caregivers ask of themselves. What possibilities and sources are there for the caregivers to find answers to their own questions of development? They can draw from the same sources as those described earlier, for these are universal. For caregivers the schooling of their personality is a help. In the professional training programmes attention is given to professionalism, the acquisition of knowledge, insight, and skills, as well as to inner attitude and personality development. Various exercises are used for this.[99] Their purpose is to develop inner balance and stay healthy in work. Working with these exercises supports the development questions of caregivers.

6.8 Evaluation

Evaluation means looking back over the caregiving process and identifying what has been achieved in the caregiving. For the client the evaluation applies to the care that was agreed out of the diagnosis based on the constitution, the classification, and the formulated perspective into the future. Following the method of dynamic judgement-formation we look back (on the cognitive phase) on the care that was provided. In this process the key elements are observation and review of what was done.

Together with the client or his representative, we evaluate whether the goals of the care have been realized and how the client is doing. To arrive at a good evaluation, the care- and treatment plan must in an earlier phase have fulfilled the following conditions:

- the goals of care and treatment, together with a feasible time period, were concretely formulated. This implies that the goals are in harmony with the possibilities of the client, his parents or representatives, and the caregivers;
- there is clarity as to who is responsible for the implementation of the care plan, respectively for the evaluation;

- in the care- or treatment plan agreements are recorded for the evaluation in relation to:
  - the timing of the evaluation, depending on the goal to be evaluated;
  - the person(s) responsible for the evaluation;
  - the evaluation criteria.

A method that is helpful for the evaluation of provided care and treatment is the *Causal method of examining effect*, developed by Helmut Kiene[100] on the basis of *Gestalt* psychology.[101] With this method a caregiver can assess the effectiveness of an action performed by him. Every action has consequences. The point is to find the specific connection between the action and the consequences. Footprints in the sand are imprints of the feet of a person and an example of a simple causal connection. Identifying the causal connection rests on identifying the agreement in image or *Gestalt*—there is a foot and an imprint of the foot in the sand. Finding the connection between singing a song or playing on the lyre and the child that stops crying or banging its head is less evident. But when this connection occurs repeatedly in time—the singing stops and the child starts to cry again; the singing resumes and the crying stops again—this connection develops a typical *Gestalt* and a causal character. In the case of the footprints in the sand, the *Gestalt* becomes visible in space; with the singing for the child it becomes visible in time. A connection can be observed in different forms.

With the evaluation the last step is made in the caregiving process, and the provision of care can be concluded. But more often it will be the case that the evaluation results in new questions for a continuation of the care, with a new round in going through the methodical steps in the caregiving process.

7 The Caregiving Methodology Scientifically Justified

Erik Baars

7.1 Introduction

In the preceding chapters the ingredients and contours of a methodology of good caregiving were discussed from the following points of view:

- anthropopsophical-ethical fundamental values (Chapter 2);
- disturbances in personal development from a spiritual-psychological perspective (Chapter 3);
- the most important elements in the practice of curative educational and social therapeutic caregiving (Chapter 4);
- the professional identity of the caregiver (Chapter 5); and
- the diverse methods used in caregiving practice (Chapter 6).

In our time, however, a description of the parts that make up a methodology is no longer sufficient. Within the healthcare sector a scientific underpinning of professional practice has been growing in the past few decades. This irreversible development is shown in terms that came into use in the 1990s as Evidence Based Medicine (EBM). Professional practice increasingly needs to be based on the best available evidence. Existing treatments need to be provided with a scientific foundation. New treatments need to be founded from the start on scientific research, and evaluated as to their effectiveness.

For this book, the consequence of this development is that, in addition to a description of the different aspects of the caregiving methodology, a scientific justification will also have to be provided. To do this we will first of all examine to what extent the various aspects of caregiving practice can be considered as formal aspects of a method (7.2). Next we will conceptually identify and test the two most conspicuous basic aspects of the caregiving methodology (7.3 and 7.4). Finally, after discussing a scientific context of the caregiving methodology (7.5) we will describe how quality control takes place regarding the acquisition and application of knowledge (7.6).

7.2 The Formal Aspects of the Caregiving Methodology

7.2.1 Formal Aspects of a Method

In science as well as in the practice of professional practitioners countless methods have been developed. Roughly these can be arranged into two categories:

1. methods to acquire knowledge (for example, diagnostic questionnaires to identify the presence of ADHD);
2. methods to apply knowledge to actions (for example, guidelines and protocols in cases of self-mutilation).

In each method we can distinguish five formal aspects:

1. A reality aspect (favourite approach or paradigmatic choice)
Methods contain conceptions of reality through which problem situations are approached. Professionals 'read' reality out of their own practice paradigm—their own favourite view or approach. In these practice paradigms are reflected first of all the experiences of the practitioners, their colleagues, and those who trained them. Secondly, methods are expressions of scientific paradigms and underlying philosophical views of the human being and society.

> Thirdly, there are societal paradigms, the general tendencies and broadly accepted strategies to identify, confront, and solve problems in society. [...]
>
> When one works methodically, methodologies or methods importantly determine the intervention. [...] First of all, a method includes an interpretation of the reality of the client, of the development that is stagnating and is therefore brought before the professional. [...] We therefore determine that from the start a rigorous limitation is taking place in the interpretation of the disturbance or, more precisely said, in the transformation of the failing, chaotic situation into a manageable problem. Some interpretations of the situation do not get a chance, others strongly dominate. This is not caused by the stagnation itself, but by the favourite view or approach of the expert practitioner. Paradigmatic choice therefore comes before a consultation of theories and even determines the direction of such consultation. [...] It is therefore our opinion that a method first of all incorporates a practice paradigm

> (a favourite way of viewing and treating problems) acquired out of accumulated personal experiences, strategies accepted in science and society to confront problems, and limitations imposed by the relative organizational framework. This combination determines, as it were, the practitioner's direction and indicates his otherwise scientifically or, at least, professionally applied solutions, including the choices he makes within those.[102]

2. An Aspect of Good Action

Every method incorporates an idea of the desired final result—of the correct theory of reality (acquisition of knowledge), or the good and successful action, of the way the situation can best continue (applying knowledge to action).

> Methodological aspects relate to the ways in which knowledge is gained and to the fundamental principles, rules, and strategies used for this. In particular, it is the question of whether, in order to arrive at the correct knowledge or concept of a certain level of organization (the level of the whole), we would have to study the underlying levels of organization (the component parts and their interactions), or the higher level itself, or perhaps its relationships to even higher levels.[103]

> A method includes not only the practice paradigm, but also a conceptual idea regarding the solution. [...] ... that when one uses a method in a capable manner, one not only delimits the stagnation and defines it as a particular kind of problem, but at the same time one brings solutions and even prescribes these. Every method therefore contains an idea about the desired end result, about good and successful action, about how things can best continue from this point. [...] A method not only reflects a favourite way of viewing a failing action, but also an idea of successful action. The idea of the 'good', as an inherent reference point of a method, therefore precedes the client situation. For, a method is a more or less standardized manner of solving problems. When one approaches a client with a particular method, one actually knows already what is good in such situations. The method communicates that—formally or in its substance.[104]

3. A Process- and Technique Aspect

A method is about the manner in which, on the one hand, knowledge is acquired and, on the other hand, knowledge is applied in giving direction to actions—the fundamental principles, rules, and strategies used for this.

> The most conspicuous element of every method is undoubtedly the aspect of inventiveness—the indications for the way one has to work to reach the intended solution, the goal anchored in the method itself. It is a set of specific actions which have to be executed with technical skill and in a specific sequence—purposeful, appropriate, effectual. And the promise is that this way of acting will lead to the intended result with an acceptable degree of probability. Usually the method indicates procedures and instruments for this.[105]

4. A Relationship Aspect

A method also includes indications as to the way the researcher and the object of research need to relate to each other for the process to 'work'.

> If a method were only a favourite way of viewing the stagnation, an idea of the good and a technique, it would be impracticable. A method only becomes useful in the hands of a caregiver who enters into a relationship with the person who is having a problem. [...] A method in people-oriented professions is a lot more than a technique to solve problems with the concomitant schematics for interpretation. It also includes directions as to the way the helping and helped persons need to relate to each other for the process to be effective.[106]

5. A Quality Aspect

The method is qualitatively so good that its use leads to obtaining *valid* knowledge or the ability to apply *usable* knowledge.

> Methodology is the science that seeks for ways to develop strategies that offer ever better guarantees for the achievement of intended goals. It occupies itself with problems around the acquisition of knowledge and makes precepts available that products have to satisfy to be considered of high scientific quality.[107]

7.2.2 Two Examples of the Specific Manner of Acquiring and Applying Knowledge

Before we proceed to a closer definition and testing of the formal aspects of the caregiving practice, we will first more closely analyse the methodical steps of acquiring and applying knowledge, for the purpose of making the definition and testing more precise. Following the methodical steps Goethe used in his research of living nature, and which we also find in many of the diagnostic methods in curative education and social therapy, we will examine the methodology of the specific mode of acquiring knowledge. We will use the descriptions from the preceding chapters for this. With the help of the example of the curative educational images, the specific way of applying knowledge to an action in a situation can be described more exactly. The result of both analyses will be brought into the definition of the formal aspects of caregiving methodology (7.2.3).

The Steps of the Specific Way of Acquiring Knowledge

Goethe's book *The Metamorphosis of Plants* may be regarded as one of the first natural scientific works in which the research result consists of 'idea' knowledge, or *Gestalt* knowledge. The way in which Goethe acquired this knowledge is an historically interesting example of the way the acquisition of knowledge is also pursued in caregiving methodology. For the method that Goethe implicitly used formed the starting point for Rudolf Steiner to provide this way of working with a better methodological and philosophical foundation. In doing so he at the same time gave a methodological and philosophical foundation to anthroposophical activities, such as the care of children and adults with developmental disabilities.

Goethe's methodical approach includes three phases, which we also recognize in the caregiving methodology described in the previous chapters. The first phase consists of exact observation while holding back any personal judgement. The result of this phase is a series of exact recollections of the observed object. These are memory pictures of, ideally, all observable aspects such as colour, form, etc., which exactly correspond with the factual appearance of the object in space and time. In the context of the attitude of 'loving acceptance' this is called in section 5.2.1 the phase of 'objective observation'. Section 6.3 about observation speaks of 'loving devotion'.

In the second phase this series of recollections—with the exclusion of all other pictures—is placed in consciousness and intensively repeated. This leads to a process that Goethe called 'inner imitation'. After a shorter or longer time we become conscious of the 'gesture' or sign language of the observed object. In caregiving methodology this phase is called 'using one's own soul as an instrument of observation of the other' (5.2.1) or 'empathetic observation' (6.3).

The last phase is characterized by the perception of the creative 'being' behind the sensory observations and soul gesture, of which we become conscious after repeatedly, intensively going through the first two phases. Section 5.2.1 describes in this context the step when the other being can express himself in the soul. In section 6.3 we find this in the characterization of the third methodical step of Goethe, when insights are gained into the being of the observed object, the being which, as it were, makes itself known and expresses itself.

From a methodological point of view the following aspects are important in this approach. In the first phase the point is exact observation and the use of a transformed kind of thinking. Our everyday kind of thinking wants to recognize things. Fairly unconsciously we walk through a world of 'things we recognize', or in more formal words, we perceive all the time through concepts we have acquired in our life. In this phase, thinking has to be transformed to so-called *perceptive thinking.* This means that thinking has to become an instrument to bring back into memory, without self-interest, the connections between observations in space and time, as these exist in the world (for instance, the specific manner of movement of a child with ADHD). From an instrument of recognition ('Oh, that is a child with ADHD') thinking becomes an instrument to let the way an object appears in space and time in the world show itself anew, but now in the cognitive consciousness of the person.

In the second phase, subjective feeling is transformed into an objective, perceptive organ of observation—*perceptive feeling*. Instead of the usually immediately arising subjective sympathy or antipathy ('Look at that child's funny movements!'), the total memory picture built up in the first phase is repeatedly brought back into consciousness. On this basis we can, through this repetition, observe with increasing clarity the lawful dynamic behind sensory perceptions through our feeling. From an instrument of subjective judgement, feeling becomes an instrument to come to know the objective, lawful dynamics behind relationships in time and space.

In the third phase our regular willing is transformed into *perceptive willing*. Usually we approach objects from the point of view of what we want with them. Perceptive willing has two sides. First of all it is used in the first and second phase. Only because I am very active in my own will does the exact memory picture arise in my consciousness, and I can observe the dynamic through my feeling. In both cases my will is acting completely in service of (the examination of) the object I am examining. When I totally hold back what I myself might want with the object, it can appear objectively in my consciousness. The other aspect of perceptive willing is the perception of the idea or being that is responsible for creating the object in nature, for its appearance in space and time.

In conclusion we may first state that the whole of thinking, feeling, and willing of the human being is the instrument to acquire 'essential or ideal knowledge'. To achieve this it is necessary that they be stripped of subjective influences, and thus receive a perceptive quality. Secondly, we may note that the process of acquiring knowledge in this context is *the imitation of nature* in cognitive consciousness, the goal being to give the creative idea or being that was *originally* connected with this the possibility to appear *inactively* in our consciousness. As a result of this, there appears the idea connected with the gesture or memory pictures of the appearance of the idea in space and time. Thirdly, we see that in this process we do not, as usual, stand only as a spectator facing a world of which we do not know how it came into being. With this form of acquiring knowledge we cross the threshold, as it were, of physical appearance, and from a physical world perceptible through the senses we come into a world in which we can follow in our own consciousness the creative activity of beings, the way beings come into existence in space and time.

The Steps of the Specific Manner of Applying Knowledge

The curative educational images (see also Appendix 1) form a typology that is related to the human constitution. This typology is a classification of jointly appearing morphological, physiological, and psychological features. The ordering principle that forms the basis of the three pairs of polar curative educational constitutional images is that of 'threefoldness'. Threefoldness is an archetypal image that works creatively like a blueprint in the development of living organisms.[108] In the human organism it creates an ordering in organ systems and functions on three levels: the nerve-sense process, the metabolic-limbs process, and the rhythmical process. These three processes work as supra-ordered and supra-sensory principles in our physical and soul development. They work throughout the human organism, but each of them has one or several principal organs.

For curative education these constitutional images were introduced by Rudolf Steiner in a lecture series for people who had taken on the care of children with developmental disabilities (*Curative Education*, CW 317). Steiner describes three pairs of polar pictures. Each pair is related to one of the processes working in the threefold organism. The polar pictures each show a one-sidedness in one of the three processes:

- the polarity of the compelling/rich-in-iron picture versus the forgetful/rich-in-sulphur picture expresses itself in one-sidedness in the development of thinking and memory and the related physical processes. Specifically, this becomes noticeable as an incapacity to forget, respectively to remember;
- the polarity of the obstructed/closed picture versus the outflowing/open picture expresses itself in one-sidedness in the emotional development of feeling and experiencing, and in the related physiological/rhythmical processes of sleeping and waking as well as breathing. The one-sidedness is observable in tendencies to closing oneself off, respectively opening and losing oneself;
- finally, the polarity of the slow/heavy picture versus the excessively mobile/light picture expresses itself in one-sidedness in the development of the movements of the child and the related physical processes. These are tendencies of being unable to come into movement, respectively of coming to rest.

The relationship between the three pairs of polar pictures was worked out by Holtzapfel.[109] He places the three as extreme forms of 'contraction' and 'expansion' in a centripetal, respectively centrifugal dynamic. On this basis he makes a difference between *peripheral* or *centrifugal* pictures that, as it were, want to move away from a point: forgetful/rich-in-sulphur, outflowing/open, and excessively mobile/light. The three other pictures show a *centripetal* dynamic and want to pull together into one point, as it were. In every human being there is a natural striving toward balance between these two extremes. Holtzapfel: 'We need the totality of these polarities; they encompass processes which together give form to our humanness. We all need rest and movement, remembering and forgetting, waking and sleeping.' The point is thus actively to realize a state of equilibrium between alternately being more peripherally and more inwardly oriented, in a harmonious rhythm.

When looked at more closely we will see threefoldness in all rhythmical processes: the two poles with a dynamic middle position in between. The active middle mediates between the two poles, for example, the proportion between anabolism (upbuilding) and catabolism (breakdown). This mediation is a prerequisite for all development. In case of a one-sidedness because of a *continual* predominance of one of the two poles, the mediation falls short, and stagnation occurs. The six constitutional images represent such one-sidedness in development, in which the equilibrium is continually pushed to one of the two poles (see also 3.4).

When for instance a child is diagnosed with one of the constitutional images, we can recognize several phases in subsequent action:

1. *Defining the problem in terms of a specific problem for the functioning of the whole*
   Out of complete insight into the relationship between pathology, physiology, and anatomy, the problem can be defined *in terms of a specific problem for the 'healthy whole' of the system*—in this case the rhythmical process between two extremes of a polarity. The definition of the problem in this form is then: there is no possibility of arriving at a rhythmic alternation between the two poles. The consequence is a dominant influence from one of the poles, which expresses itself in one-sidedness in the physiology, morphology, and soul functions.
2. *Formulating a general direction for action*
   Based on phase 1 a general direction for action can be formulated: creating the possibility that the one-sidedness is neutralized as much as possible, and the healthy, dynamic middle position between the two poles is reached. In principle, this step is made completely in the realm of purely conceptual thinking.
3. *Translating the general direction for action into a specific action plan*
   In the next step the general direction for action is converted into a *specific* action plan for the situation. Theoretically, this may be done in an infinite number of ways. First, one could think of stimulating the weak pole, inhibiting the working of the dominant pole, or strengthening the balance-creating middle. In the second instance, each of these three approaches can be made concrete and specific in countless ways. For example, for a child with a forgetful (rich-in-sulphur) constitution that has difficulties in making things its own and remembering events, the weak pole of the constitution may be stimulated by the rhythmic repetition of activities (such as washing, getting dressed, or a verse), always in virtually the same manner. The specific circumstances of a situation (the facts and the available

means) then determine the change from the general direction for action into a specific action plan. In this phase, however, we are still only dealing with a conceptual conversion to a specific action plan, not its actual implementation.

4. *The good implementation of the specific action plan*
   In the last phase the specific action plan that was chosen has to be implemented. This may be a one-time intervention or a series of interventions. The caregiver involved has to fulfil certain requirements to convert the specific action plan into a *good* specific action. In our example, the stimuli have to be given by someone who is familiar with the curative educational images, who can give the stimuli precisely and, in the process, can take the specific circumstances of the child into account. The action becomes 'good' because in this way all mutual connections are taken into account (see also 2.9.1):
   a those between the specific problem and the healthy condition, and
   b those relating to the goal, the means, and the unique features of the situation.
5. *The result of the good action*
   The result of a good action is that the 'healthy whole' of a healthy system can manifest *in a form*. In this example it is the healthy rhythmic alternation between the two poles, without either becoming dominant. In many cases this ideal will in actual practice not be fully reached. Most often the final result will be a lesser, but still present, dominance of the stronger pole.

On the basis of this analysis of the different phases, we can now first of all establish that the general direction for action proceeds from the 'encounter' of the problem with 'the idea of the healthy condition'. Secondly, we realize that this general direction for action is an idea; it might 'appear' in all kinds of forms. Thirdly, it becomes clear that the situation (the facts and the means) is determinative for the choice of a specific action plan which, in itself, is still but an idea. Fourthly, the conclusion has to be that, if the 'idea of a specific action plan' is to be converted into a factual, specific action, the experience of an expert is required. Finally, we see that the effect of a good action is a final condition in which the healthy whole can manifest *in a form*.

7.2.3 The Formal Aspects of the Caregiving Methodology

When we review the preceding chapters as a whole, it is possible to distil from them the five formal aspects of a method.

The Reality Aspect

The reality aspect, the favourite, paradigmatic view and/or approach to the caregiving methodology described here, is without a doubt anthroposophy. On the one hand, anthroposophy provides us with the three fundamental values that give direction to the core concepts, namely equality, sense of service, and spiritual presence of mind; the professional attitude; and the processes of acquiring and applying knowledge in our actions. On the other hand, it provides us with concepts through which situations are evaluated and approached to arrive at solutions, such as the 'threefold and fourfold human being', human development in seven-year periods, et cetera.

The Good Action Aspect

This aspect indicates that a method contains, more or less explicitly, an idea regarding the desired end situation—an idea about the correct theory of reality (the acquisition of knowledge) or the good and successful action, about how the situation can best proceed (applying knowledge in action). With regard to the correct theory of reality, following the methodological works of Goethe and Rudolf Steiner, the caregiving methodology takes an ontological position (see also 7.3.1 and Appendix 1) that corresponds with that of anthroposophy. Whereas science today generally considers theory as a sort of subjective 'imprint' or 'reflection' of the reality outside us, here theory is considered as the appearance of the being of the examined object in the cognitive consciousness of the human being. In this context section 5.2.1 speaks of loving acceptance as the cognitive instrument through which the other being can express itself in the soul. In 6.3 we find this in the characterization of Goethe's third methodical step, when insights regarding the being of the observed object are obtained, the being makes itself known and expresses itself, as it were, and the object is perceived in 'what it wants (to be)'. Bortoft describes this point of view in his work about Goethe's method.

> We consider knowledge as the subjective condition of the cognizing person, a change in consciousness that has no influence whatever on the cognized phenomenon, which stays the same, whether it is known or not. Goethe considered the cognition of the phenomenon as closely connected with the phenomenon itself, for in his view, the condition of 'having become cognized' has to be understood as a higher level of the phenomenon itself. [...] With the right attitude of consciousness, it

> becomes the medium in which the phenomenon becomes present. From a more encompassing view, however, it is the phenomenon itself that appears in the consciousness when it is cognized. The process of acquiring knowledge is an evolutionary disclosure of the phenomenon, not a subjective activity of the human being. That is the ontological significance of intuitive knowledge. The true significance of 'theory' now becomes clear. When the phenomenon becomes its own theory, this is a higher level of the phenomenon itself.[110]

Caregiving methodology here follows an old tradition of scientific theory that was expressed, among other ways, in the *Universalia* of the medieval Scholastics. At that time the so-called Realists distinguished three 'levels of existence' of 'creative ideas', the *Universalia*:

1. The *Universalia ante rem*: the ideas that 'exist in themselves,' in other words, before (*ante*) they work in a 'thing' (*res*) that has become visible, and thus have not yet become manifest in the sensory world. The word *res* means here a visible thing.
2. The *Universalia in re*: the ideas as they are *creatively working* and are manifested *in* the things of the world that can be observed through the senses.
3. The *Universalia post rem*: the ideas which, after (*post*) having worked in visible nature, appear *not-working* in the thinking consciousness of the human being who has studied visible nature, and who has therefore gained insight and knowledge regarding the *Universalia*.

In the context of caregiving methodology, the *correct theory* of reality must thus be viewed as the *Universalia post rem* condition.

The idea of *good action* has already been described in a general sense in 7.2.2. When we apply this to caregiving methodology we can state that the general direction for action lies in many cases in the idea that the client ideally will develop toward a condition of freedom. To this end, the structural and situational conditions and potential are created in spiritual presence of mind (specifically through encounters with other people, in work life, through elements of culture, and living in community), in order to enable the child or adult to go through this development, if necessary with care and support.

The Process and Technique Aspect

The instrument that is used in the caregiving methodology for acquiring and applying knowledge is the specially schooled objective judgement of the individual. The way knowledge is acquired is through the process of forming an objective empathetic image of the client in his situation. One's own subjectivity (prejudices, etc.) are held back so that the built-up image or memory picture ideally corresponds exactly with the observations of the client and his situation. On the basis of this image or memory picture, through one's perceptive feeling, after it has been transformed into an objective cognitive organ, the dynamic of the image can be identified. Finally, on the basis of the previous steps and through one's perceptive will, after this has been transformed into an objective cognitive organ, the idea, the essential nature of the situation can be identified. This is therefore a process of gaining knowledge of the way in which ideal-essential principles are working in the situation under examination (see also 7.2.2).

The way in which in caregiving methodology *knowledge is applied to giving direction to action* is by means of the unexpected situation, expertise (unconscious experience-based knowledge), or the consciously present experience-based knowledge, which give direction to action. This is an intervention choice that is consciously or unconsciously based on the steps made in one's actions undertaken in a situation, as described in 7.2.2. Explicitly or implicitly, in this process a specific action plan is chosen based on a general direction for action, and brought to actual realization through competent action. The result of this process-based intervention is ideally and ultimately the adequately appearing 'ideal' working principle.

In both cases therefore, the activity of the schooled good judgement of the individual co-workers is key, so that the 'ideal' working principle can make its appearance. In the first case of the acquisition of knowledge it appears in the consciousness of the co-worker; in the case of the application of the knowledge it appears in the reality of the situation.

The Relationship Aspect

The relationship aspect of *the acquisition of knowledge* is the opposite of what in the concept of experimental science was already formulated by Francis Bacon in the sixteenth century: 'Nature has to be put on the rack to make it give up its secrets.' The random double-blind experiment is the big example of this approach, in which the greatest possible distance between object and subject is maintained.

In caregiving methodology the relationship between 'examining co-worker' and 'object of examination' is diametrically different from this. The key here is love as a cognitive organ. Through the loving projecting, cognitive activity of the 'examining person' the essential being of the other can express itself in him. We can also call this the methodical side of the virtues belonging to the fundamental value of sense of service (see 2.7.2).

How subject and object of the examination have to relate to each other to 'make it all work', involves entering into a real encounter, in which the being of the patient and his developmental question are key and are the starting point for an adequate professional act in the situation. In conclusion we quote Petersen who in 1982 already so beautifully described the core of the professional encounter:

> Transformation comes forth from the encounter. In the word *dialogue* we can already hear something of the secret of transformation: the 'in-between word' (Greek *dia-logos*), the word that arises as something new, as a third (person) between you and me. The form of this third in the dialogue depends on our therapeutic work. For the music therapist it is the right tone, for the curative eurythmist the right gesture, for the psychotherapist the telling concept, and for the speech therapist the relaxing poem. This third is always born from the necessity of the moment, the here and now; it is never precalculated and planned, even though as a therapist I preferably have to have a large number of medications at my disposal. Certainly, as a therapist I should have learned as many therapeutic recipes as possible—the manuals of all therapeutic institutions are full of them; and it is the task of therapeutic schools to teach the exact applications of therapeutic techniques. The therapy-artist has to master craftmanship and knowledge. Still, I can never precisely determine which therapeutic remedy I am actually going to apply; that would cause the danger of therapy becoming manipulation. Every conversation runs aground if it is planned ahead. The therapist is also always willing to let go of his preconceived plans, in order to make space for what wants to come to manifestation in the space between him and his patient. Transformation becomes possible by taking distance. Not to make something—to let the new arise in the space out of the enormous tension between you and me. You can't stage therapy, just as you can't make a conversation.[111]

The Quality Aspect

The *quality aspect* indicates whether a method is qualitatively good enough so that its use leads to the acquisition of *valid* knowledge, or the ability to apply *useful* knowledge. Of key importance for the maintenance of quality in caregiving methodology is the development of specific virtues, which prevent distortion by subjective influences from the examining person in the processes of acquiring and applying knowledge. Some of these virtues, which are prerequisites for arriving at valid knowledge, are: open-mindedness, patience, perseverance, exact observation, thinking and recollecting, and empathy. In addition, the soul functions have to be strictly disciplined; it is necessary to learn to reflect on one's own experiences, recognize and restrain one's own prejudices, control one's emotions and other vices. This creates the potential for a person to act freely, intuitively in a situation. Instead of objectifying things by excluding the subjective—as is done in the usual scientific approach—this is a path of objectifying the subjective (see also 7.6).

7.2.4 Conclusions Regarding the Formal Aspects of the Caregiving Methodology

On the basis of the preceding analysis, we can conclude that the aspects of the caregiving methodology described in earlier chapters may formally be regarded as elements of a method. This satisfies a first scientific foundation of the methodology. It is, however, also evident that it is not an ordinary methodology, because its formal aspects rather deviate from usual practice.

The first prominent aspect of the methodology is the key importance of individual judgement in the professional shaping of the acquisition of knowledge and its application in action, as well as the quality control on this process. The second prominent aspect of the method is that the reality aspect is anthroposophy. Scientifically, anthroposophy can be viewed as an ontological, non-atomistic, holistic vision of reality (see also Appendix 1). What is meant with this is that anthroposophy recognizes and acknowledges the presence of non-material (non-atomistic) layers of reality (ontological), which give direction to forms, functions, and matter of living organisms, and which are to be distinguished from these material elements (holistic). Examples of this that were described in preceding chapters are 'the three- and fourfold human being' and the seven-year periods.

By contrast, the current scientific view is that the individual and his judgement have to be excluded as much as possible in the processes of acquiring and applying knowledge (viz. the use of diagnostic questionnaires and protocols for action). It is also generally reductionist. For these reasons it is necessary to make another step in the context of scientific justification, namely to test the most important deviating theoretical points of view. The key question then is whether the theories of the role of individual judgement in the acquisition and application of knowledge, and non-atomistic holism, are tenable from a scientific point of view.

As a generality, whether concepts are tenable is assessed by examining whether theories:

a. are inherently consistent (internal conceptual test);
b. are consistent with other theories developed in science (external conceptual test);
c. are consistent with empirical reality.

Concretely this means that to test the above theoretical aspects of the caregiving methodology we will answer the following questions:

1. To what extent are there indications of the validity of individual judgement in the acquisition of knowledge and its application in action, and of the quality control involved? (7.3 and 7.5.2)
2. To what extent are there indications for the validity of an ontological, non-atomistic, holistic view of reality? (7.4)

7.3 The Validity of Individual Judgement In the Acquisition and Application of Knowledge

This section describes which indications there are for the validity of individual judgement in the acquisition of knowledge and its application in action. After a brief sketch of the usual exclusion of the individual and his judgement in science, we will discuss the manner of acquiring and applying knowledge by experts by means of pattern recognition and its quality. In conclusion we will examine how we can understand pattern recognition.

7.3.1 Exclusion of the Subject in Experiments and Protocols

Both in regard to the acquisition and the application of knowledge in action the historical development of science has led to excluding the individual and his judgement as much as possible. Ever since the very beginning of scientific experiments in acquiring valid knowledge in the sixteenth century, it has been the intention to eliminate the influence of the human being as much as possible. In recent centuries experimental research has been further refined and is regarded by many as the 'golden standard' for the acquisition of valid knowledge. Ideally, in experiments the influence of the subjective individual and his judgement in the acquisition of knowledge are completely eliminated.

On the other hand, in the valid application of knowledge in professional action we see the influence of a developing Evidence Based Medicine. Professional action needs to be increasingly based on the best available evidence. New actions need to be founded from the start on scientific research, and assessed on their effectiveness. Worldwide there are such enormous and ever growing amounts of knowledge available that an individual can hardly keep up with it.

This situation has caused many professional groups to draw up guidelines and protocols for professional action, in which all this knowledge is incorporated. Guidelines describe in broad terms the 'how' of an action, followed by indications for its concrete implementation. Protocols prescribe the 'what' of the action in detail. Within this development there is a tendency that strives to base all professional action on the results of random double-blind experiments in the form of protocols. Just as in the development of the acquisition of experimental knowledge, we notice here also that in actions based on protocols the influence of the subject is eliminated—the 'implementing person' is irrelevant.

It is clearly the intention of the use of both experiments and protocols to arrive at *valid* knowledge, respectively at a *useful* application of knowledge. In these ways of working it may be necessary to *exclude* the subject. In this context, however, the question is whether there are also different, so-called *subject-integrating* ways of working that generate equally valid and useful knowledge. We find the answer to this in the literature about expertise and pattern recognition.

7.3.2 The Way Experts Process Information

Experts, experienced workers, have learned in their specialized work to deal with its inherent rules and situations (experiential knowledge, expertise, tacit knowledge, clinical look, skill, green thumb). Experts in 'chicken sexing,' for example, are able to determine the sex of a first-day chick. When asked how they do it, they have no idea! They 'simply' look at the hind part of the little animal and 'see' whether it is male or female.

Experiential knowledge produces valid and useful knowledge in many cases.[112] Experts are able on the basis of their experience to generate knowledge within their field of experience regarding the 'what' (diagnosis/insight into the problem) and the 'how' (choice of intervention to solve the problem at hand). They will recognize 'prototypical situations' on the basis of pattern recognition, will view problems in this light, and out of understanding and insight into their inherent nature and the situation, will act appropiately.[113] Sufficient knowledge of the inherent lawfulness reigning in their type of work, and the way this has to be handled in different situations, lead to the development of self-regulation, based on 'attuned action' in which 'knowing what and knowing how' are adequately applied to the unique situation. Self-regulation can here be formulated as 'adaptive use of skill across changing personal and environmental conditions'. [114] This knowledge of experts (expertise) is represented in an in-between level of abstraction called 'moderately abstract conceptual representation' (MACR). This level is a compromise between abstractions, such as comparisons in physics or chemistry, and concrete specific problems.[115]

The conscious handling of unique patterns makes it possible to create causal connections on the basis of individual observations and out of a whole (*Gestalt*), in which we make use of identifying the correspondence in unique patterns between intervention and the arising effect. This completes the whole sequence of information processing (diagnostics, intervention choice, and evaluation of the intervention's effect).

7.3.3 Pattern Recognition

Theories of Pattern Recognition

The core of 'expert performance' is therefore the ability to recognize meaningful patterns. Although the approach may differ, the various scientific explanatory models agree that pattern recognition is a process of matching (for example) visual stimuli and information in the brain. There are three kinds of theories that try to understand the phenomenon of pattern recognition:[116]

1. *Template Matching Theories*
   These suggest that patterns are recognized when the incoming sensory stimuli match a 'template' or copy of the pattern in long-term memory.
2. *Feature Detection Theories*
   These suggest that the sensory stimuli are analysed into simple features. Every pattern is then a combination of these features, and pattern recognition consists of the identification of this combination.
3. *Prototype Theories*
   These suggest that pattern recognition consists of comparing the sensory stimuli with the idealized mental form or prototype of the pattern.

The Influence of the Context, Expectation and Expertise

However, none of these theories is able to explain all phenomena. This is especially true for the influence of the context, expectations, and experience, although many examples show that pattern recognition is influenced by these.[117]

For instance, in Figs. 9 and 10 below the assignment is to name the middle figure. When Fig. 9 is autonomously evaluated, most people will recognize a B. An autonomous evaluation of Fig. 10 usually results in the number 13.

Fig. 9

Fig. 10

Finally, Fig. 11 shows that in both cases the exact same figure stands in the middle. It is therefore the context that determines a match with either the B or the 13, although the stimulus is the same and has the same features. However, all theories of pattern recognition predict that the figure will always be perceived as the same letter or the same number!

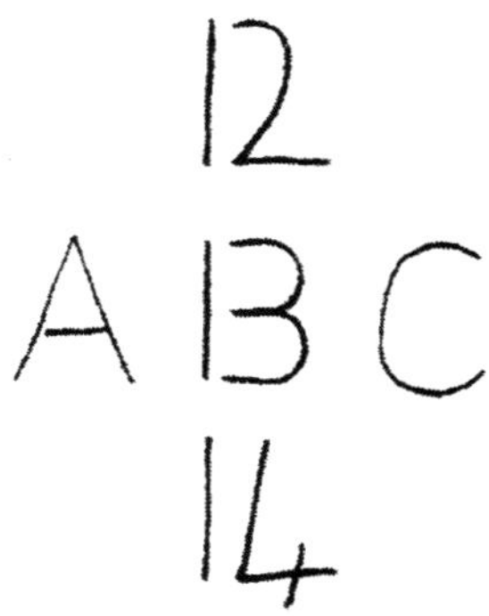

Fig. 11

In the well-known Figs. 12 and 13 we see the same problem. Even though the stimulus is the same, built up from the exact same parts in the same connection, we can perceive two objects in both pictures. In Fig. 12 we recognize alternately the young and the old woman. In Fig. 13 the grey surface is alternately the front and the back of the cube. Research shows that when people first are only shown the young woman and then Fig. 12, they will more readily recognize the young woman than the old one. Expectation and experience therefore also play a role in the kind of match that is made.

Fig. 12

(and)

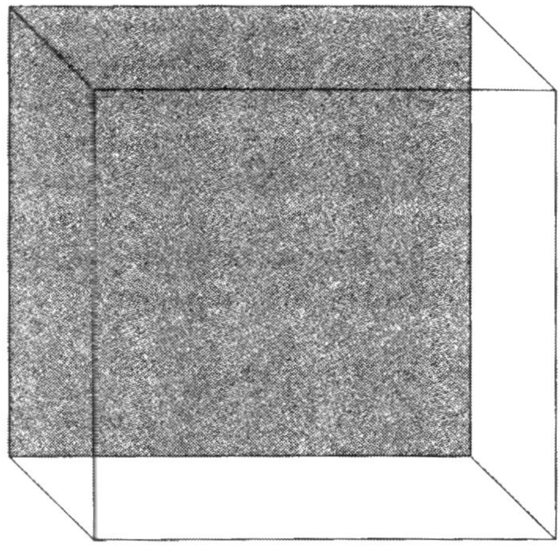

Fig. 13

A last example relates to the specific role of experience in pattern recognition. Research into the judgement-forming process of chess masters has shown that experience is manifested in recognizing *meaningful relationships between the chess pieces*:

> On the basis of the protocols of chess matches of grandmasters it was argued that grandmasters observed and recognized the characteristics of a chess position, and evaluated possible moves, more by falling back on their enormous experience than by calculating and considering these possible moves. [...] ... shows that the superior memory activity of the grandmaster rests on the presence of meaningful relationships between the chess pieces...[118]

In his above-referenced book, Lund describes that the influence of context, expectation, and experience can probably best be explained by the so-called top-down theories of perception, which state that recognition takes place from the whole (top) to the parts (down).

We can understand the influence of the context when we consider the knowledge of case study methodology.[119] For this theory teaches that the identification of causal relationships through matching becomes possible when we make a pattern more unique by creating more so-called data points, such as the number of predictions of a theory. By making it more unique we can distinguish the examined pattern from other patterns. In this light, the influence of the context becomes understandable as a situation in which there appear more data points, so that the match can ultimately only take place with one unique pattern.

The role of prior experience and knowledge can be understood based on the theory of expertise, and especially the development of the MACRs (mentioned in 7.3.2) in memory. Experts recognize the relationship between the observed phenomena and the unique patterns through the development of these MACRs. In this regard, MACRs can be regarded as the developed skill to recognize the universal in the specific (in acquiring knowledge) and to give form to the universal in changing circumstances (in applying knowledge).

What Matches What?

An important question that now arises is: What matches what? Two examples may help us here. When I sing a melody, and then sing it five tones higher while not repeating any of the notes of the first time, it is clear that there is not a single part in both melodies the same. And yet, we know that it is the exact same melody in both cases. Another example is that people are able to recognize patterns they have learned in a particular domain, also in another domain. This is the case, for instance, with many scientific discoveries.[120]

The only explanation is that, in the recognition of the melody or pattern in a new domain, that which lives between the parts, or the specific relationship between the parts (for instance in space and time), is recognized between the parts (for instance the tones in a melody). This theory is confirmed by the results of research into the development of self-regulating skills of experts in which, as was mentioned before, pattern recognition plays a key role.

There are several models that describe the development of self-regulation. Glaser[121] describes a three-phase model: external support, transitional, self-regulatory. The first phase is the one in which the novice receives support from parents, teachers, or coaches who help structure the environment and enable the novice to learn. In the second phase the support is gradually removed. The learning person develops self-monitoring and self-regulating skills, and determines the criteria for a high level of performance. In the third and last phase the learning and regulating of the performance is under the control of the learning person.

In the context of acquiring self-regulating skills Boekaerts describes a four-phase model:[122]

1. *model:* understanding the model;
2. *emulation*: repeating the principal features in the presence of the model;

3. *self-control*: training the skills in the absence of the model under highly structured circumstances;
4. *self-regulation*: the continual accommodated use of the skill under changing personal and environmental circumstances.

The general picture is here that a model is internalized and can ultimately be applied under changing circumstances.

Finally, Schumacher & Czerwinski[123] describe a three-phase model focusing on the development of memory pictures. The first, *pre-theoretical*, stage is recollecting specific cases based on superficial features of the current situation and of the cases that are stored in memory. This works when the superficial features are correlated with the underlying structural features of the system. In the *experiential stage* understanding appears of causal relationships that are fundamental to the system. In the *expert stage* the learning person can make abstractions through various system representations. The knowledge so acquired is therefore transferable.

When we review the three models of the development of self-regulating capacities together, we see a development of expertise on the basis of internalization of a model that is founded on knowledge of the systematic relationships of the system, and the occurrence of a match between this inner knowledge (in memory) on the one hand, and every form in which these specific causal relationships appear, on the other. For in the phase of self-regulation we see an adaptive use of skill across *changing* personal and environmental conditions, in other words, the possibility to recognize a pattern in any form of manifestation (in the process of acquiring knowledge).

Forms of Matching the Universal and the Specific

In conclusion we can determine that pattern recognition has to consist of a match of, on the one hand, the universal relationship in itself and, on the other hand, the specifically observed relationships between specifically observed data points. In philosophical terms, it is a match between the universal and the specific in which the universal appears and provides the relationship. In practice, this can occur in three ways:

1. *The Discovery of New Concepts*

   As a *eureka* moment of 'coincidental' and 'inspired' new insight in which there is a match between the observed relationship among observed parts, and a new concept.[124]

2. *The Unconscious Application of Known Concepts on New Observations (acquiring knowledge) and New Situations (applying knowledge)*
   As an implicit and unconscious match in the context of the 'clinical look' or 'tacit knowledge', expressing itself in 'knowing what' in combination with 'knowing how', and based on the presence of implicit experiential knowledge or expertise.
3. *The Fully Conscious Application of Ideal or* Gestalt *Knowledge on Known Images*
   As an explicit and conscious match between universal, plastic *Gestalt* knowledge and the specific forms of appearance, such as described in Goethean phenomenology (see 6.3), and the application of the knowledge of curative educational images (see 7.2.2) as an example of the application of knowledge.

The Circle and the Circles: an Example of the Relationship between the Universal and the Specific Forms of Appearance

More insight into how we can understand the universal can be found in the work of Ziegler about the relationship between mathematics and spiritual science.[125] On the basis of an experiment we can in the first place gain experiences in thinking that can help us get to know the universal better. In this so-called thought experiment the idea is to gain experience in the process of letting the one circle blend into the other one in our mind (see Fig. 14). In the second place we include the fact that it is possible to give several correct definitions of 'the circle' (see below). In our context an exact description of the experiment and the resulting experiences would take us too far; we therefore refer to Ziegler's book.

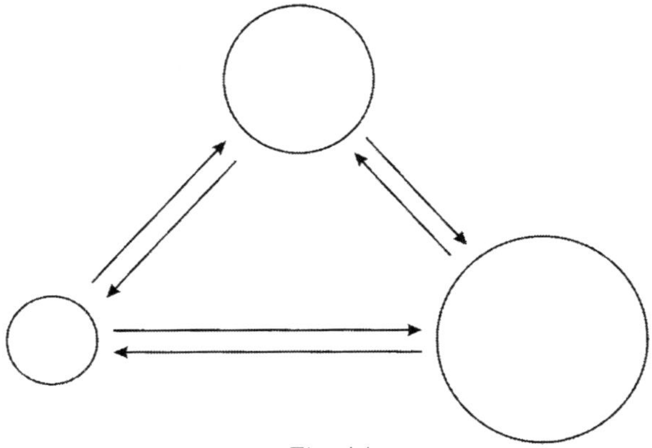

Fig. 14

Definitions of a Circle:

- A circle is a geometric figure of which all points lie in one surface and have a fixed distance to a point on this surface, the centre.
- A circle consists of the collection of all points on a surface, of which the radius from each point always has a constant length.
- A circle is the geometric place of all points, in which the distances between two fixed points have a constant quotient.

In summary, from this thought experiment we can gain the experience that we ourselves have to be active to let one picture of the circle blend into the other. However, in the background it is the idea of the circle itself which (following its own inherent lawfulness) *gives direction* to the form of the relationship between the parts (such as the centre, the radius, the surface). In the experiment we are in theory able to let all possible forms of appearance of 'the circle' manifest in our consciousness. But each image is then *one* manifestation of the *universal* circle. The universal circle is the plastic 'substance' that gives the specific relationship between the parts (following its inherent lawfulness).

This also explains that there can be several correct definitions of the circle. For in each definition there are (partly) different parts which, however, are brought together into a specific relationship by the same relationship-causing principle (*the* circle). As a result, new forms of manifestations of *the* circle make their appearance, now however, not with parts originating from observation—as in images (see Fig. 14)—but with conceptual parts as formulated in the definitions.

7.3.4 Conclusion Regarding the Validity of Individual Judgement

Based on the foregoing we can give a positive answer to the first question of section 7.2.4. There are clear indications for the validity of individual judgement in the acquisition of knowledge and its application in action. For this is the case with experts who, on the basis of their experiential knowledge, are able to recognize patterns. This conclusion forms a contribution to a scientific foundation of the key element of the caregiving methodology: individual judgement in the professional shaping of the acquisition of knowledge and its application in action. It is also a contribution to the scientific foundation of the process- and technique aspect of the caregiving methodology.

7.4 *The Validity of a Non-Atomistic, Holistic View of Reality*

In this section the second question of section 7.2.4 will be answered: To what extent are there indications for the validity of an ontological, non-atomistic, holistic view of reality? Indirectly, this will include an answer to the question of whether anthroposophy is scientifically defensible as the reality aspect of the caregiving methodology. Since anthroposophy is based on the presence of non-material (non-atomistic) layers of reality (ontological), which give direction to forms, functions, and matter of living organisms, and which are to be distinguished from these material parts (holistic), anthroposophy can scientifically be regarded as an ontological, non-atomistic, holistic view of reality.

7.4.1 Reductionism and Holism

In scientific theory, reductionism is usually placed opposite holism or organicism. 'An organism is essentially nothing but a complex set of atoms and molecules' is a statement that touches on the core of reductionism. The statements 'You cannot simply reduce an organism to a sack of molecules' and 'The whole is more than the sum of the parts' characterize holism. The reductionist model states that all characteristics and other features of living organisms, their morphology, physiology, behaviour, and ecology, can ultimately be completely and exclusively explained by their physical-chemical particles (DNA, proteins, etc.) of which they consist. Reductionism is based on the idea that the laws, concepts, and theories that are formulated for a higher level of organization in biology (for instance the level of the organism) can be explained by theories that were developed for a lower level of organization, such as the level of organs, tissues, or cells. This means that all biological concepts, laws, and theories can ultimately be reduced to physical-chemical ones.

Ever since the Middle Ages reductionist and holistic descriptions and theories have alternated in science. Verhoog[126] summarized this development as follows:

> In the medieval concept of reading the Book of Nature, nature is viewed as an organism, as the body of Mother Earth, a harmonious and self-regulating whole, that is treated with respect. In the sixteenth century this concept of nature is replaced by that of 'fallen nature'.

Nature is now viewed as disorderly, chaotic; the 'blind' nature forces have to be controlled by the human intellect. The human being is therefore no longer viewed as an intrinsic element of a God-created nature. Nature becomes objective and material during the scientific revolution of the sixteenth and seventeenth centuries. In a nature that is no longer guided by divine providence, the human being becomes free to manipulate it and use it as an instrument. Experimental natural science provided the means to reach this goal. Philosophy professor Gloy[127] described the development of organicism as a development in phases. Nature magic in the Renaissance (fifteenth and sixteenth centuries), the Monadology of Leibniz, the nature philosophy of German Idealism and Romanticism, and the vitalistic and holistic concepts of the early twentieth century are the precursors of the ecological thinking of today. It is evident that reductionism predominates in current social and scientific thinking.

7.4.2 The Validity of the Theory of Reductionism

The validity of a theory, thus also that of reductionism, is tested by determining whether the theory:

a. is consistent in itself (internal conceptual test);
b. is consistent with other theories developed in science (external conceptual test); and
c. is consistent with empirical reality.

Should a theory be inconsistent in itself, be inconsistent with other theories, and unable to explain empirical phenomena, then a serious question has to arise whether it is tenable. In this section the validity of the theory of reductionism is tested by example. This means that only a few of many arguments are used as examples.

Reductionism Falls Short in the Internal Conceptual Test

As was mentioned before, reductionism is based on the view that all characteristics and other features of living organisms can ultimately be completely and exclusively explained by the physical-chemical particles (DNA, proteins, etc.) from which they are built up. This therefore also holds true for the thinking of the human being! With every effort to explain how reality is put together, however, one has to begin by forming thoughts about the phenomena in the world.

Ontological reductionism, therefore, begins with thoughts about matter. This means that it places itself in fact before two different realms: the material world and the thoughts about it. It tries to understand the latter by viewing them as purely material processes. It maintains that thinking in the brain comes about in approximately the same way as digestion in the organs of the metabolism. Just as ontological reductionism ascribes mechanical and organic effects to matter, it also ascribes to matter the capacity, under certain conditions, to think. It forgets, however, that it has now only shifted the problem. Instead of to the human being, ontological reductionism ascribes the capacity to think to matter. And that brings it back to its point of departure. How can matter think about its own nature? Why is it not simply content in itself and accepts its lot? The ontological reductionistic view is not able to solve this problem; it can only shift it.[128]

In her previously mentioned book Professor Gloy also puts two big question marks by the internal consistency of reductionism. First of all she indicates that there is a contradiction in the theory between the postulate of the smallest indivisible particles and the assumption of expansion into space, which implies divisibility. Secondly, she points out the fact that within this theory reductionist thinking and teleological thinking cannot be connected with each other.

Reductionism Falls Short in the External Conceptual Test

Based on his scientific research into the human brain, famous Nobel Prize recipient and neuro-physiologist Eccles[129] described that reductionist science cannot give an explanation for our spiritual existence. He comes to the conclusion that mental events can cause neuronal effects. And over time more and more other scientists have also questioned the theory that mental 'substances' can be reduced to physical matter: 'Mental properties are now widely regarded by philosophers as epistemologically irreducible to their physical ones.' [130] This statement confirms theories formed in connection with near-death experiences, from which it has in recent years become increasingly plausible that human consciousness cannot be reduced to physical human features.

Reductionism Falls Short on Empirical Grounds

The question remains whether, on the basis of the fundamental factors of the reductionist world picture (matter, space, movement, and moving material forces), a man-made product can ever duplicate living nature. So far the only successful thing has been the cloning of new beings out of *living* beings. No one has yet succeeded in doing this out of dead matter alone.

Properties or behaviour of the parts of an organism can mostly only be explained in terms of their functions in the whole. Such functional explanations are unavoidable in biology. And because they don't occur in physics and chemistry, they form an important argument to make a positive distinction of biology as compared with these other sciences.[131] Researchers of the morphological changes in living organisms also point to the function of the whole:

> It is clear that what the parts (molecules and ions) are doing and the patterns they form are what they are because of their incorporation into the system-as-a-whole; in fact, these are patterns within the system in question. The parts would not be behaving as observed if they were not parts of that particular system (the 'whole'). The state of a system-as-a-whole is affecting (i.e., acting like a cause on) what the parts, the constituents, actually do. Many examples of this kind could be taken from the literature on, for instance, self-organizing and dissipative systems.[132]

Countless research results demonstrate the limitations of genetic reductionist thinking. For example, there are some old paradigms of genetics that are consistent with reductionism:

1. DNA (and in some viruses RNA) is the genetic material;
2. the genetic flow of information runs from DNA to RNA to protein;
3. the base sequence of DNA runs via RNA, exactly to the amino acid sequence of polypeptides.

All these paradigms have been relativized or disproved. Also the assumption that a gene contains a code for a protein has been disproved in many respects. All options are open: one gene or many genes may contain codes for one protein or many proteins.[133]

In the heredity of genetic information, more takes place than just a transfer of DNA; frequently it is a question of 'epigenetic inheritance'.[134] The assumption that the base sequence of DNA runs, via RNA, exactly to the amino acid sequence of polypeptides, has also been disproved.[135]

Similarly, the genetic reductionist assumption that in the base sequence of DNA the construction and function of organic forms and their component parts lie programmed is not tenable. Transplantation of DNA cores of highly specialized cells into another environment shows that the function of that environment and that developmental phase is adopted.[136] Ontogenesis and morphogenesis of organisms show that beyond DNA, there have to be other sources of information and ordering, other streams of heredity.[137] Genetically identical cells differentiate themselves lawfully into distinguishable cell types and distinguishable protein substances, and therefore distinguishable genetic expressions.

This raises the question of how the various genes are turned on and off when the genetic 'equipment', the 'genetic programme,' is the same everywhere. It is the so-called logical dilemma of developmental biology.[138] The cause, therefore, has to be found outside DNA, in other words, it has to be epigenetic. In humans and animals supra-cellular forms and patterns come into being, such as arms and legs, with identical types of cells (skin cells, bone cells, etc.); the supra-cellular form, the arrangement in space of identical cells, is thus independent of the genetic expression.[139]

In conclusion we quote Service who concludes on the basis of research into the complexity of organisms: 'When we get to a certain network complexity, we completely fail to understand how it works.'[140]

7.4.3 Conclusion Regarding the Validity of a Non-Atomistic, Holistic View of Reality

On internal conceptual, external conceptual, and empirical grounds, we may draw the conclusion that there are clear indications that reductionism falls short as an explanatory model of reality. A variety of scientists in a variety of scientific realms have come to the conclusion, independently of each other, that there are clear indications that the whole directs the parts. This at the same time gives form to a scientific foundation for a non-atomistic, holistic view of reality.

With this finding we can also cautiously provide a positive answer to the second question. There are clear indications that the theory of ontological, non-atomistic holism might be plausible. Indirectly this also makes a contribution to the scientific foundation of anthroposophy as the reality aspect of the caregiving methodology.

7.5 The Scientific Context of the Caregiving Methodology

Since we have now, with the conclusions of sections 7.3 and 7.4, established that the caregiving methodology satisfies the formal demands of a method, we can thereupon place this method in a scientific context. First of all we will describe that the scientific view, within which the caregiving methodology can be placed, is that of experiential knowledge (7.5.1). Next we will show that, as a method, it is consistent with, among others, the Aristotelian doctrine of *phronesis*, qualitative research methods, case study methodology, and the presence approach (7.5.2).

7.5.1 Experiential Science

Methods are used in the context of a particular scientific view. For example, the alpha, beta, and gamma sciences use different research methods that are consistent with the underlying scientific paradigms. The scientific view that is consistent with the caregiving methodology is that of experiential science.[141]

Like every form of science, the objective of experiential science is to develop knowledge. The particular characteristic of experiential science, however, is that it aims for a specific form of knowledge, namely experiential knowledge or expertise. To begin with, this is available to the individual experiential expert in the form of *Gestalt* knowledge, and because of its flexibility it offers the ability to recognize the general in the specific, as well as to give form to the specific out of the general when acting in a situation. It is characteristic for the way information is processed that in the first instance it takes place unconsciously and implicitly. The change from experiential expertise to experiential science is represented by the change from implicitly and unconsciously handling *Gestalt* knowledge to handling it explicitly, consciously, and methodically. When this occurs in the correct manner, the experiential expert becomes an experiential scientist.

Whereas most science focuses on abstract, general knowledge and therefore has difficulties in learning and handling uniqueness and complexity, experiential science adds to this by its knowledge of the relationship between the universal and the specific, and its application in unique and complex situations. De Vries[142] puts these two forms of knowledge side by side as personal knowledge and systematized knowledge:

Personal knowledge	*Systematized knowledge*
knowledge	information
experiential or implicit knowledge	explicit knowledge
ability	knowledge
practical wisdom	scientific knowledge
practice	theory
situational knowledge	general knowledge

Characteristics of the first form of knowledge are that the knowledge is person-bound, concrete, embedded in an environment or related to a position, and mobile or dynamic. By contrast, formal knowledge is impersonal, abstract, and static.

7.5.2 Methodical Consistency

The Methodically Worked-Out Virtue of Practical Insight

The caregiving methodology connects in the history of science with a specific virtue described by Aristotle, *phronesis*, often called practical insight or practical wisdom. Aristotle distinguished five virtues to discover truth; in addition to practical insight these are expertise, scientific knowledge, philosophical wisdom, and the intellect. Gadamer[143] describes *phronesis* as a work process in which during the work itself decisions are made that could not have been specified ahead of time from a code. Goudsmit[144] describes it as the kind of knowledge needed by a general physician to be able to go back and forth between the everyday phenomena of the patient and professional knowledge, both in the diagnostic process (acquisition of knowledge) and in the treatment (application of knowledge).

> General physicians increasingly base their treatments on the outcomes of scientific research. But there are moments when that is not quite possible. For the GP moves in his work between two discourses: that of everyday phenomena and that of the professional thought model. The first has to be converted into the second, and the reverse. In the first, everyday discourse belong the ordinary 'unscientific' impressions the patient makes on him; also the story of the patient, his experiences, and the experiences of the doctor himself belong to this discourse. The transitions between these two discourses are crucial to the work, but in themselves they do not fit

> within either of the two. These are moments when a decision is made as to which available knowledge is 'activated', and which is not. Such a decision cannot be pre-cooked, and therefore does not exist as theoretical or technical knowledge.
>
> [...]
>
> The transition from everyday discourse to professional discourse means that the doctor has to choose which professional conceptual model he considers applicable. This choice is a decision the doctor has to make himself; he has to say: this diagnosis seems to me most fitting with these phenomena and with this story. Choices like this cannot be described in medical manuals, and also cannot be obviated by the use of advanced testing equipment, procedures, or any existing guidelines, protocols, or standards. It is always the doctor who decides to use a particular theoretical concept, an instrument, or certain procedures, and at which moment to switch to another instrument or protocol.
>
> The same is true for the other transition, from the professional to the everyday discourse. Given the outcome of a professional line of argument—the outcome of the conceptual model—it is the general physician's task to translate this into the terms of a treatment plan. Here too, choices have to be made that do not lie ready-made within the conceptual model, for these depend on the specific circumstances of the moment.[145]

The caregiving methodology described in this book may be regarded as the methodically elaborated and employable virtue of *phronesis*.

Qualitative Research Methods

The caregiving methodology is also consistent with qualitative research methods, because these have first of all to do with the nature and properties of the phenomena, with qualities therefore, and not with quantities such as how much, how big, the frequency or extent of occurrence of something or someone. Secondly, just as the caregiving methodology, qualitative research methods are used, among others, in situations when the particularities, the unusual aspects are described of a person, a case, or a phenomenon.[146]

Case Study Methodology

The methodical core of the caregiving methodology is consistent with the core of the case study methodology: applying the process of pattern recognition in the acquisition and application of knowledge. In the context of identifying causal connections in case studies, Swanborn writes about this:

> Historians have altogether formulated at least 25 explanations of the reasons why the French Revolution happened. We could say that there are more explanations than facts. This an example of the basic weakness of, and critique on this branch of methodology: the material of a case study allows for a lot of interpretations, and we do not possess the possibilities to make a responsible choice out of this abundance. In other words, we do not know which theory gives the correct explanation of the facts.[147]

Swanborn's solution of this problem lies in increasing the number of data points. According to the author this can be done by increasing the number of 'measuring points' or the number of predictions. Through this 'intervention' a situation is created in which more facts have to be explained by a theory.

> There are then, as it were, more possibilities that a theory does not fit; it becomes difficult to find a fitting theory that is yet not excessively complicated. [...] In brief, by collecting more data we create the possibility to make a choice for the theory that can best explain the facts that were found. We can then make this choice because a theory has to fit; facts and explanatory theory have to correspond.[148]

How this works concretely becomes clear, among others, in the way 'increasing the number of predictions' is worked out. Swanborn again:

> From every theory, from every model, a larger or smaller number of predictions can be derived that can be tested by the data of the cases themselves. [...] If in addition one devises some alternative interpretations ahead of time, and also pours their consequences into predictions, one has a strong position if these predictions do not work out. When such a pattern occurs, it becomes difficult to ascribe the changes to something other than the intervention. [...] The more independent predictions prove to work out, and the fewer predictions out of alternative theories prove to work out, the better a causal interpretation is grounded.[149]

The analysis of this methodology is called pattern matching. What it amounts to is that 'the score pattern on a number of variables together is compared with a previously predicted pattern. [...] The more extensive the predicted pattern is, the stronger is the challenge to the hypothesis.'

The Presence Approach

The presence theory was developed by Baart[150] based on long-term research into the practices of pastors in underdeveloped neighbourhoods, a world of poverty, marginal people, violence, loneliness, and the work of the neighbourhood pastor there. It wants to come up with a theory of and for that kind of work and to that end intensive research took place for seven years in the field, in particular in the city of Utrecht, Netherlands, with two pastors. But similar research was also done in about ten other places, where church workers were following a presence-like approach in their connections with neighbourhood people. The most important methodological characteristics of presence practice are:

1. it actively follows the other: the professional follows the other—instead of the other way around;
2. it works out of one vision (integralism)—instead of fragmentation and specialization;
3. it connects with life as it is lived—instead of schematic bureaucratization;
4. it puts the good of the other first and foremost—instead of one's own good intentions;
5. the other is important to at least one—acknowledgement and relationship are foremost.

> A very brief description of presence practice is the following. It is a practice in which the caregiver enters into a relationship of attention and devotion with the other, in order to discover what the issue is with the other—from longings to anxiety and fear—and, as a result, comes to understand what could be done in the situation, and in the process, who he or she can be for the other. What can be done is then indeed done. It is a way of working and being that can only be achieved with a feeling of subtlety, expertise, with practical wisdom and loving faithfulness.
>
> Remarkable, for example, is the sequence in which the described (helping, caregiving) actions unfold. First, the relationship is entered into in a specific, intensive manner (attention, devotion); only then, or as a result, it can become apparent who the caregiver can be for the other, what longing or what need there is, and what care is needed. The relationship therefore comes first, problem-solving action is postponed, and the identity of the caregiver ('Who can I be for you?') is not fixed, but forms itself in a shared learning process. This deviates from what we usually see; usually it is predetermined who and what the caregiver has to be for the other, and what will be the issues in the relationship.[151]

It is not hard to recognize the five characteristics of the method of the presence approach in the key aspects of the caregiving methodology:

Presence Approach	*Caregiving Methodology*
Actively follows the other	1. The care team meeting, including all methodical steps 2. Acting in the situation
Works out of one vision (integralism)	1. The holistic concept of the human being of anthroposophy 2. The joint work of the caregivers based on the care team meeting and the shared concept of the human being
It connects with life as it is lived, schooled	Spiritual presence of mind based on individual judgement
Puts the good of the other first and foremost	Sense of service
The other is important to at least one	Equality

7.5.3 Conclusion

Based on the foregoing, we may conclude that the caregiving methodology can be regarded as a method of experiential science consistent with the Aristotelian doctrine of practical insight, as well as current research methods such as qualitative research, the case study method, and the method of presence approach.

7.6 Quality Control on Pattern Recognition in the Diagnostic Phase and Choice of Intervention

As has been described, in science today quality control in the processes of the acquisition and application of knowledge wants to eliminate, respectively exclude, the subject(ive). The way in which *valid* knowledge is acquired within experiential science and *useful* knowledge is applied consists of three kinds of activities in which the subject is an integral part; the subjective is not excluded but objectified.

1. *Preventive Activities*
   This refers to the schooling of thinking, feeling, and the will into a measuring instrument for the observation of the Universals. To this end Rudolf Steiner gave many exercises in the context of the anthroposophical path of schooling. The result of this path of development is the totality of perceptive thinking, perceptive feeling, and perceptive will. Examples are the six so-called subsidiary exercises,[152] and the exercises in the context of the practical development of thinking.[153] This instrument can be used both in the acquisition and application of knowledge (see also 7.2.2).
2. *Activities in the Moment*
   This is the activity of reflecting in the moment on the process of coming to a judgement, the ability (ideally) to follow the process of coming to a judgement in complete consciousness in the moment when it takes place. In its essence, this is about the ability to directly relate the universal to the specific. This activity can be used in diagnostic processes, the pursuit of therapy processes, and the evaluation of effects.
3. *Retrospective Activities*
   This is the process in which one reflects in a methodical way on 'flash experiences', implicit acquisition of knowledge and/or its application on the basis of 'tacit knowledge', and unexpectedly successful action. In all such cases the universal has to be made explicit based on reflection on the specific manifestation of the universal.

In all three activities the methodically justified positive identification of the universal in the specific is the key factor.

Appendix 1

Syllabus

Anthroposophical Care and Caregiving

In several chapters of this book anthroposophical care and caregiving are mentioned. What is meant is that there is a method of providing care for people with developmental disabilities that is based on knowledge from anthroposophical spiritual science, besides knowledge from 'conventional health care'. Anthroposophical caregivers are usually people who have followed the conventional training and have, in addition, received supplemental anthroposophical training. Anthroposophical care can therefore be considered as an extension of the possibilities of 'regular care'.

The Anthroposophical Concept of 'Type'

The anthroposophical concept of 'type' has its origin in the natural scientific work of Johann Wolfgang von Goethe[154] and the philosophical-methodical underpinning of this in the work of Rudolf Steiner.[155] The type is for living or organic nature what natural laws (for instance, gravity) are for dead or inorganic nature. It is a creative, dynamic archetypal image, not perceptible to the physical senses (for instance the archetypal plant or animal), from which all species, subspecies, and separate organisms have come forth and can be 'lawfully' derived. This creative archetypal image cannot be known from the separate organisms perceptible through the senses; each of the latter shows only one form of manifestation of the type. Only by comparing ideally all forms of manifestation can we ultimately, beyond sensory perception, come to know this creative archetypal organism.

The Threefold and Fourfold Human Being

The development of the child begins already before birth. The non-material spiritual individuality connects itself with a hereditary stream, the fertilized egg cell. At conception heredity is a given which has to be transformed by the individuality of the child into the child's own physical instrument—as much as is possible, and under the influence of the environment—especially in the first seven years of life. The name used for this physical instrument is 'physical body'. It is related to the mineral world, and subject to the laws of the physical world, to gravity. This physical instrument is under the influence of life processes, such as metabolism, growth and maturity, in a continual biological development. In the well-known 'biological clock' we can experience that this biological development takes place in time. The life processes are directed by the 'life body' or 'etheric body' (see hereafter). This 'body' is a structure of forces that are not visible as such. However, the result of the working of these forces is visible, for example, in physical growth. The etheric body has a relationship with the world of plants.

In a first confrontation between individuality and heredity, early in the pregnancy already, the as yet unborn child reacts to the environment. This marks the beginning of the development of the soul. The soul is carried by a structure of forces that has the name 'astral body'. In the development the astral body first contributes to the forming and functioning of organs such as the heart, lungs, liver, kidneys, and nerve system. Subsequently it separates itself in part from this for the development of psycho-social functions of feeling, will, and thinking.

For this reason, the threefold anthroposophical view of the human being distinguishes three bio-psychosocial functions:

1. The nerve-sense system, which is poor in vital forces, forms the physical basis for perception and thinking, through images, thoughts, and memory. These functions require an awake consciousness.
2. The rhythmically working middle area, with the breathing lungs and the beating heart, is the physical basis for the development of feeling and experiencing. In these functions consciousness is of a dreaming nature.
3. The vital and mobile organ system of the metabolism and the limbs forms the physical basis for the development of the will and action, with passions and desires, impulses of will, wishes and intentions. In the regions of the metabolism and will, consciousness is of a sleeping nature.

(A different form of threefoldness used in anthroposophical literature is that of body, soul, and spirit. It is described in detail in section 2.4.2.)

The origin of the individuality lies in the spiritual world. It is this non-material individuality that incarnates into the hereditary stream.

As 'I-organization' it is first active in biological development, for example in the development of the human form, standing and walking erect, and speech. Gradually the individuality frees itself from this and becomes perceptible in the development of the personality. The working of the I in the three layers of the soul leads to I-consciousness in thinking, I-experience in feeling, and I-realization in deeds. The development of the personality becomes visible in the biography.

Physical Body

The physical body is a structure that is perceptible through the senses, filled with material substance, and limited in space. It has a surface, an exterior, which is visible and touchable in its contours. The surface forms the boundary between inner and outer world, and at that boundary its substance is perceptible. Also when, as is done in research into physical substance, one cuts into it so that the parts can only be viewed through a microscope, one still sees in the cutting surfaces only a surface, an exterior. The physical body has a spatial structure and follows the laws of gravity.

It can be known through weighing and measuring; in this respect, contour, space, and substance are core concepts. Characteristic for a physical substance is the fact that out of itself it cannot change; change is only possible through influences working in from outside.

In the diagnostic process the physical body is examined for the following:

- the substances from which the physical organism is formed: earth, water, air, warmth;
- the physical proportions, for instance, the size of the head in relation to the limbs;
- the presence of physical handicaps; for instance blindness or paralysis are phenomena showing that the etheric body (see below) is not or hardly working in those places.

Etheric Body

Permeating the physical world and the physical body works an etheric world through the etheric or life body. In nature all living organisms are carriers of an etheric body, and the human being also has an etheric body. The etheric body as such cannot be perceived through the senses, unless the needed clairvoyant capacities have been developed for this. It is indirectly perceptible via the life cycles. The plant has a life cycle of germinating, growing, blossoming, bearing fruit, and dying. Similar processes can be observed in human beings in growth, vitality, illness and recovery, and living and dying. The etheric body keeps a plant, animal and human being together as an integral living whole, with forces that work from the inside out and 'mould' or form the cohesion of the physical body. For this reason, the etheric body is also called the body of formative forces. Physical substances are formed in this structure of forces.

The etheric body brings about growth and development, it fosters health and recovery from illness. At death it withdraws from the organism. What then remains is physical substance, dead and subject to decay through external forces.

The etheric body causes substances that are taken up from the outside world to be transformed into an inner world. What is taken up is sustenance for the human being: warmth, light, food, and nourishment for the senses. In the first years of life this sustenance brings about physical growth and development. In the seventh year of life the organism of the child has become sufficiently independent that the etheric body is partly freed and can support the development of thinking, learning, and the growth of memory. In the course of life the forces of the etheric body decline and with it our vitality and health.

Life Processes

With seven life processes the etheric body (with the help of the astral body) looks after the life of the human being, by transforming the outside world into the inside world. These life processes are the following:

1 To absorb 7 To create (renew)

2 To adapt 6 To grow

3 To break down 5 To maintain

4 To separate (internalize and excrete)

The first three processes are related to the outside world:

1. to absorb the substances needed for breathing and nourishment. What we absorb through our senses may in this connection be considered as 'observation substance'. In the child this nourishment has to be

2. adapted by chewing and warming or cooling in the mouth, to be
3. broken down and digested.

Of key importance in the life processes are:

1. separating—separating in and out. On the one hand, the body takes in what it needs for
2. its maintenance,
3. its growth, and ultimately for
4. bringing about something new, such as sexual maturity.

On the other hand, excretion takes place: bowel movement, urine, perspiration, carbon dioxide, menstruation, ejaculation, phlegm.

The first three processes belong to active day-consciousness. Maintenance and growth happen especially during sleep; recovery and growth belong to the night.

In the diagnostic process a doctor will, concerning the etheric body, observe:

- the form of the body, its hollow and rounded forms, how it is 'moulded';
- the vitality, the degree of health, the capacity to recover from illness;
- the life processes.

The effects of the forces that come (partly) free around age seven:

- coherence in the nerve-sense system resulting in cohesion between thinking, memory and learning capacity;
- in the rhythmic system: habit forming;
- in the metabolism: contentment and liveliness in the moods.

Astral Body

The astral body is the carrier of the soul; through it we are related to the animals. Characteristics of animals are their movement, perception, and consciousness. In nature we can see how animals move, feed, create their own spot, nest or territory, make sounds, communicate, and procreate. Their movements have a direction, toward or away from something; their perception shows as an expression of lust or disgust, a fight-or-flight reaction. Self-generated movement and perception assume the presence of consciousness, and the degree to which this is present depends on the degree to which this has developed in the different animal species.

A typical difference between animal and plant life lies in gas-exchange. While in plants this occurs through diffusion, higher animals have lungs and breathe, they are 'in-spired' and are as such 'ensouled'.

The astral body is here described following the soul functions of thinking, feeling and the will. The threefoldness of corporeality—upper pole (nerve-sense system), middle area (rhythmic system with respiration and blood circulation), and lower pole (metabolic-limbs system)—colours the soul in the qualities of, respectively, observation and thinking, feeling and experiencing, and the will and action.

The characteristic phenomena of the inworking of the astral body—moving, perceiving, consciousness—express themselves as polarities: exertion and relaxation, sympathy and antipathy, inner and outer.

In the diagnostic process the astral body is examined for:

- Consciousness
  - in the soul: awake perception, thinking, comprehending;
  - in the body: illness, pain, breakdown processes.

- Experience
  - in the soul: the dreamy consciousness of experiencing and feeling;
  - in the body: the dynamic of respiration and heartbeat.

- Movement
  - in the soul: passions, impulses;
  - in the body: instincts, muscle tension.

The I

The incarnated individuality is called and experienced as 'I' by each of us. Characteristic for human beings are their self-consciousness and capacity to develop; these features distinguish them from the animal world. Animals are born and are 'trapped' in specific skills, such as spiders that spin their webs and wrap their prey in it. A spider instinctively knows how to do this from birth, but is not free to decide someday to learn a different way of behaving; human beings, on the other hand, have to learn an incredible amount once they are born; they can make choices, and can freely and permanently develop themselves.

The human I works on different levels; on the physical level, for example, through posture and speech, on the soul level in control of perception and thinking, experiencing and feeling. On the social level the I expresses itself in its ability to be conscious and to experience itself and others, as well as in its ability to make choices. Morality, conscience, self-consciousness, possessing ideals and wishes, and building perspective in life, are also functions that can come to development out of the I.

In the diagnostic process the I is examined for:

- Posture and manner of movement
- Speech
- Dealing with warmth processes
- Ability to hold back and reflect
- Action and conscience
- Freedom and personal perspective
- Ability to make choices
- Self-regulation and autonomy
- The biography.

The Curative Educational Constitutional Images

The curative constitutional images were introduced by Rudolf Steiner in 1924 in a lecture series for people who had undertaken the care of children with developmental disabilities.[156] He sketched three pairs of polar images; together they form a coherent picture of six constitutional images. With the aid of these images, the developmental dynamic in a person, and especially any one-sidedness in it, can be characterized.

All development, physiological and physical, but also soul development, is characterized by rhythmic processes. A rhythmic process moves between two poles, such as forming and dissolving, building up and breaking down, remembering and forgetting, waking and sleeping, movement and rest, sympathy and antipathy. Rhythmic alternation between the two poles is a prerequisite for development. When looking at this more closely, we can observe in all rhythmic processes a threefoldness: the two poles and a dynamic middle position in between.

The dynamic of the middle is an important phenomenon. It mediates and shows the relationship between the two poles following which development takes place, for instance, the relationship between building up and breaking down. This mediation between the two poles is necessary for development to proceed. Stagnation occurs when development runs aground in one-sidedness at one of the poles. The six constitutional images represent such one-sidedness in development, when a rhythmic process falters and is stuck at one of the poles. For example, the development gets stuck in being awake without being able to sleep, or in mobility that never stops.

compulsive/rich in iron	versus	forgetful/rich in sulphur
obstructed/closed	versus	flowing/open
immobile/heavy	versus	too mobile/light

These images show one-sidedness in development on three levels. The first level consists of the nerve-sense processes, which are located mostly in the head, and form the basis for perception, thinking, and memory. The two poles are: remembering and forgetting. If the rhythmic process between the two poles comes to a halt, one-sidedness arises:

Creating densified form with sharp conours, inability to forget	versus	Suppressing form, dissolving contours, forgetting, inability to remember

The second level consists of the rhythmic processes of breathing and blood circulation, which have their centre in the chest, and form the basis for empathy and feeling. The two poles are: connecting and letting go. One-sidedness:

Closing off and obstructing	versus	Opening and losing oneself

The third level consists of the metabolic and movement processes primarily located in the abdomen and the limbs; they form the basis for the will and for action, deeds. The two poles are: moving and resting. When the process comes to a halt, one-sidedness arises:

Unintended retarding and inability to come into movement	versus	Unrestrained acceleration and inability to come to rest

The Concept of Health

The anthroposophical practice paradigm is holistic in nature and works with, in summary, some basic, theretical assumptions:

1. Health is the result of a continual activity of keeping the different constitutional levels dynamically in balance: the organic, psychological, and biographical.

2. The principles that actively maintain the balance are self-regulating capacities on the levels of the body, soul, and spirit.
3. The self-regulating capacities can be therapeutically addressed and, if need be, strengthened. Ideally, the result of this is that, provided the required means are available, health comes about as the final state, or is restored.

A more formal definition of health is that it is the dynamic final state of an autonomous, self-regulating structure (without explicit pressure of involvement from outside the system) in time, and sometimes also in space. Within this structure, perceptions, judgements, decisions, and actions are ordered in such a way that a specific function can be performed. On the one hand, this structure is cognitively able to recognize the general pattern in the specific (matching) and, on the other hand, also able out of the general pattern to adopt a specific form of action: 'knowing how' in combination with 'knowing what'. It is therefore a flowing picture that enables one to do justice to the various aspects of the situation, both from a cognitive and from an action point of view. This structure has its origin in (experiential) knowledge of the inherent relationships in the relative domain.

The *physically* oriented self-regulating activity always tries to restore the balance between the organism and its environment, the balance between sub-systems in the organism itself, and thus the form and function of the whole organism.

The psycho-socially oriented self-regulating activity always tries, on the basis of developed self-regulating capacities, to be able, in changing circumstances, to give a meaningful direction to one's own life.

In the scientific literature there are, among others, three important theories that are consistent with the concept of psycho-social self-regulation: autonomy, meaning-in-life, and salutogenesis. In the process of the self-regulating maintenance of the physical organism, two 'systems' are of key importance: the immune system (perhaps supported by the fever reaction), and the chrono-biological rhythmic system.

Autonomy

The concept of autonomy literally means 'to set your own laws for yourself'. In other words, an autonomous person has the wherewithal to set his own rules and boundaries, and is not dependent on others for this. Bekker distinguishes three domains of autonomy:[157]

1. self-consciousness: the degree of awareness of one's own wishes, needs, views, and the ability to manifest these;
2. sensitivity to others: the degree of independence and sensitivity to, and being preoccupied with the judgement, look, wishes of others; the degree of empathy; the need and ability to be close; affection and separation;
3. the ability to handle new situations: the ability to maintain oneself in new situations and autonomously initiate new activities; tendency to explore; (in)dependence with regard to familiar structures.

Salutogenesis

A concept of heath that is consistent with that of autonomy is the concept of salutogenesis or self-healing, which originated with Professor of Medical Sociology A. Antonovsky.[158] In connection with the threats and destruction of the Nazi era and countless other wars in our time, Antonovsky wondered what enables some people to survive, and even enables them to be unexpectedly healthy, in spite of going through experiences like fear of confrontation with death, hunger, torture. His research into what formed the basis of this ability of some people to be healthy led to his formulating 'Sense of Coherence'. According to the author, human beings possess sources from which they derive their health. These 'generalized resistance resources' are among others: a favourable social-economic background, knowledge and intelligence, a strong I, a social support system, a healthy way of life, and a circumscribed cultural background. These sources come into being based on earlier life experiences and genetic make-up. In this way, through consistent and repeated experiences, a 'sense of coherence' (a capacity to integrate) is built up, which reaches its apex around the thirtieth year of life. According to Antonovsky it is a unique human characteristic to be able to integrate conflicting experiences, and give them meaning. Within the concept of 'sense of coherence' we can distinguish three core properties:

1. *comprehensibility*: the ability to order, make consistent, structure, and clarify incoming information;
2. *manageability*: the degree to which one has the skills to handle situations adequately;
3. *meaningfulness*: the experience of being an active participant in giving form to one's own life.

Meaning in Life

In his dissertation *Meaning in Life*, Debats[159] describes that within the theories that have the greatest influence in clinical psychology there is, despite the differences, agreement on the importance of values as guiding principles in the process of giving meaning to personal existence. In the relativistic perspective on *Meaning in Life* by Battista and Almond, it is stated that persons who experience their lives as meaningful are characterized by two factors: (a) they are able to contemplate their life from a meaningful perspective and from this they derive a number of objectives for their life; and (b) they experience themselves as persons who have achieved these objectives or are in the process of achieving them. In Debats' own study the crucial role of the interpersonal dimension in the process of creating meaning also came to the fore: meaningfulness was characterized by a variety of forms of contact—with oneself, others, and the world—whereas meaninglessness was characterized by various types of isolation—of oneself, others, and the world.

The concepts of autonomy, sense of coherence, and meaning in life can without any problem be recognized as self-regulating 'structures'. Without explicit pressure or involvement from outside the system, within this structure perceptions, judgements, decisions, and actions are ordered in such a way that a specific function can be performed.

The Holism-vs-Reductionism Question

Looijen[160] points out that in regard to the reductionism-vs-holism problem a distinction has to be made between three aspects: ontological, epistemological, and methodological aspects.

Ontological aspects have to do with the question from which entities, things, or substances it is assumed that reality (nature) is made, what properties are ascribed to these things or entities, and what relationships and functions are assumed to exist among them.

Epistemological aspects relate to our knowledge of reality, to the manner in which this knowledge is expressed in (among others) theories, and on logical relationships between theories. They apply especially to relationships between theories that were developed for different domains of reality, or for different levels of organization.

Methodological aspects have to do with the ways in which knowledge is acquired, and with the fundamental principles, rules, and strategies used in the process. Here the focus is on the question whether, in order to arrive at the 'correct' knowledge or concept of a certain level of organization (the level of the whole), we would have to study the underlying levels of organization (the component parts and their interactions), or the higher level itself, or perhaps its relationships with possibly even higher levels.

Intellectual Limitation, Intellectual Handicap, and Developmental Disability

In this book the terms intellectual handicap, intellectual limitation, and developmental disability are all used. The terms intellectual handicap and intellectual limitation are used especially to follow today's customary terminology. In curative education and social therapy the terms developmental problems and developmental disability are customary. Developmental problems are regarded as easier to influence and change, while developmental disabilities, because they are more difficult to influence, go more in the direction of an intellectual limitation or handicap. With the term developmental disability is meant that the person does not develop in accordance with general patterns of development.

In this regard, a very important point of view from anthroposophical spiritual science is that learning and development are always possible. A life with a handicap is, besides all the problems it comes with, *also* a life full of development potential.

Senses and Sense Organs

For the achievement of sensory perception four conditions have to be satisfied:

1. an intact organ - physical level
2. a healthy organ - etheric level
3. an awake soul - astral level
4. a will to observe - I-level.

Items 1 and 2 form the instrumental side of perception; 3 and 4 the functional side.[161]

In the anthroposophical conception of the human being a distinction is made between the physical *sense organs* (such as the ear, eye, nose) and the non-physical *senses*. There are twelve senses that can be grouped as follows:

1. The body-related or lower senses:
   sense of touch
   sense of life
   sense of movement
   sense of balance.
2. The environment-related or middle senses:
   sense of smell
   sense of taste
   sense of colour
   sense of warmth.
3. The spirit-related or higher senses:
   sense of tone
   sense of word
   sense of thought
   sense of I.

The senses can be used in the process of perception by different sense organs. For instance, in the observation of a painting through the eye as the sense organ, the consistency/structure (sense of touch), the vitality (sense of life), the dynamic (sense of movement), and the arrangement of the composition (sense of balance) may all be observed.

Appendix 2

Summary

In this book, ethical premises and methodological aspects of good care are described from an anthroposophical perspective. The book was written in the context of a development in society of the past few decades in which the advancement of the quality of health care has received great emphasis. Clients want to receive ever better care. Caregivers want to provide good, and ever better care. This development has led to the introduction of large numbers of quality projects in health care. Forms of care and treatment methods are being made explicit, quality norms are being set, and the quality, including the effect, is periodically assessed. This approach has led to an unceasing tendency toward the optimization of care.

Within curative education (the anthroposophically grounded care of children and youths with developmental disabilities) and social therapy (for persons with a developmental disability 18 years and older), a specific care methodology is used in practice. So far, however, no fundamental explicit descriptions and scientific justification have appeared of the features of the methodology, including its ethical premises. This book aims to fill this hiatus, consistent with the spirit of the time. The leading question throughout this book is therefore: What are the characteristics of the anthroposophical caregiving methodology that are needed, and are also accountable, for responsible, 'good' care?

In *Chapter 2* the question is addressed what the fundamental values are that guide anthroposophical care of children and adults with developmental disabilities, and how these values can lead persons to providing 'good care'. Three fundamental values are introduced: equality, sense of service, and spiritual presence of mind. Regarding equality two levels of reality are identified: that of the essential being—all human beings are spiritual entities—and that of the appearance—all human beings go through an individual path of development through many incarnations. This conception of reality is determinative for the anthroposophical care of the handicapped. The unity of being-and-appearance forms the basis and gives content to the fundamental value of equality.

The awareness that people are equal as spiritual beings also provides the basis for the second fundamental value in the care of the handicapped: sense of service. Sense of service is a readiness to help a person especially in his development, out of a consciousness of a karmic connection into a distant future. We humans have to do with each other; my development is connected with yours, and the other way around. My destiny is related to that of all other humans. Sense of service means entering into a relationship out of an awareness of a karmic connection.

Spiritual presence of mind shows in a person's action in specific situations as a result of being professionally 'awake', so that an intuitive action can come into being. This ability to act intuitively in such a manner in spiritual presence of mind is the height of caregiving out of a sense of service.

The three fundamental values are each time connected with a number of practical virtues, which gives the ethics also a methodological significance. In conclusion, this chapter discusses the subjects of professionalism and good care.

In *Chapter 3* spiritual-psychological conceptions are presented to understand the person with a developmental disability. The basic premise is that the individuality has to work in life with the combination of forces he has brought with him from the spiritual world and what comes out of heredity and the environment.

Everything we notice in persons with developmental disabilities can also be observed in 'normal' people, only in them it is present in more subtle and covered forms. Therefore, in order to understand a person with a developmental disability it is important first to be familiar with the course of normal development, so that one can then understand what steps and tasks in the development were missed or happened in a one-sided, retarded, or accelerated way.

For these reasons, in this chapter first the normal course of development of the first three seven-year periods is described, when the emphasis is, respectively, on learning by imitation, learning to learn, and learning to work. Next, normal development in adulthood is described in phases of 21 years.

The anthroposophical conception of health as a balance-creating process between opposite poles in a threefold human being is sketched, to show how developmental disabilities can be understood as one-sidedness within this threefoldness. Then the three factors of constitution, heredity, and environment are discussed from which a developmental disability may grow. One-sided tendencies in our culture and society are indicated which, as negative factors from the environment, may cause or aggravate developmental disabilities. Curative education and social therapy are described as positive environmental factors that aim to have a healing effect on developmental disabilities, among others, by working toward creating a culture of the heart. Finally, characteristics of children of our time are examined, as well as questions as to the meaning of things.

In *Chapter 4* the most important elements of the caregiving practice of curative education and social therapy are described. The principal objectives that curative education and social therapy strive for are:

- looking for the individual development question;
- doing justice to the universal equality of human beings in practical deeds and treatment;
- awakening the healing forces in the child and adult through education and the arrangement of the living, learning, and working environment, so that they can develop and maintain themselves as harmoniously as possible, in body, soul, and spirit;
- forming carrying social communities or networks in which interpersonal relationships support both individual and community development.

In anthroposophical caregiving the personal encounter is key. It is regarded as the means through which, on the one hand, mutual experiences between people and, on the other hand, individual experiences in the surrounding learning, working, or living environment are gained. Learning, working, and living together bring insight in one's own actions, and can thus lead to continued development in the individual. Inner sources of strength are described—salutogenesis.

The aspects of anthroposophical care are described in relation to learning, treatment, culture, and life, leading to the significance of social networks and relationships, rhythm, and art. Within curative education and social therapy the social field is formed by the individuals who need care and their caregivers who made a choice to share their humanness with them and make their professional capacities available to them. The social organism—meaning the total environment in which living together, work, and cultural and religious life are all having their effect—thus becomes the vehicle for anthroposophical care.

In *Chapter 5*, the professional identity of professional caregivers is described. This identity encompasses the whole of the core concepts of professional educators in curative education and social therapy and their competencies; in other words, the whole of knowledge, insight, skills, and attitude aspects that belong to the profession. Professional caregivers work with five core concepts that help guide their professional actions. These concepts have to do with human driving forces, the fundamental values that underlie caregiving, the person of the caregiver, the caregiving and treatment process, and the methods of education and treatment.

In addition, there are two aspects that form the basis of the attitude of professional caregivers: the attitude of loving acceptance, and inner listening and openness as a basis for action. The core concepts and attitude aspects of the professional identity lead to focused forms of schooling that are also consistent with the core values of equality, sense of service, and spiritual presence of mind. Moreover, they are not only of importance in the direct professional interaction with persons who are in need of care. They are just as important in the cooperation with colleagues. In conclusion, and further emphasizing the professional identity, the position of the professional caregiver is described vis-à-vis that of the parents and family in regard to their developmentally disabled child.

In *Chapter 6* the caregiving process is described from a methodological point of view. The basis of the caregiving process is the client's need for care. Besides clarifying the need for care, methodological imagery based on empathetic observation points the way to the diagnostic process on three levels: diagnosis on the basis of the constitution, classification, and the perspective or will of the client. This threefold diagnostic process leads to the care plan, which guides the care and treatment, and also to the evaluation. There are three categories:

1. realizing the perspective and will of the client;
2. supporting the developmental dynamic;
3. minimizing the consequences of the developmental disability.

Means and measures that can be used to realize the goals are the human capacity of self-healing, creating a healthy living climate, art, and spirituality. The application of the means can be attuned to the person involved through trained judgement. At the end of the chapter, some possibilities for evaluation are given.

In *Chapter* 7 the caregiving methodology described in the book is scientifically justified. For this purpose, first the formal aspects of a method are discussed, namely the reality aspect, the aspect of good action, the process and technique aspect, the rational aspect, and the quality aspect. Next, the question is examined, and answered positively, how the caregiving methodology satisfies the formal requirements of a method. Two unusual key aspects of the methodology, namely individual judgement and the holistic practice paradigm, are then tested for their theoretical tenability, again with positive results.

The conclusion is that the caregiving methodology can be regarded as an experiential-scientific method that is consistent with the Aristotelian doctrine of practical insight and with conventional research methods, such as qualitative research, the case study method, and the method of the practice of presence. The chapter ends with a description of subject-integrated quality control in the acquisition and application of knowledge, and of quality assessment by means of the methodically responsible positive identification of the universal in the specific (pattern recognition).

Notes

1 Rudolf Steiner, *Curative Education*, CW 317; all references in this section.
2 P. Singer, *Practical Ethics*, Cambridge 1979.
3 H. Vos, *Filosofie van de moraal. Inzicht in moraal en ethiek* (Philosophy of Morality. Insight into Morality and Ethics), Spectrum 1995. He writes: 'The principle of beneficence is in itself a very abstract value. In different contexts it therefore receives different meanings. That is because we are of course not responsible for the well-being of relatives and friends. In those cases beneficence quickly means care, friendship, love. Vis-à-vis others our involvement is more distant. Solidarity then forms the appropriate figure of beneficence. These moral values are not separately named because they are implied in beneficence.'
4 J. S. Reinders, *Ethiek in de zorg voor mensen met een verstandelijke handicap* (Ethics in the Care of People with Intellectual Handicaps), Amsterdam 2000.
5 F.W.A. Brom et al., *Beleid en ethiek* (Policy and Ethics), Van Gorcum 1993. The authors differentiate between minimum standards (required standards) and goal-standards. They write: 'This dual structure implies that, besides legal rules, the right of caregiving also has to offer a merely marginally regulated space for freedom or professional autonomy.' And: 'When personal characteristics or virtues are involved, there is a clear difference from mandatory legal standards.'
6 Op. cit., note 4.
7 H. P. Meininger, Doctoral Thesis 1998, University Utrecht.
8 J. Tronto, *Moral Boundaries*, New York/London 1993.
9 H. Manschot & M. Verkerk, *Ethiek van de zorg. Een discussie* (Ethics of Caregiving. A discussion), Amsterdam 1997.
10 Ibid.
11 Ibid.
12 Ibid.
13 J. Stolk (ed.), *Gebroken wereld. Zwakzinnigenzorg en de vraag naar euthanasie* (Broken World. Care of the Handicapped and the Demand for Euthanasia), Kampen 1988.
14 H. Dupuis, *Op het scherp van de snede* (On the Edge of the Knife), Amsterdam 1998.
15 Rudolf Steiner, *The Philosophy of Freedom*, CW 4, Chapter 13. An example Steiner gives is the striving to climb a mountaintop to enjoy the wonderful view. As long as this striving has strength, you accept all the effort of the climb and all the weight of your backpack.
16 P. Bavastro (ed.), *Individualität und Ethik*, Stuttgart 1997.

17 Op. cit., note 14.

18 A. H. Vedder, *De ontologie van de person* (The Ontology of the Person) in: F.W.A.Brom et al., *Beleid en ethiek* (Policy and Ethics), Van Gorcum 1993.

19 R. Spaemann, *Personen. Versuch über den Unterschied zwischen 'etwas' und 'jemand'*. Stuttgart 1996.

20 See Rudolf Steiner, *Theosophy*, CW 9, *How to Know Higher Worlds*, CW 10, and *An Outline of Esoteric Science*, CW 13.

21 Frank Teichmann, *The Origins of the Anthroposophical Society in the Light of the Ancient Mysteries*, Temple Lodge 2020.

22 Understanding a development presumes the capacity to observe as many forms of appearance as possible and in the review let them shade off into each other. This is the capacity to picture the stages of development in the form of memory pictures, one after the other, in such a way that you inwardly learn to make the invisible changes. Thus the capacity can be developed to form an inner image of the unity in this multiplicity, by thinking the laws of the whole. The original being encompasses all forms of appearance and is imagined in an 'archetypal image'. A number of researchers have included this spiritual concept of development in their spiritual research: besides Goethe and Steiner, among others, Julius, Bockemühl, Van der Bie, Van Tellingen.

23 Rudolf Steiner, *Karmic Relationships*, Vol. I–VIII, CW 235–240.

24 G. E. Lessing, *The Education of Humankind*.

25 H. Poppelbaum, *Man and Animal*, London 1960.

26 This ideal can be found in Camphill organizations (with an anthroposophical signature) and in Ark organizations (with a Christian signature). Camphill goes back to anthroposophical physician Karl König, Ark to the movement *L'Arche* of the Dominican Jean Vanier.

27 See Rudolf Steiner, *How to Know Higher Worlds*, CW 10, Chapter 3.

28 We can focus our cognitive capacity on ourselves. The generally accepted philosophical view is now that those who do this inevitably get caught in their own subjectivity: you can make yourself into an object, but that can never be objective. Those who say this forget that they contradict themselves by objectively declaring that everything is subjective. If I am already caught in my subjectivity, what then enables me to still look at myself?

29 In our time we grow up with the prejudice that our soul functions, and our cognitive functions, are generated by neural processes in our brain. In our brain we are supposed to be able to find the explanation of how the human psyche functions. This view rests on a confusion of two different kinds of causes. Brains are necessary: without a brain we cannot function. But maintaining that human beings observe, remember, think, feel, etc. because they have brains is like saying that a car moves because it has wheels. Without brains human beings cannot function just as a car cannot move without

wheels. In the wheels, however, we do not find a driver, ignition, engine or fuel. And in the brain we also do not find an I, an intention, observation and thought. This fact should be sufficient to reject the idea that brain and mind are the same.

30 Rudolf Steiner, *The Philosophy of Freedom*, CW 4.

31 Rudolf Steiner, *How to Know Higher Worlds*, CW 10.

32 See Charles Taylor, *The Malaise of Modernity*, Toronto 1998.

33 Rudolf Steiner, *How to Know Higher Worlds*, CW 10.

34 The basic exercises were originally intended for meditation. This inner harmony is in the care of the handicapped, and in caregiving in general, of great importance, because caregivers often have the upper hand and power over their clients, which not infrequently leads to their manipulation. Persons with impairments often do not put up verbal opposition. They work on the other not so much through their cognitive reactions, more through their 'being'. To communicate with them, caregivers have to find new ways. In that process the caregivers run into their own limitations. They thus experience their own (communicative) incapacities, and may experience themselves as limited, impaired. We might call this the 'dialectic of impairment'. At first, only the others were impaired; but then the caregivers turn out to have limitations, for they do not understand the others. Both are then impaired, and therefore the contrast has become relative. The relationship then also becomes symmetrical. In order to handle this dialectic, the caregivers have to harmonize their soul functions.

35 Besides compassion we should also mention 'wonder' as a virtue that can strengthen observation. In anthroposophical literature we find many references to Rudolf Steiner's mention of wonder, compassion, and conscience.

36 For Rudolf Steiner the concept of initiate has a specific meaning; a clairvoyant person need not be an initiate. Steiner also considered the evangelists as initiates. The general principle of education is also present in spiritual schooling: the teacher gives lesson material (meditations) to the student; the teacher knows which material is appropriate to make good progress. According to Steiner, a personal teacher is no longer necessary. See also *How to Know Higher Worlds*.

37 Rudolf Steiner, *An Outline of Esoteric Science*, CW 13, Chapter 5.

38 Rudolf Steiner, *How to Know Higher Worlds*, CW 10, Chapter 1.

39 Rudolf Steiner, *Friedrich Nietzsche, Fighter for Freedom*, CW 5.

40 H. Philipse, *Atheistisch Manifest*, Amsterdam 2004.

41 Rudolf Steiner, *The Philosophy of Freedom*, CW 4.

42 Ibid.

43 K. M. Dietz (ed.), *Rudolf Steiners 'Philosophie der Freiheit'*, Stuttgart 1994.

44 J. Tronto, *Moral Boundaries*, New York/London 1993.

45 With the cooperation of Willem de Koning. Section 3.3 was written by A. Dekkers and H. Dekkers-Appel.

46 Rudolf Steiner, *Curative Education*, CW 317.

47 Anthroposophy describes that human development proceeds throughout life in phases of seven years each. Physically, for example, every cell in the body has been renewed after seven years.

48 Rudolf Steiner, *Curative Education*, CW 317.

49 Rudolf Steiner, *Zur Sinneslehre. Themen aus dem Gesamtwerk 3*, Stuttgart 1980.

50 Rudolf Steiner, *Educating Children Today*, CW 34.

51 Rudolf Steiner, *Curative Education*, CW 317.

52 Ibid.

53 Ibid.

54 J. Sleigh, *Seelenpflege in Heilpedagogik und Sozialtherapie*, Dornach 1996.

55 Rudolf Steiner, *Founding a Science of the Spirit*, Rudolf Steiner Press 1999.

56 George Kühlewind et al., *Star Children*, Temple Lodge 2004.

57 L. Carroll & J. Tober, *The Indigo Children,* Hay House 1999.

58 Rudolf Steiner, *Curative Education*, CW 317.

59 As a picture we might think here of Grimm's fairy tale of Frau Holle, which shows that the spiritual world is waiting for aptitudes that are acquired on earth, in order to metamorphose them into new talents with 'Frau Holle'.

60 R. Normann, *Service Management, Strategy and Leadership in Service Business*, Chichester 1988.

61 J. Denger, *Lebensformen in der sozialtherapeutische Arbeit*, Stuttgart 1995.

62 B. C. J. Lievegoed, *Samenwerkingsvormen* (Forms of Collaboration), Zeist 1988.

63 B. C. J. Lievegoed, *Phases. The Spiritual Rhythms in Adult Life*, Rudolf Steiner Press 1998.

64 M. Fennis, *Inrichten van zorginstellingen* (Designing Caregiving Institutions), Apeldoorn 2003.

65 G. Douma & G. Wiegers, *De ouder wordende mens,* (The Ageing Person), Schoorl 2002.

66 Rudolf Steiner, *Theosophy*, CW 9.

67 Karl König in H. Müller-Wiedemann, *Karl König. Eine mitteleuropäische Biographie im 20. Jahrhundert*, Stuttgart. 1992.

68 Ibid.

69 Bank-Mikkelsen in W. Thimm, *Das Normalisierungsprinzip, eine Einführung*, 1988.

70 H. Kistner, *Arbeit und schwere Behinderung*, Dornach 2003.

71 M. Schubert, *Verhaltensstörungen und Sinnesstörungen* in: *Erziehungskunst, 11*, 1988.

72 With the cooperation of Willem de Koning.

73 Rudolf Steiner, *Theosophy*, CW 9, and *An Outline of Esoteric Science*, CW 13.

74 B. C. J. Lievegoed, *Samenwerkingsvormen* (Forms of Collaboration), Zeist 1988.

75 J. Krausen, *Gesprek voeren met mensen die niet kunnen praten* (Conversing with People who Cannot Talk), Arnhem 1996.

76 A. Fischer, *Vom Betreuen zum Begleiten; Facetten der sozialtherapeutische Arbeit.* Dornach 2004.

77 Ibid.

78 M. J. Lambert & A. E. Bergin, *The Effectiveness of Psychotherapy*, in: A. E. Bergin & S. L. Garfield (eds.), *Handbook of Psychotherapy and Behavior Change*, New York 1994.

79 L. Sjoukes & F. Wessels, *De prognose voorbij, mogelijkheden voor een klein kind in de heilpedagogie* (Beyond the Prognosis, Possibilities for a Small Child in Curative Pedagogy), Bilthoven 1993.

80 In his description of this law, Steiner used the following nomenclature for these elements: (1) spirit self (this is the spiritual element that can become active especially through the community and in the social context), (2) the I, (3) the astral body, and (4) the etheric body.

81 B. Sellin, *Berichten uit een autistische kerker* (Messages from an Autistic Dungeon), Bussum 1993.

82 H. P. Meininger, Doctoral Thesis 1998, University Utrecht.

83 Summarized from: W. von Eschenbach, *Parsifal.*

84 *Handbuch: Ausbildung in der Heilpädagogik und Sozialtherapie*, Dornach 2001.

85 Rudolf Steiner, *Curative Education*, CW 317.

86 J. Isarin, *De eigen ander: moeders, deskundigen en gehandicapte kinderen; filosofie van ervaring* (The True Other: Mothers, Experts, and Handicapped Children; Philosophy of Experience), Amsterdam 2002.

87 A. H. Bos et al., *Oordeelsvorming, een weg naar innerlijke vrijheid* (Judgement Forming, a Way toward Inner Freedom), Assen 2003.

88 J. W. Goethe, *The Metamorphosis of Plants*, Wyoming RI, 1978.

89 Rudolf Steiner, *Goethean Science*, Mercury Press 1988.

90 Rudolf Steiner, *How to Know Higher Worlds*, CW 13.

91 M. Domeijer, *Zum Begriff der inneren Intuition im heilpädagogischen Kurs Rudolf Steiner*, Dornach 2003.

92 R. van Zijl (ed.), *Kinderbespreking. Het kind als inspiratiebron* (Child discussion. The Child as Source of Inspiration), Zeist 2002.

93 M. Niemeijer & E. Baars, *Instrument voor de beeldvormende diagnostiek van de kinderlijke constitutie* (Instrument for the Image-Forming Diagnostic Process of the Constitution of the Child), Driebergen 2004.

94 P. Heusser (ed.), *Akademische Forschung in der Anthroposophischen Medizin*, Bern 1999.

95 A. Antonovsky, *Salutogenese. Zur Entmystifizierung der Gesundheit*, Tübingen 2004.

96 M. Glöckler: *Salutogenese*, Dornach 2002.
97 E. Golombek et al., *Anthroposophische Kunsttherapie*, Stuttgart 2000.
98 A. Baart, *Een theorie van de presentie* (A Theory of Presence), Utrecht 2004.
99 Rudolf Steiner, *An Outline of Esoteric Science*, CW 13; and J. van Dam, *Het zesvoudige pad, basis oefeningen voor spirituele ontwikkeling* (The Sixfold Path, Basic Exercises for Spiritual Development), Zeist 1999.
100 H. Kiene, *Single-case Causality Assessment as a Basis for Clinical Judgement*, in: *Alternative Therapies*, 4, 1998.
101 K. Duncker, *Zur Psychologie des produktiven Denkens*, Berlin 1935.
102 A. Baart, *Een theorie van presentie* (A Theory of Presence), Utrecht 2004.
103 R. Looijen, *Holism and Reductionism in Biology and Ecology. The Mutual Dependence of Higher and Lower Levels of Research Programmes*, Groningen 1998.
104 A. Baart, *Een theorie van presentie* (A Theory of Presence), Utrecht 2004.
105 A. Baart, *Een theorie van presentie* (A Theory of Presence), Utrecht 2004.
106 Ibid.
107 A. Reuling, *Methodologieen. Een inleiding in onderzoeksstrategieen* (Methodologies. An Introduction into Research Strategies), Baarn 1986.
108 Rudolf Steiner, *Riddles of the Soul*, CW 21.
109 W. Holtzapfel, *Heilende Erziehung: Vom Wesen seelenpflegebedürftiger Kinder und deren heilpädagogischer Förderung*, Stuttgart 1998.
110 H. Bortoft, *Goethes naturwissenschaftliche Methode*, Stuttgart 1995.
111 P. Petersen, *Therapie als kunst. De essentie van genezing.* (Therapy as Art. The Essence of Healing), Zeist 1990.
112 T. S. Kuhn, *Die Entstehung des Neuen—Studien zur Struktur der Wissenschaftsgeschichte*, Frankfurt 1977; A. de Groot, *Thought and Choice in Chess*, The Hague 1979; I. Robertson, *Problem Solving*, University of Luton 2001.
113 W. Brouwer, *De psychologie van de aandacht* (The Psychology of Attention), Lisse 1994.
114 M. Boekaerts et al., *Handbook of Self-Regulation*, San Diego 2000.
115 C. M. Zeitz, *Some Concrete Advantages of Abstraction*, Cambridge 1997.
116 N. Lund, *Attention and Pattern Recognition*, East Sussex 2001.
117 I. Robertson, *Problem Solving*, University of Luton 2001.
118 K. A. Ericsson & J. Smith, *Toward a General Theory of Expertise: Prospects and Limits*, Cambridge 1994.
119 P.G. Swanborn, *Evalueren*, Amsterdam 1999.
120 G. H. van der Bie, *What is behind the Great Discoveries?,* Lunteren 2003.
121 R. Glaser, *Changing the Agency for Learning: Acquiring Expert Performance*, Mahwah 1996.
122 M. Boekaerts et al., *Handbook of Self-Regulation*, San Diego 2000.
123 R. Schumacher & R. Czerwinski, *Mental Models and the Acquisition of Expert Knowledge*, New York 1992.

124 R. Davis-Floyd & P. Sven-Arvidson, *Intuition*, London 1997; G. H. van der Bie, op. cit., note 118.

125 R. Ziegler, *Mathematik und Geisteswissenschaft*, Dornach 1992.

126 H.Verhoog, *Reductionistisch en organistisch denken in de wetenschap* (Reductionist and Organistic Thinking in Science), Driebergen 1993.

127 K. Gloy, *Das Verständnis der Natur. Die Geshcichte des gansheitlichen Denkens*, Munich 1996.

128 Rudolf Steiner, *The Philosophy of Freedom*, CW 4.

129 J. C. Eccles, *How the Self Controls Its Brain,* Berlin 1994.

130 A. Peacocke, *Complexity, Emergence, and Divine Creativity*, Oxford 2003.

131 R. Looijen, *Holism and Reductionism in Biology and Ecology. The Mutual Dependence of Higher and Lower Level Research Programmes*, Groningen 1998.

132 A. Peacocke, *Complexity, Emergence, and Divine Creativity*, Oxford 2003.

133 M. W. Ho, *Das Geschäft mit den Genen: Genetic Engineering—Traum oder Alptraum*, Munich 1999.

134 E. Jablonka & M. J. Lamb, *Epigenetic Inheritance and evolution*, Oxford 1993; V. E. A. Russo et al, *Epigenetic Mechanisms of Gene Regulation*, New York 1996.

135 M. W. Ho, *Das Geschäft mit den Genen: Genetic Engineering—Traum oder Alptraum*, Munich 1999.

136 G. S. Kienle & H. Kiene, *Die Mistel in der Onkologie—Fakten und konzeptionelle Grundlagen*, Stuttgart 2003.

137 Ibid.

138 M. Hamburgh, *Theories of Differentiation*, London 1971.

139 W. A. Müller & M. Hassel, *Entwicklungsbiologie der Tiere und des Menschen*, Berlin 1999.

140 R. F. Service, *Exploring the Systems of Life*, in: *Science* 284, 1999.

141 T. Baars & A. de Vries, *De boer als ervaringswetenschapper* (The Farmer as Experiential Scientist), Doetinchem 1999.

142 A. de Vries, *Ervaringsleren cultiveren. Onderzoek in eigen werk* (Cultivating Experiential Learning. Research into One's Own Work), Delft 2004.

143 H. G. Gadamer, *Wahrheit und Methode*, Tübingen 1960.

144 A. L. Goudsmit, *De plaats ven 'phronese' in de huisartsengeneeskunde* (The Place of 'phronesis' in General Medicine), 2005.

145 Ibid.

146 D. B. Baarda et al., *Kwalitatief onderzoek* (Qualitative Research), Houten 1996.

147 P. G. Swanborn, *Case studies. Wat, wanneer en hoe?* (Case Studies. What, When, and How?), Amsterdam 2000.

148 Ibid.

149 Ibid.

150 A. Baart, *Een theorie van presentie* (A Theory of Presence), Utrecht 2004.

151 Ibid.

152 Rudolf Steiner, *How to Know Higher Worlds*, CW 13.

153 Rudolf Steiner, *Practical Training in Thought*, Karlsruhe, 1/18/1909, from CW 108.

154 J.W. Goethe, *The Metamorphosis of Plants*, Wyoming RI, 1978.

155 Rudolf Steiner, *Goethe the Scientist*, CW 1.

156 Rudolf Steiner, *Curative Education*, CW 317.

157 Bekker, *Autonomie Lijst* (Autonomy List), Lisse, 1991.

158 A. Antonovsky, *Unraveling the Mystery of Health: How People Manage Stress and Stay Well*, Ann Arbor 1987.

159 D. L. Debats, *Meaning in Life. Psychometric, Clinical, and Phenomenological Aspects*, Groningen 1996.

160 R. Looijen, *Holism and Reductionism in Biology and Ecology. The Mutual Dependence of Higher and Lower Level Research Programmes*, Groningen 1998.

161 E. P. S. Schoorel, *De eerste zeven jaar. Kinderfysiologie* (The First Seven Years. Child Physiology), Zeist 1998.